Writings of
Rosa Luxemburg

by Rosa Luxemburg

Red and Black Publishers, St Petersburg, Florida

Library of Congress Cataloging-in-Publication Data

Luxemburg, Rosa, 1871-1919.
   [Selections. English. 2010]
   Writings of Rosa Luxemburg / by Rosa Luxemburg.
      p. cm.
   ISBN 978-1-934941-91-1
1. Socialism--Germany. 2. Communism--Germany. 3. Luxemburg, Rosa, 1871-
1919. I. Title.
   HX273.L83313 2010
   335.43092--dc22

                                                                2010015087

Red and Black Publishers, PO Box 7542, St Petersburg, Florida, 33734

Contact us at: info@RedandBlackPublishers.com

         Printed and manufactured in the United States of America

Contents

The Polish Question at the International Congress in London
(1896)

Thirty-two years ago, when what was later to become the International met for the first time in London, it opened its proceedings with a protest against the subjugation of Poland, which just then was engaged, for the third time, in a fruitless struggle for independence. In a few weeks the International Workers' Congress will meet, also in London, and will be presented with a resolution in support of Polish independence. The similarity of circumstances quite naturally suggests a comparison of these two events in the life of the international proletariat.

The proletariat has come a long way in its development over these past thirty-two years. Progress is evident in every regard, and many aspects of the working-class struggle look quite different from the way they did thirty-two years ago. But the essential element in this entire development lies in the following: from a sect of ideologues, socialists have grown into a major unified party capable of handling its own affairs. Then, they barely existed in isolated little groups outside the mainstream of political life in every country; today, they represent the dominant factor in the life of society. This is particularly true in the major civilized countries; but in every country they are an element to be taken seriously and to be reckoned with at every step by government and ruling class alike. Then, it was a question of merely spreading the new message; today, the paramount question is how the struggle of the vast popular masses, now thoroughly imbued with the gospel of socialism, can best be led toward its goal.

The International Workers' Congress has undergone corresponding changes. In its beginning, the International was more of a council that met to formulate the basic principles of the new movement; today, it is primarily, even exclusively, a body for practical deliberations by the conscious proletariat on the urgent questions of its day to day struggle. All tasks and objectives are here subjected to rigorous evaluation as to their practicability; those, however, that appear to exceed the forces of the proletariat are laid aside, regardless of how attractive or appealing they may sound. This is the essential difference between the conference this year in St. Martin's Hall and the one that took place thirty-two years ago, and it is from this perspective that the resolution laid before the Congress must be examined.

The resolution on the restoration of Poland to be presented at the London Congress reads as follows.

"Whereas, the subjugation of one nation by another can serve only the interests of capitalists and despots, while for working people in both oppressed and oppressor nation it is equally pernicious; and whereas, in particular, the Russian tsardom, which owes its internal strength and its external significance to the subjugation and partition of Poland, constitutes a permanent threat to the development of the international workers' movement, the Congress hereby resolves: that the independence of Poland represents an imperative political demand both for the Polish proletariat and for the international labor movement as a whole."

The demand for the political independence of Poland is supported by two arguments: first, the general perniciousness of annexations from the point of view of the interests of the proletariat; and second, the special significance of the subjugation of Poland for the continued existence of the Russian tsardom, and thus, by implication, the significance of Polish independence for its downfall.

Let us take the second point first.

The Russian tsardom derives neither its inner strength nor its external significance from the subjugation of Poland. This assertion in the resolution is false from A to Z. The Russian tsardom derives its inner strength from the social relations within Russia itself. The historical basis of Russian absolutism is a natural economy resting on the archaic communal-property relations of the peasantry. The remains of this backward social structure—and there are many such remains still to be found in Russia today—along with the total configuration of other social factors, constitute the basis of the Russian tsardom. The nobility is kept under the tsar's thumb by an endless flow of handouts paid for by taxing the peasantry. Foreign policy is conducted to benefit the bourgeoisie with the opening of new markets as its main objective, while customs policy puts the Russian consumer at the mercy of the manufacturers. Finally, even the domestic activity of the tsardom is in the service of capital: the organization of industrial expositions, the construction of the Siberian railroad, and other projects of a similar nature are all carried out with a view to advancing the interests of capitalism. In general, under the tsardom the bourgeoisie plays an inordinately important role in shaping domestic and foreign policy, a role which its numerical inconsequence would never permit it to play without the tsar. This, then, is the combination of factors which gives the tsardom its strength internally. So it continues to vegetate, because the obsolete social forms have not yet completely disappeared, and the embryonic class relations of a modern society have not yet fully developed and crystallized.

Again: the strength of the tsardom abroad derives not from the partition of Poland, but from the particular features of the Russian Empire. Its vast human masses provide an unlimited source of financial and military resources, available almost on command, which elevates Russia to the level of a first-rate European power. Its vastness and geographic position give Russia a very special interest in the Eastern question, in which it vies with the other nations that are also involved in that part of the world. At the same time, Russia borders on the British possessions in Asia, which is leading it toward an inevitable confrontation with England. In Europe, too, Russia is deeply involved in the most vital concerns of the European powers. Especially in the nineteenth century, the revolutionary class struggles just now emerging have put the tsardom in the role of guardian of reaction in Europe, which fact also contributes to its stature abroad.

But above all, in speaking of Russia's foreign position, especially over the last few decades, it is not the partition of Poland but solely and exclusively the annexation of Alsace-Lorraine that lends it its power: by dividing Europe into two hostile camps, by creating a permanent threat of war, and by driving France further and further into the arms of Russia.

From false premises come false conclusions: as if the existence of an independent Poland could deprive Russia of its powers at home or abroad. The restoration of Poland could bring about the downfall of Russian absolutism only if it simultaneously abolished the social basis of the tsardom within Russia itself, i.e., the remains of the old peasant economy and the importance of the tsardom for both the nobility and the bourgeoisie. But of course this is arrant nonsense: it makes no difference — with or without Poland these relations remain unchanged. The hope of breaking the hold of Russian omnipotence through the restoration of Poland is an anachronism stemming from that bygone time when there seemed to be no hope that forces within Russia itself would ever be capable of achieving the destruction of the tsardom. The Russia of that time, a land of natural economy, seemed, as did all such countries, to be mired in total social stagnation. But since the sixties it has set a course toward the development of a modern economy and in so doing has sown the seeds for a solution to the problem of Russian absolutism. The tsardom finds itself forced to support a capitalist economy, but in so doing it is sawing off the limb on which it sits.

Through its financial policies it is destroying whatever remains of the old agricultural-communal relationships, and is thus eliminating any basis for conservative modes of thought among the peasantry. What is more, in its plundering of the peasantry, the tsardom is undermining its own material foundations and destroying the resources with which it purchased the loyalty of the nobility. Finally, the tsardom has apparently made it its special task to ruin the major class of consumers at the bourgeoisie's expense, thus leaving with its pockets empty the very class to whose pecuniary interests it sacrificed the interests of the nation as a whole. Once a useful agent of the bourgeois economy, the ponderous bureaucracy has become its fetters. The result is the accelerated growth of the industrial proletariat, the one social force with which the tsardom cannot ally itself and to which it cannot give ground without jeopardizing its own existence.

These, then, are the social contradictions whose solution involves the downfall of absolutism. The tsardom is driving forward to that fatal moment like a rolling stone on a steep hill. The hill is the development of capitalism, and at its foot the iron fists of the working class are waiting. Only the political struggle of the proletariat throughout the entire Russian empire can accelerate this process. The independence of Poland has comparatively little to do with the fall of the tsardom, just as the partition of Poland had little to do with its continued existence.

Let us take now the first point of the resolution. "The subjugation of one nation by another," we read, "can serve only the interests of capitalists and despots, while for working people in both oppressed and oppressor nation it is equally pernicious ..." On the basis of this proposition the independence of Poland is supposed to become an imperative demand of the proletariat. Here we have one of those great truths, so great, in fact, as to be one of the greatest of commonplaces, and as such it can lead to no practical conclusions whatsoever. If, from the assertion that the subjugation of one nation by another is in the interests of capitalists and despots, it is therefore concluded that all annexations are unjust or can be eliminated within the capitalist system, then this we hold to be absurd, for it makes no allowance for the basic principles of the existing order.

It is interesting to note that this point in the resolution is almost identical with the argument in support of the notorious Dutch resolution: "Since the subjugation and control of one nation by another can lie only in the interests of the ruling classes ... ," the proletariat is supposed to bring about the end of the war with the aid of the striking military. Both resolutions are based on the naive belief that it is enough to recognize any circumstance benefiting despots to the detriment of working people in order to do away with it immediately. The similarity goes further. The evil that must be rooted out is, in principle, the same in both resolutions: the Dutch resolution proposes to prevent future annexations by ending the war, while the Polish resolution intends to undo past wars by abolishing annexations. In both cases, the proletariat is supposed to eliminate war and annexations under capitalism without eliminating capitalism itself, though both, in fact, are part of the very essence of capitalism.

Granted that the truism just cited does not give any basis for the general abolition of annexations, it provides even less of a reason for abolishing the existing Polish annexation. In this case especially, without a critical assessment of the concrete historical conditions, nothing of value can be contributed to the problem. But on this point, on the question of how — and if — the proletariat can liberate Poland, the resolution maintains a deep silence. The Dutch resolution is more sophisticated in this respect: it at least proposes a specific means — a secret accord with the military — which allows us to see the utopian aspect of the resolution. The Polish resolution is more modest and contents itself with a "demand," although it is not any less utopian on that account than the other.

How is the Polish proletariat to build a classless state? In the face of the three governments ruling Poland; in the face of the bourgeoisie of the Polish congress pandering to the throne in Petersburg and recoiling from any thought of a restored Poland as a crime and a plot against its own pocket-book; in the face of the large Galician landholdings in the person of the governing Badani, who watches over the unity of the Austrian monarchy (that is: guarantees the partition of Poland) and finally, in the face of the Prussian-Polish Junkers who provide the military budget and more supplies of bayonets to safeguard the Polish annexation — in the face of all these factors, what can the Polish proletariat do? Any rebellion would be bloodily suppressed. But if no rebellion is attempted, nothing at all can be done, since armed rebellion is the only way that Polish independence can be achieved. Certainly none of these states can be expected to voluntarily relinquish its provinces, which they have now ruled for a long hundred years. But under existing conditions, any rebellion of the proletariat would be crushed — there could be no other result. Perhaps then, the international proletariat would help? It, however, is in less of a position to act than the Polish proletariat; at most it can declare its sympathy. But suppose the entire campaign in support of the restoration of Poland limits itself to peaceful demonstrations? Well, then, in that case, of course, the partition states can continue to rule over Poland in all tranquility. So if the international proletariat makes the restoration of Poland its political demand — as the resolution requires — it will have done no more than utter a pious wish. If one "demands" something, one must do something to achieve that demand. If one can do nothing, the empty "demand" may well make the air tremble, but it will certainly not shake the states ruling over Poland.

The adoption of the social-patriotic resolution by the International Congress could, however, have further-reaching implications than might be obvious at first glance. First and foremost, it would go in the face of the decisions of the previous Congress, especially those on the

Dutch resolution about the military strike. In the light of their essentially parallel arguments and identical content, the adoption of the social-patriotic resolution would let the Dutch one in, once again, through the back door. How the Polish delegates, who voted against the Nieuwenhuis resolution, have now managed to propose what is essentially an identical resolution on that question, we shall not discuss for the moment. In any case, it would be worse if the entire Congress were to fall into such a contradiction with itself.

Secondly, this resolution, if adopted, would have an import for the Polish movement that the delegates to the up-coming Congress have surely not even dared to imagine. For the past three years—as I discussed at length in my essay in *Neue Zeit*, numbers 32 and 33—the attempt has been made to impose on Polish Socialists a program for the restoration of Poland; the intention is to separate them from their German, Austrian, and Russian comrades by uniting them in a Polish party organized along nationalist lines. Given the utopianism of this program and the contradiction between it and any effective political struggle, the promoters of this tendency have not yet been able to provide any argument for the planned nationalist turn strong enough to withstand criticism. And so they have, up to now, been rather circumspect about any open disclosure of this tendency. While the Polish parties in the Prussian and Austrian sectors have not yet included the point concerning the restoration of Poland in their program, the advance guard of the nationalist tendency, the London group calling itself Zwiazek Zagraniczny Socjalistow Polskich, has been working hard to arouse sympathy in the Western European parties, especially through the paper Bulletin Officiel and in countless articles: Socialist Poland, The Poland of the Workers, Democratic Poland, The Independent Republic of Poland, etc. These and similar slogans have been praised in Polish, German, and French by turns. The way is being prepared for the adoption of a Polish class state into the program. The crowning touch to this entire process is to be the London congress, and through the adoption of the resolution the nationalist position is to be smuggled in under the international banner. The international proletariat is presumably supposed to run up the red flag, with its own hand, on the nationalist edifice, and so consecrate it as a temple of internationalism. Moreover, the sanction by the representatives of the international proletariat is meant to provide an effective cover for social patriotism's total lack of any scientific basis and raise it to the level of a dogma, where it will be immune to criticism of any sort. Finally, this sanction is meant to encourage the Polish parties to adopt, once and for all, the nationalist program and organize themselves along national lines.

The adoption of the social-patriotic resolution would establish an important precedent for the socialist movement in other countries. What is good for one is purchased cheaply by the other. If the national liberation of Poland is elevated to a political goal of the international proletariat, why not also the liberation of Czechoslovakia, Ireland, and Alsace-Lorraine? All these objectives are equally utopian, and are no less justified than the liberation of Poland. The liberation of Alsace-Lorraine, in particular, would be far more important for the international proletariat, and far more likely at that; behind Alsace-Lorraine stand four million French bayonets, and in questions of bourgeois annexations, bayonets carry more weight than moralistic demonstrations. And if the Poles in the three partitioned sectors organize themselves along nationalist lines for the liberation of Poland, why should the other nationalities in Austria not also do the same, why should the Alsatians not organize themselves with the French? In a word, the door would be opened wide to national struggles and nationalist organizations. Rather than a working class organized in accordance with political realities, there would be an espousal of organization along national lines, which often goes astray from the start. Instead of political programs, nationalist programs would be drawn up. Instead of a coherent political struggle of the proletariat in every country, its disintegration through a series of fruitless national struggles would be virtually assured.

Here lies the greatest significance of the social-patriotic resolution, if adopted. We stated at the beginning that the greatest forward step that the proletariat has made since the days of the International is its development from a number of small sectarian groups into a major party capable of handling its own affairs. But to what does the proletariat owe this progress? Solely to its ability to understand the primacy of the political struggle in its activity. The old International gave way to parties organized in each country in conformity with the political conditions peculiar to that country, without, on that account, having regard for the nationality of the workers. Only, political struggle in line with this principle makes the working class strong and powerful. But the social-patriotic resolution pursues a course in diametric opposition to this principle. Its adoption by the Congress would repudiate thirty-two years of the proletariat's accumulated experience and theoretical education.

The social-patriotic resolution was formulated quite cleverly: behind the protest against the tsardom lay the protest against annexation — after all, the demand for Poland's independence is raised against Austria and Prussia as well as against Russia: it sanctions nationalist tendencies with international interests; it tries to obtain backing for a practical program on the basis of a general moral demonstration. But the weakness of its argument is even greater than the artfulness of its formulation: a few commonplaces about the perniciousness of annexations and some nonsense about Poland's importance for the tsardom — this and no more — is all that this resolution is capable of offering.

Reform or Revolution

Introduction

At first view the title of this work may be found surprising. Can the Social-Democracy be against reforms? Can we contrapose the social revolution, the transformation of the existing order, our final goal, to social reforms? Certainly not. The daily struggle for reforms, for the amelioration of the condition of the workers within the framework of the existing social order, and for democratic institutions, offers to the Social-Democracy an indissoluble tie. The struggle for reforms is its means; the social revolution, its aim.

It is in Eduard Bernstein's theory, presented in his articles on "Problems of Socialism", *Neue Zeit* of 1897-98, and in his book *Die Voraussetzungen des Socialismus und die Aufgaben der Sozialdemokratie* (English title; "*Evolutionay Socialism*") that we find, for the first time, the opposition of the two factors of the labour movement. His theory tends to counsel us to renounce the social transformation, the final goal of Social-Democracy and, inversely, to make of social reforms, the means of the class struggle, its aim. Bernstein himself has very clearly and characteristically formulated this viewpoint when he wrote: "The Final goal, no matter what it is, is nothing; the movement is everything."

But since the final goal of socialism constitutes the only decisive factor distinguishing the Social-Democratic movement from bourgeois democracy and from bourgeois radicalism, the only factor transforming the entire labour movement from a vain effort to repair the capitalist order into a class struggle against this order, for the suppression of this order—the question: "Reform or Revolution?" as it is posed by Bernstein, equals for the Social-Democracy the question: "To be or not to be?" In the controversy with Bernstein and his followers, everybody in the Party ought to understand clearly it is not a question of this or that method of struggle, or the use of this or that set of tactics, but of the very existence of the Social-Democratic movement.

Upon a casual consideration of Bernstein's theory, this may appear like an exaggeration. Does he not continually mention the Social-Democracy and its aims? Does he not repeat again and again, in very explicit language, that he too strives toward the final goal of socialism, but in another way? Does he not stress particularly that he fully approves of the present practice of the Social-Democracy?

That is all true, to be sure. It is also true that every new movement, when it first elaborates its theory and policy, begins by finding support in the preceding movement, though it may be in direct contradiction with the latter. It begins by suiting itself to the forms found at hand and by speaking the language spoken hereto. In time the new grain breaks through the old husk. The new movement finds its forms and its own language.

To expect an opposition against scientific socialism at its very beginning, to express itself clearly, fully and to the last consequence on the subject of its real content: to expect it to deny openly and bluntly the theoretic basis of the Social-Democracy—would amount to underrating the power of scientific socialism. Today he who wants to pass as a socialist, and at the same time declare war on Marxian doctrine, the most stupendous product of the human mind in the century, must begin with involuntary esteem for Marx. He must begin by acknowledging himself to be his disciple, by seeking in Marx's own teachings the points of support for an attack on the latter, while he represents this attack as a further development of Marxian doctrine. On this account, we must, unconcerned by its outer forms, pick out the sheathed kernel of Bernstein's theory. This is a matter of urgent necessity for the broad layers of the industrial proletariat in our Party.

No coarser insult, no baser aspersion, can be thrown against the workers than the remarks: "Theocratic controversies are only for academicians." Some time ago Lassalle said: "Only when science and the workers, these opposite poles of society, become one, will they crush in their arms of steel all obstacles to culture." The entire strength of the modern labour movement rests on theoretic knowledge.

But doubly important is this knowledge for the workers in the present case, because it is precisely they and their influence in the movement that are in the balance here. It is their skin that is being brought to market. The opportunist theory in the Party, the theory formulated by Bernstein, is nothing else than an unconscious attempt to assure predominance to the petty-bourgeois elements that have entered our Party, to change the policy and aims of our Party in their direction. The question of reform or revolution, of the final goal and the movement, is basically, in another form, but the question of the petty-bourgeois or proletarian character of the labour movement.

It is, therefore, in the interest of the proletarian mass of the Party to become acquainted, actively and in detail, with the present theoretic knowledge remains the privilege of a handful of "academicians" in the Party, the latter will face the danger of going astray. Only when the great mass of workers take the keen and dependable weapons of scientific socialism in their own hands, will all the petty-bourgeois inclinations, all the opportunistic currents, come to naught. The movement will then find itself on sure and firm ground. "Quantity will do it".

Rosa Luxemburg

Chapter I. The Opportunist Method

If it is true that theories are only the images of the phenomena of the exterior world in the human consciousness, it must be added, concerning Eduard Bernstein's system, that theories are sometimes inverted images. Think of a theory of instituting socialism by means of social reforms in the face of the complete stagnation of the reform movement in Germany. Think of a theory of trade union control. Consider the theory of winning a majority in Parliament, after the revision of the constitution of Saxony and in view of the most recent attempts against universal suffrage. However, the pivotal point of Bernstein's system is not located in his conception of the practical tasks of the Social-Democracy. It is found in his stand on the course of the objective development of capitalist society, which, in turn is closely bound to his conception of the practical tasks of the Social-Democracy.

According to Bernstein, a general decline of capitalism seems to be increasingly improbable because, on the one hand, capitalism shows a greater capacity of adaptation, and, on the other hand, capitalist production becomes more and more varied.

The capacity of capitalism to adapt itself, says Bernstein, is manifested first in the disappearance of general crises, resulting from the development of the credit system, employers' organisations, wider means of communication and informational services. It shows itself secondly, in the tenacity of the middle classes, which hails from the growing differentiation of the branches of production and the elevation of vast layers of the proletariat to the level of the middle class. It is furthermore proved, argues Bernstein, by the amelioration of the economic and political situation of the proletariat as a result of its trade union activity.

From this theoretic stand is derived the following general conclusion about the practical work of the Social-Democracy. The latter must not direct its daily activity toward the conquest of political power, but toward the betterment of the condition of the working class, within the existing order. It must not expect to institute socialism as a result of a political and social crisis, but should build socialism by means of the progressive extension of social control and the gradual application of the principle of co-operation.

Bernstein himself sees nothing new in his theories. On the contrary, he believes them to be in agreement with certain declarations of Marx and Engels. Nevertheless, it seems to us that it is difficult to deny that they are in formal contradiction with the conceptions of scientific socialism.

If Bernstein's revisionism merely consisted in affirming that the march of capitalist development is slower than was thought before, he would merely be presenting an argument for adjourning the conquest of power by the proletariat, on which everybody agreed up to now. Its only consequence would be a slowing up of the pace of the struggle.

But that is not the case. What Bernstein questions is not the rapidity of the development of capitalist society, but the march of the development itself and, consequently, the very possibility of a change to socialism.

Socialist theory up to now declared that the point of departure for a transformation to socialism would be a general and catastrophic crisis. We must distinguish in this outlook two things: the fundamental idea and its exterior form.

The fundamental idea consists of the affirmation that capitalism, as a result of its own inner contradictions, moves toward a point when it will be unbalanced, when it will simply become impossible. There were good reasons for conceiving that juncture in the form of a catastrophic general commercial crisis. But that is of secondary importance when the fundamental idea is considered.

The scientific basis of socialism rests, as is well known, on three principal results of capitalist development. First, on the growing anarchy of capitalist economy, leading inevitably to its ruin. Second, on the progressive socialisation of the process of production, which creates the germs of the future social order. And third, on the increased organisation and consciousness of the proletarian class, which constitutes the active factor in the coming revolution.

Bernstein pulls away from the first of the three fundamental supports of scientific socialism. He says that capitalist development does not lead to a general economic collapse.

He does not merely reject a certain form of the collapse. He rejects the very possibility of collapse. He says textually: "One could claim that by collapse of the present society is meant something else than a general commercial crisis, worse than all others, that is a complete collapse of the capitalist system brought about as a result of its own contradictions." And to this he replies: "With the growing development of society a complete and almost general collapse of the present system of production becomes more and more improbable, because capitalist development increases on the one hand the capacity of adaptation and, on the other—that is at the same time, the differentiation of industry."

But then the question arises: Why and how, in that case, can we attain the final goal? According to scientific socialism, the historic necessity of the socialist revolution manifests itself above all in the growing anarchy of capitalism, which drives the system into an impasse. But if one admits with Bernstein that capitalist development does not move in the direction of its own ruin, then socialism ceases to be objectively necessary. There remain the other two mainstays of the scientific explanation of socialism, which are also said to be consequences of capitalism itself: the socialisation of the process of production and the growing consciousness of the proletariat. It is these two matters that Bernstein has in mind when he says: "The suppression of the theory of collapse does not in any way deprive socialist doctrine of the power of persuasion. For, examined closely, what are all factors enumerated by us that make for the suppression or the modification of the former crises? Nothing else, in fact, than the conditions, or even in party the germs, of the socialisation of production and exchange."

Very little reflection is needed to understand that here too we face a false conclusion. Where lies the importance of all the phenomena that are said by Bernstein to be the means of capitalist adaptation — cartels, the credit system, the development of means of communication, the amelioration of the situation of the working class, etc.? Obviously, in that they suppress or, at least, attenuate the internal contradictions of capitalist economy, and stop the development or the aggravation of these contradictions. Thus the suppression of crises can only mean the suppression of the antagonism between production and exchange on the capitalist base. The amelioration of the situation of the working class, or the penetration of certain fractions of the class into middle layers, can only mean the attenuation of the antagonism between Capital and Labour. But if the mention factors suppress the capitalist contradictions and consequently save the system from ruin, if they enable capitalism to maintain itself — and that is why Bernstein calls them "means of adaptation" — how can cartels, the credit system, trade unions, etc., be at the same time "the conditions and even, in part, the germs" of socialism? Obviously only in the sense that they express most clearly the social character of production.

But by presenting it in its capitalist form, the same factors render superfluous, inversely, in the same measure, the transformation of this socialised production into socialist production. That is why they can be the germs or conditions of a socialist order only in a theoretic sense and not in an historic sense. They are phenomena which, in the light of our conception of socialism, we know to be related to socialism but which, in fact, not only do not lead to a socialist revolution but render it, on the contrary, superfluous.

There remains one force making for socialism — the class consciousness of the proletariat. But it, too, is in the given case no the simple intellectual reflection of the growing contradictions of capitalism and its approaching decline. It is now no more than an ideal whose force of persuasion rests only on the perfection attributed to it.

We have here, in brief, the explanation of the socialist programme by means of "pure reason." We have here, to use simpler language, an idealist explanation of socialism. The objective necessity of socialism, the explanation of socialism as the result of the material development of society, falls to the ground.

Revisionist theory thus places itself in a dilemma. Either the socialist transformation is, as was admitted up to now, the consequence of the internal contradictions of capitalism, and with the growth of capitalism will develop its inner contradictions, resulting inevitably, at some point, in its collapse, (in that case the "means of adaptation" are ineffective and the theory of collapse is correct); or the "means of adaptation" will really stop the collapse of the capitalist system and thereby enable capitalism to maintain itself by suppressing its own contradictions. In that case socialism ceases to be an historic necessity. It then becomes anything you want to call it, but it is no longer the result of the material development of society.

The dilemma leads to another. Either revisionism is correct in its position on the course of capitalist development, and therefore the socialist transformation of society is only a utopia, or socialism is not a utopia, and the theory of "means of adaptation" is false. There is the question in a nutshell.

Chapter II. The Adaptation of Capital

According to Bernstein, the credit system, the perfected means of communication and the new capitalist combines are the important factors that forward the adaptation of capitalist economy.

Credit has diverse applications in capitalism. Its two most important functions are to extend production and to facilitate exchange. When the inner tendency of capitalist production to extend boundlessly strikes against the restricted dimensions of private property, credit appears as a means of surmounting these limits in a particular capitalist manner. Credit, through shareholding, combines in one magnitude of capital a large number of individual capitals. It makes available to each capitalist the use of other capitalists' money —

form of industrial credit. As commercial credit it accelerates the exchange of commodities and therefore the return of capital into production, and thus aids the entire cycle of the process of production. The manner in which these two principle functions of credit influence the formation of crises is quite obvious. If it is true that crises appear as a result of the contradiction existing between the capacity of extension, the tendency of production to increase, and the restricted consumption capacity of the market, credit is precisely, in view of what was stated above, the specific means that makes this contradiction break out as often as possible. To begin with, it increases disproportionately the capacity of the extension of production and thus constitutes an inner motive force that is constantly pushing production to exceed the limits of the market. But credit strikes from two sides. After having (as a factor of the process of production) provoked overproduction, credit (as a factor of exchange) destroys, during the crisis, the very productive forces it itself created. At the first symptom of the crisis, credit melts away. It abandons exchange where it would still be found indispensable, and appearing instead, ineffective and useless, there where some exchange still continues, it reduces to a minimum the consumption capacity of the market.

Besides having these two principal results, credit also influences the formation of crises in the following ways. It constitutes the technical means of making available to an entrepreneur the capital of other owners. It stimulates at the same time the bold and unscrupulous utilisation of the property of others. That is, it leads to speculation. Credit not only aggravates the crisis in its capacity as a dissembled means of exchange, it also helps to bring and extend the crisis by transforming all exchange into an extremely complex and artificial mechanism that, having a minimum of metallic money as a real base, is easily disarranged at the slightest occasion.

We see that credit, instead of being an instrument for the suppression or the attenuation of crises, is on the contrary a particularly mighty instrument for the formation of crises. It cannot be anything else. Credit eliminates the remaining rigidity of capitalist relationships. It introduces everywhere the greatest elasticity possible. It renders all capitalist forces extensible, relative and mutually sensitive to the highest degree. Doing this, it facilitates and aggravates crises, which are nothing more or less than the periodic collisions of the contradictory forces of capitalist economy.

That leads us to another question. Why does credit generally have the appearance of a "means of adaptation" of capitalism? No matter what the relation or form in which this "adaptation" is represented by certain people, it can obviously consist only of the power to suppress one of the several antagonistic relations of capitalist economy, that is, of the power to suppress or weaken one of these contradictions, and allow liberty of movement, at one point or another, to the other fettered productive forces. In fact, it is precisely credit that aggravates these contradictions to the highest degree. It aggravates the antagonism between the mode of production and the mode of exchange by stretching production to the limit and at the same time paralysing exchange at the smallest pretext. It aggravates the antagonism between the mode of production and the mode of appropriation by separating production from ownership, that is, by transforming the capital employed in production into "social" capital and at the same time transforming a part of the profit, in the form of interest on capital, into a simple title of ownership. It aggravates the antagonism existing between the property relations (ownership) and the relations of production by putting into a small number of hands immense productive forces and expropriating large numbers of small capitalists. Lastly, it aggravates the antagonism existing between social character of production and private capitalist ownership by rendering necessary the intervention of the State in production.

In short, credit reproduces all the fundamental antagonisms of the capitalist world. It accentuates them. It precipitates their development and thus pushes the capitalist world forward to its own destruction. The prime act of capitalist adaptation, as far as credit is concerned, should really consist in breaking and suppressing credit. In fact, credit is far from being a means of capitalist adaptation. It is, on the contrary, a means of destruction of the most extreme revolutionary significance. Has not this revolutionary character of credit actually inspired plans of "socialist" reform? As such, it has had some distinguished proponents, some of whom (Isaac Pereira in France), were, as Marx put it, half prophets, half rogues.

Just as fragile is the second "means of adaptation": employers' organisations. According to Bernstein, such organisations will put an end to anarchy of production and do away with crises through their regulation of production. The multiple repercussions of the development of cartels and trusts have not been considered too carefully up to now. But they predict a problem that can only be solved with the aid of Marxist theory.

One thing is certain. We could speak of a damming up of capitalist anarchy through the agency of capitalist combines only in the measure that cartels, trusts, etc., become, even approximately, the dominant form of production. But such a possibility is excluded by the very nature of cartles. The final economic aim and result of combines is the following. Through the suppression of competition in a given branch of production, the distribution of the mass of profit realised on the market is influenced in such a manner that there is an increase of the share going to this branch of industry. Such organisation of the field can increase the rate of profit in one branch of industry at the expense of another. That is precisely why it cannot be generalised, for when it is extended to all important branches of industry, this tendency suppresses its own influence.

Furthermore, within the limits of their practical application the result of combines is the very opposite of suppression of industrial anarchy. Cartels ordinarily succeed in obtaining an increase of profit, in the home market, by producing at a lower rate of profit for the foreign market, thus utilising the supplementary portions of capital which they cannot utilise for domestic needs. That is to say, they sell abroad cheaper than at home. The result is the sharpening of competition abroad — the very opposite of what certain people want to find. That is well demonstrated by the history of the world sugar industry.

Generally speaking, combines treated as a manifestation of the capitalist mode of production, can only be considered a definite phase of capitalist development. Cartels are fundamentally nothing else than a means resorted to by the capitalist mode of production for the purpose of holding back the fatal fall of the rate of profit in certain branches of production. What method do cartels employ for this end? That of keeping inactive a part of the accumulated capital. That is, they use the same method which in another form is employed in crises. The remedy and the illness resemble each other like two drops of water. Indeed the first can be considered the lesser evil only up to a certain point. When the outlets of disposal begin to shrink, and the world market has been extended to its limit and has become exhausted through the competition of the capitalist countries — and sooner or later that is bound to come — then the forced partial idleness of capital will reach such dimensions that the remedy will become transformed into a malady, and capital, already pretty much "socialised" through regulation, will tend to revert again to the form of individual capital. In the face of the increased difficulties of finding markets, each individual portion of capital will prefer to take its chances alone. At that time, the large regulating organisations will burst like soap bubbles and give way to aggravated competition.

In a general way, cartels, just like credit, appear therefore as a determined phase of capitalist development, which in the last analysis aggravates the anarchy of the capitalist world and expresses and ripens its internal contradictions. Cartels aggravate the antagonism existing between the mode of production and exchange by sharpening the struggle between the producer and consumer, as is the case especially in the United States. They aggravate, furthermore, the antagonism existing between the mode of production and the mode of appropriation by opposing, in the most brutal fashion, to the working class the superior force of organised capital, and thus increasing the antagonism between Capital and Labour.

Finally, capitalist combinations aggravate the contradiction existing between the international character of capitalist world economy and the national character of the State—insofar as they are always accompanied by a general tariff war, which sharpens the differences among the capitalist States. We must add to this the decidedly revolutionary influence exercised by cartels on the concentration of production, technical progress, etc.

In other words, when evaluated from the angle of their final effect on capitalist economy, cartels and trusts fail as "means of adaptation." They fail to attenuate the contradictions of capitalism. On the contrary, they appear to be an instrument of greater anarchy. They encourage the further development of the internal contradictions of capitalism. They accelerate the coming of a general decline of capitalism.

But if the credit system, cartels, and the rest do not suppress the anarchy of capitalism, why have we not had a major commercial crisis for two decades, since 1873? Is this not a sign that, contrary to Marx's analysis the capitalist mode of production has adapted itself—at least, in a general way—to the needs of society? Hardly had Bernstein rejected, in 1898, Marx's theory of crises, when a profound general crisis broke out in 1900, while seven years later, a new crisis beginning in the United States, hit the world market. Facts proved the theory of "adaptation" to be false. They showed at the same time that the people who abandoned Marx's theory of crisis only because no crisis occurred within a certain space of time merely confused the essence of this theory with one of its secondary exterior aspects—the ten-year cycle. The description of the cycle of modern capitalist industry as a ten-year period was to Marx and Engels, in 1860 and 1870, only a simple statement of facts. It was not based on a natural law but on a series of given historic circumstances that were connected with the rapidly spreading activity of young capitalism.

The crisis of 1825 was in effect, the result of extensive investment of capital in the construction of roads, canals, gas works, which took place during the preceding decade, particularly in England, where the crisis broke out. The following crisis of 1836-1839 was similarly the result of heavy investments in the construction of means of transportation. The crisis of 1847 was provoked by the feverish building of railroads in England (from 1844 to 1847, in three years, the British Parliament gave railway concessions to the value of 15 billion dollars). In each of the three mentioned cases, a crisis came after new bases for capitalist development were established. In 1857, the same result was brought by the abrupt opening of new markets for European industry in America and Australia, after the discovery of the gold mines, and the extensive construction of railway lines, especially in France, where the example of England was then closely imitated. (From 1852 to 1856, new railway lines to the value of 1,250 million francs were built in France alone). And finally we have the great crisis of 1873—a direct consequence of the firm boom of large industry in Germany and Austria, which followed the political events of 1866 and 1871.

So that up to now, the sudden extension of the domain of capitalist economy, and not its shrinking, was each time the cause of the commercial crisis. That the international crisis repeated themselves precisely every ten years was a purely exterior fact, a matter of chance. The Marxist formula for crises as presented by Engels in Anti-Dühring and by Marx in the first and third volumes of Capital, applies to all crises only in the measure that it uncovers their international mechanism and their general basic causes.

Crises may repeat themselves every five or ten years, or even every eight or twenty years. But what proves best the falseness of Bernstein's theory is that it is in the countries having the greatest development of the famous "means of adaptation"—credit, perfected communications and trusts—that the last crisis (1907-1908) was most violent.

The belief that capitalist production could "adapt" itself to exchange presupposes one of two things: either the world market can spread unlimitedly, or on the contrary the development of the productive forces is so fettered that it cannot pass beyond the bounds of the market. The first hypothesis constitutes a material impossibility. The second is rendered just as impossible by the constant technical progress that daily creates new productive forces in all branches.

There remains still another phenomenon which, says Bernstein, contradicts the course of capitalist development as it is indicated above. In the "steadfast phalanx" of middle-size enterprises, Bernstein sees a sign that the development of large industry does not move in a revolutionary direction, and is not as effective from the angle of the concentration of industry as was expected by the "theory" of collapse. He is here, however, the victim of his own lack of understanding. For to see the progressive disappearance of large industry is to misunderstand sadly the nature of this process.

According to Marxist theory, small capitalists play in the general course of capitalist development the role of pioneers of technical change. They possess that role in a double sense. They initiate new methods of production in well-established branches of industry; they are instrumental in the creation of new branches of production not yet exploited by the big capitalist. It is false to imagine that the history of the middle-size capitalist establishments proceeds rectilinearly in the direction of their progressive disappearance. The course of this development is on the contrary purely dialectical and moves constantly among contradictions. The middle capitalist layers find themselves, just like the workers, under the influence of two antagonistic tendencies, one ascendant, the other descendant. In this case, the descendent tendency is the continued rise of the scale of production, which overflows periodically the dimensions of the average size parcels of capital and removes them repeatedly from the terrain of world competition.

The ascendant tendency is, first, the periodic depreciation of the existing capital, which lowers again, for a certain time, the scale of production in proportion to the value of the necessary minimum amount of capital. It is represented, besides, by the penetration of capitalist production into new spheres. The struggle of the average size enterprise against big Capital cannot be considered a regularly proceeding battle in which the troops of the weaker party continue to melt away directly and quantitatively. It should be rather regarded as a periodic mowing down of the small enterprises, which rapidly grow up again, only to be mowed down once more by large industry. The two tendencies play ball with the middle capitalist layers. The descending tendency must win in the end.

The very opposite is true about the development of the working class. The victory of the descending tendency must not necessarily show itself in an absolute numerical diminution of the middle-size enterprises. It must show itself, first in the progressive increase of the minimum amount of capital necessary for the functioning of the enterprises in the old branches of production; second in the constant diminution of the interval of time during which the small capitalists conserve the opportunity to exploit the new branches of production. The result as far as the small capitalist is concerned, is a progressively shorter duration of his stay in the new industry and a progressively more rapid change in the methods of production as a field for investment. For the average capitalist strata, taken as a whole, there is a process of more and more rapid social assimilation and dissimilation.

Bernstein knows this perfectly well. He himself comments on this. But what he seems to forget is that this very thing is the law of the movement of the average capitalist enterprise. If one admits that small capitalists are pioneers of technical progress, and if it true that the latter is the vital pulse of the capitalist economy, then it is manifest that small capitalists are an integral part of capitalist development, which can only disappear together with capitalist development. The progressive disappearance of the middle-size enterprise—in the absolute sense considered by Bernstein—means not, as he things, the revolutionary course of capitalist development, but precisely the contrary, the cessation, the slowing up of development. "The rate of profit, that is to say, the relative increase of capital," said Marx, "is important first of all for new investors of capital, grouping themselves independently. And as soon as the formation of capital falls exclusively into a handful of big capitalists, the revivifying fire of production is extinguished. It dies away."

Chapter III.   The Realisation of Socialism through Social Reforms

Bernstein rejects the "theory of collapse" as an historic road toward socialism. Now what is the way to a socialist society that is proposed by his "theory of adaptation to capitalism"? Bernstein answers this question only by allusion. Konrad Schmidt, however, attempts to deal with this detail in the manner of Bernstein. According to him, "the trade union struggle for hours and wages and the political struggle for reforms will lead to a progressively more extensive control over the conditions of production," and "as the rights of the capitalist proprietor will be diminished through legislation, he will be reduced in time to the role of a simple administrator." "The capitalist will see his property lose more and more value to himself" till finally "the direction and administration of exploitation will be taken from him entirely" and "collective exploitation" instituted.

Therefore trade unions, social reforms and, adds Bernstein, the political democratisation of the State are the means of the progressive realisation of socialism.

But the fact is that the principal function of trade unions (and this was best explained by Bernstein himself in *Neue Zeit* in 1891) consists in providing the workers with a means of realising the capitalist law of wages, that is to say, the sale of their labour power at current market prices. Trade unions enable the proletariat to utilise at each instant, the conjuncture of the market. But these conjunctures — (1) the labour demand determined by the state of production, (2) the labour supply created by the proletarianisation of the middle strata of society and the natural reproduction of the working classes, and (3) the momentary degree of productivity of labour — these remain outside of the sphere of influence of the trade unions. Trade unions cannot suppress the law of wages. Under the most favourable circumstances, the best they can do is to impose on capitalist exploitation the "normal" limit of the moment. They have not, however, the power to suppress exploitation itself, not even gradually.

Schmidt, it is true, sees the present trade union movement in a "feeble initial stage." He hopes that "in the future" the "trade union movement will exercise a progressively increased influence over the regulation of production." But by the regulation of production we can only understand two things: intervention in the technical domain of the process of production and fixing the scale of production itself. What is the nature of the influence exercised by trade unions in these two departments? It is clear that in the technique of production, the interest of the capitalist agrees, up to a certain point, with the progress and development of capitalist economy. It is his own interest that pushes him to make technical improvements. But the isolated worker finds himself in a decidedly different position. Each technical transformation contradicts his interests. It aggravates his helpless situation by depreciating the value of his labour power and rendering his work more intense, more monotonous and more difficult.

Insofar as trade unions can intervene in the technical department of production, they can only oppose technical innovation. But here they do not act in the interest of the entire working class and its emancipation, which accords rather with technical progress and, therefore, with the interest of the isolated capitalist. They act here in a reactionary direction. And in fact, we find efforts on the part of workers to intervene in the technical part of production not in the future, where Schmidt looks for it, but in the past of the trade union movement. Such efforts characterised the old phase of English trade unionism (up to 1860), when the British organisations were still tied to medieval "corporative" vestiges and found inspiration in the outworn principle of "a fair day's wage for a fair day's labour," as expressed by Webb in his *History of Trade Unionism*.

On the other hand, the effort of the labour unions to fix the scale of production and the prices of commodities is a recent phenomenon. Only recently have we witnessed such attempts—and again in England. In their nature and tendencies, these efforts resemble those dealt with above. What does the active participation of trade unions in fixing the scale and cost of production amount to? It amounts to a cartel of the workers and entrepreneurs in a common stand against the consumer and especially rival entrepreneurs. In no way is the effect of this any different from that of ordinary employers' associations. Basically we no longer have here a struggle between Labour and Capital, but the solidarity of Capital and Labour against the total consumers. Considered for its social worth, it is seen to be a reactionary move that cannot be a stage in the struggle for the emancipation of the proletariat, because it connotes the very opposite of the class struggle. Considered from the angle of practical application, it is found to be a utopia which, as shown by a rapid examination, cannot be extended to the large branches of industry producing for the world market.

So that the scope of trade unions is limited essentially to a struggle for an increase of wages and the reduction of labour time, that is to say, to efforts at regulating capitalist exploitation as they are made necessary by the momentary situation of the old world market. But labour unions can in no way influence the process of production itself. Moreover, trade union development moves—contrary to what is asserted by Konrad Schmidt—in the direction of a complete detachment of the labour market from any immediate relation to the rest of the market.

That is shown by the fact that even attempts to relate labour contracts to the general situation of production by means of a system of sliding wage scales have been outmoded with historic development. The British labour unions are moving farther and farther away from such efforts.

Even within the effective boundaries of its activity the trade union movement cannot spread in the unlimited way claimed for it by the theory of adaptation. On the contrary, if we examine the large factors of social development, we see that we are not moving toward an epoch marked by a victorious development of trade unions, but rather toward a time when the hardships of labour unions will increase. Once industrial development has attained its highest possible pint and capitalism has entered its descending phase on the world market, the trade union struggle will become doubly difficult. In the first place, the objective conjuncture of the market will be less favourable to the sellers of labour power, because the demand for labour power will increase at a slower rate and labour supply more rapidly than at present. In the second place, the capitalists themselves, in order to make up for losses suffered on the world market, will make even greater efforts than at present to reduce the part of the total product going to the workers (in the form of wages). The reduction of wages is, as pointed out by Marx, one of the principal means of retarding the fall of profit. The situation in England already offers us a picture of the beginning of the second stage of trade union development. Trade union action is reduced of necessity to the simple defence of already realised gains, and even that is becoming more and more difficult. Such is the general trend of things in our society. The counterpart of this tendency should be the development of the political side of the class struggle.

Konrad Schmidt commits the same error of historic perspective when he deals with social reforms. He expects that social reforms, like trade union organisations, will "dictate to the capitalists the only conditions under which they will be able to employ labour power."

Seeing reform in this light, Bernstein calls labour legislation a piece of "social control," and as such, a piece of socialism. Similarly, Konrad Schmidt always uses the term "social control" when he refers to labour protection laws. Once he has thus happily transformed the State into society, he confidently adds: "That is to say, the rising working class." As a result of this trick of substitution, the innocent labour laws enacted by the German Federal Council are transformed into transitory socialist measures supposedly enacted by the German proletariat.

The mystification is obvious. We know that the present State is not "society" representing the "rising working class." It is itself the representative of capitalist society. It is a class state. Therefore its reform measures are not an application of "social control," that is, the control of society working freely in its own labour process. They are forms of control applied by the class organisation of Capital to the production of Capital. The so-called social reforms are enacted in the interests of Capital. Yes, Bernstein and Konrad Schmidt see at present only "feeble beginnings" of this control. They hope to see a long succession of reforms in the future, all favouring the working class. But here they commit a mistake similar to their belief in the unlimited development of the trade union movement.

A basic condition for the theory of the gradual realisation of socialism through social reforms is a certain objective development of capitalist property and of the State. Konrad Schmidt says that the capitalist proprietor tends to lose his special rights with historic development, and is reduced to the role of a simple administrator. He thinks that the expropriation of the means of production cannot possibly be effected as a single historic act. He therefore resorts to the theory of expropriation by stages. With this in mind, he divides the right to property into (1) the right of "sovereignty" (ownership) — which he attributes to a thing called "society" and which he wants to extend — and (2) its opposite, the simple right of use, held by the capitalist, but which is supposedly being reduced in the hands of the capitalists to the mere administration of their enterprises.

This interpretation is either a simple play on words, and in that case the theory of gradual expropriation has no real basis, or it is a true picture of judicial development, in which case, as we shall see, the theory of gradual expropriation is entirely false.

The division of the right of property into several component rights, an arrangement serving Konrad Schmidt as a shelter wherein he may construct his theory of "expropriation by stages," characterised feudal society, founded on natural economy. In feudalism, the total product was shared among the social classes of the time on the basis of the personal relations existing between the feudal lord and his serfs or tenants. The decomposition of property into several partial rights reflected the manner of distribution of the social wealth of that period. With the passage to the production of commodities and the dissolution of all personal bonds among the participants in the process of production, the relation between men and things (that is to say, private property) became reciprocally stronger. Since the division is no longer made on the basis of personal relations but through exchange, the different rights to a share in the social wealth are no longer measured as fragments of property rights having a common interest. They are measured according to the values brought by each on the market.

The first change introduced into juridical relations with the advance of commodity production in the medieval city communes, was the development of absolute private property. The latter appeared in the very midst of the feudal juridical relations. This development has progressed at a rapid pace in capitalist production. The more the process of production is socialised, the more the process of distribution (division of wealth) rests on exchange. And the more private property becomes inviolable and closed, the more capitalist property becomes transformed from the right to the product of one's own labour to the simple right to appropriate somebody else's labour. As long as the capitalist himself manages his own factory, distribution is still, up to a certain point, tied to his personal participation in the process of production. But as the personal management on the part of the capitalist becomes superfluous—which is the case in the share-holding societies today—the property of capital, so far as its right to share in the distribution (division of wealth) is concerned, becomes separated from any personal relation with production. It now appears in its purest form. The capitalist right to property reaches its most complete development in capital held in the shape of shares and industrial credit.

So that Konrad Schmidt's historic schema, tracing the transformation of the capitalist "from a proprietor to a simple administrator," belies the real historic development. In historic reality, on the contrary, the capitalist tends to change from a proprietor and administrator to a simple proprietor. What happens here to Konrad Schmidt, happened to Goethe:

"What is, he sees as in a dream.

What no longer is, becomes for him reality."

Just as Schmidt's historic schema travels, economically, backwards from a modern share-holding society to an artisan's shop, so, juridically, he wishes to lead back the capitalist world into the old feudal shell of the Middle Ages.

Also from this point of view, "social control" appears in reality under a different aspect than seen by Konrad Schmidt. What functions today as "social control" – labour legislation, the control of industrial organisations through share holding, etc. – has absolutely nothing to do with his "supreme ownership." Far from being, as Schmidt believes, a reduction of capitalist ownership, his "social control," is, on the contrary, a protection of such ownership. Or, expressed from the economic viewpoint, it is not a threat to capitalist exploitation, but simply the regulation of exploitation. When Bernstein asks if there is more or less of socialism in a labour protective law, we can assure him that, in the best of labour protective laws, there is no more "socialism" than in a municipal ordinance regulating the cleaning of streets or the lighting of street lamps.

Chapter IV. Capitalism and the State

The second condition of the gradual realisation of socialism is according to Bernstein, the evolution of the State in society. It has become a commonplace to say that the present State is a class State. This, too, like referring to capitalist society, should not be understood in a rigorous absolute manner, but dialectically.

The State became capitalist with the political victory of the bourgeoisie. Capitalist development modifies essentially the nature of the State, widening its sphere of action, constantly imposing on it new functions (especially those affecting economic life), making more and more necessary its intervention and control in society. In this sense, capitalist development prepares little by little the future fusion of the State to society. It prepares, so to say, the return of the function of the state to society. Following this line of thought, one can speak of an evolution of the capitalist State into society, and it is undoubtedly what Marx had in mind when he referred to labour legislation as the first conscious intervention of "society" in the vital social process, a phrase upon which Bernstein leans heavily.

But on the other hand the same capitalist development realises another transformation in the nature of the State. The present State is, first of all, an organisation of the ruling class. It assumes functions favouring social developments specifically because, and in the measure that, these interests and social developments coincide, in a general fashion, with the interests of the dominant class. Labour legislation is enacted as much in the immediate interest of the capitalist class as in the interest of society in general. But this harmony endures only up to a certain point of capitalist development. When capitalist development has reached a certain level, the interests of the bourgeoisie, as a class, and the needs of economic progress begin to clash even in the capitalist sense. We believe that this phase has already begun. It shows itself in two extremely important phenomena of contemporary social life: on the one hand, the policy of tariff barriers, and on the other, militarism. These two phenomena have played an indispensable, and in that sense a progressive and revolutionary role in the history of capitalism. Without tariff protection the development of large industry would have been impossible in several countries. But now the situation is different.

At present, protection does not serve so much to develop young industry as to maintain artificially certain aged forms of production.

From the angle of capitalist development, that is, from the point of view of world economy, it matters little whether Germany exports more merchandise into England or England exports more merchandise into Germany. From the viewpoint of this development it may be said that the blackamoor has done his work and it is time for him to go his way. Given the condition of reciprocal dependence in which the various branches of industry find themselves, a protectionist tariff on any commodity necessarily results in raising the cost of production of other commodities inside the country. It therefore impedes industrial development. But this is not so from the viewpoint of the interests of the capitalist class. While industry does not need tariff barriers for its development, the entrepreneurs need tariffs to protect their markets. This signifies that at present tariffs no longer serve as a means of protecting a developing capitalist section against a more advanced section. They are now the arm used by one national group of capitalists against another group. Furthermore, tariffs are no longer necessary as an instrument of protection for industry in its movement to create and conquer the home market. They are now indispensable means for the cartelisation of industry, that is, means used in the struggle of capitalist producers against consuming society in the aggregate. What brings out in an emphatic manner the specific character of contemporary customs policies is the fact that today not industry, but agriculture plays the predominant role in the making of tariffs. The policy of customs protection has become a tool for converting and expressing the feudal interests in capitalist form.

The same change has taken place in militarism. If we consider history as it was—not as it could have been or should have been—we must agree that war has been an indispensable feature of capitalist development. The United States, Germany, Italy, the Balkan States, Poland, all owe the condition or the rise of their capitalist development to wars, whether resulting in victory or defeat. As long as there were countries marked by internal political division or economic isolation which had to be destroyed, militarism played a revolutionary role, considered from the viewpoint of capitalism. But at present the situation is different. If world politics have become the stage of menacing conflicts, it is not so much a question of the opening of new countries to capitalism. It is a question of already existing European antagonisms, which, transported into other lands, have exploded there. The armed opponents we see today in Europe and on other continents do not range themselves as capitalist countries on one side and backward countries on the other. They are States pushed to war especially as a result of their similarly advanced capitalist development. In view of this, an explosion is certain to be fatal to this development, in the sense that it must provoke an extremely profound disturbance and transformation of economic life in all countries.

However, the matter appears entirely different when considered from the standpoint of the capitalist class. For the latter militarism has become indispensable. First, as a means of struggle for the defence of "national" interests in competition against other "national" groups. Second, as a method of placement for financial and industrial capital. Third, as an instrument of class domination over the labouring population inside the country. In themselves, these interests have nothing in common with the development of the capitalist mode of production. What demonstrates best the specific character of present day militarism is the fact that it develops generally in all countries as an effect, so to speak, of its own internal, mechanical, motive power, a phenomenon that was completely unknown several decades ago. We recognise this in the fatal character of the impending explosion which is inevitable in spite of the complete impending explosion which is inevitable in spite of the complete indecisiveness of the objectives and motives of the conflict. From a motor of capitalist development militarism has changed into a capitalist malady.

In the clash between capitalist development and the interest of the dominant class, the State takes a position alongside of the latter. Its policy, like that of the bourgeoisie, comes into conflict with social development. It thus loses more and more of its character as a representative of the whole of society and is transformed, at the same rate into a pure class state. Or, to speak more exactly, these two qualities distinguish themselves more from each other and find themselves in a contradictory relation in the very nature of the State. This contradiction becomes progressively sharper. For on one hand, we have the growth of the functions of a general interest on the part of the State, its intervention in social life, its "control" over society. But on the other hand, its class character obliges the State to move the pivot of its activity and its means of coercion more and more into domains which are useful only to the class character of the bourgeoisie and have for society as a whole only a negative importance, as in the case of militarism and tariff and colonial policies. Moreover, the "social control" exercised by this State is at the same time penetrated with and dominated by its class character (see how labour legislation is applied in all countries).

The extension of democracy, which Bernstein sees as a means of realising socialism by degrees, does not contradict but, on the contrary, corresponds perfectly to the transformation realised in the nature of the State.

Konrad Schmidt declares that the conquest of a social-democratic majority in Parliament leads directly to the gradual "socialisation" of society. Now, the democratic forms of political life are without a question a phenomenon expressing clearly the evolution of the State in society. They constitute, to that extent, a move toward a socialist transformation. But the conflict within the capitalist State, described above, manifests itself even more emphatically in modern parliamentarism. Indeed, in accordance with its form, parliamentarism serves to express, within the organisation of the State, the interests of the whole society. But what parliamentarism expresses here is capitalist society, that is to say, a society in which capitalist interests predominate. In this society, the representative institutions, democratic in form, are in content the instruments of the interests of the ruling class. This manifests itself in a tangible fashion in the fact that as soon as democracy shows the tendency to negate its class character and become transformed into an instrument of the real interests of the population, the democratic forms are sacrificed by the bourgeoisie, and by its State representatives. That is why the idea of the conquest of a parliamentary reformist majority is a calculation which, entirely in the spirit of bourgeois liberalism, pre-occupies itself only with one side — the formal side — of democracy, but does not take into account the other side, its real content. All in all, parliamentarism is not a directly socialist element impregnating gradually the whole capitalist society. It is, on the contrary, a specific form of the bourgeois class State, helping to ripen and develop the existing antagonisms of capitalism.

In the light of the history of the objective development of the State, Bernstein's and Konrad Schmidt's belief that increased "social control" results in the direct introduction of socialism is transformed into a formula that finds itself from day to day in greater contradiction with reality.

The theory of the gradual introduction of socialism proposes progressive reform of capitalist property and the capitalist State in the direction of socialism. But in consequence of the objective laws of existing society, one and the other develop in a precisely opposite direction. The process of production is increasingly socialised, and State intervention, the control of the State over the process of production, is extended. But at the same time, private property becomes more and more the form of open capitalist exploitation of the labour of others, and State control is penetrated with the exclusive interests of the ruling class. The State, that is to say the political organisation of capitalism, and the property relations, that is to say the juridical organisation of capitalism, become more capitalist and not more socialist, opposing to the theory of the progressive introduction of socialism two insurmountable difficulties.

Fourier's scheme of changing, by means of a system of phalansteries, the water of all the seas into tasty lemonade was surely a fantastic idea. But Bernstein, proposing to change the sea of capitalist bitterness into a sea of socialist sweetness, by progressively pouring into it bottles of social reformist lemonade, presents an idea that is merely more insipid but no less fantastic.

The production relations of capitalist society approach more and more the production relations of socialist society. But on the other hand, its political and juridical relations established between capitalist society and socialist society a steadily rising wall. This wall is not overthrown, but is on the contrary strengthened and consolidated by the development of social reforms and the course of democracy. Only the hammer blow of revolution, that is to day, the conquest of political power by the proletariat can break down this wall.

Chapter V. The Consequences of Social Reformism and General Nature of Reformism

In the first chapter we aimed to show that Bernstein's theory lifted the program of the socialist movement off its material base and tried to place it on an idealist base. How does this theory fare when translated into practice?

Upon the first comparison, the party practice resulting from Bernstein's theory does not seem to differ from the practice followed by the Social Democracy up to now. Formerly, the activity of the Social-Democratic Party consisted of trade union work, of agitation for social reforms and the democratisation of existing political institutions. The difference is not in the what, but in the how.

At present, the trade union struggle and parliamentary practice are considered to be the means of guiding and educating the proletariat in preparation for the task of taking over power. From the revisionist standpoint, this conquest of power is at the same time impossible or useless. And therefore, trade union and parliamentary activity are to be carried on by the party only for their immediate results, that is, for the purpose of bettering the present situation of the workers, for the gradual reduction of capitalist exploitation, for the extension of social control.

So that if we don not consider momentarily the immediate amelioration of the workers' condition — an objective common to our party program as well as to revisionism — the difference between the two outlooks is, in brief, the following. According to the present conception of the party, trade-union and parliamentary activity are important for the socialist movement because such activity prepares the proletariat, that is to say, creates the subjective factor of the socialist transformation, for the task of realising socialism. But according to Bernstein, trade-unions and parliamentary activity gradually reduce capitalist exploitation itself. They remove from capitalist society its capitalist character. They realise objectively the desired social change.

Examining the matter closely, we see that the two conceptions are diametrically opposed. Viewing the situation from the current standpoint of our party, we say that as a result of its trade union and parliamentary struggles, the proletariat becomes convinced, of the impossibility of accomplishing a fundamental social change through such activity and arrives at the understanding that the conquest of power is unavoidable. Bernstein's theory, however, begins by declaring that this conquest is impossible. It concludes by affirming that socialism can only be introduced as a result of the trade-union struggle and parliamentary activity. For as seen by Bernstein, trade union and parliamentary action has a socialist character because it exercises a progressively socialising influence on capitalist economy.

We tried to show that this influence is purely imaginary. The relations between capitalist property and the capitalist State develop in entirely opposite directions, so that the daily practical activity of the present Social Democracy loses, in the last analysis, all connection with work for socialism. From the viewpoint of a movement for socialism, the trade-union struggle and our parliamentary practice are vastly important in so far as they make socialistic the awareness, the consciousness, of the proletariat and help to organise it as a class. But once they are considered as instruments of the direct socialisation of capitalist economy, they lose out not only their usual effectiveness but also cease being means of preparing the working class for the conquest of power. Eduard Bernstein and Konrad Schmidt suffer from a complete misunderstanding when they console themselves with the belief that even though the program of the party is reduced to work for social reforms and ordinary trade-union work, the final objective of the labour movement is not thereby discarded, for each forward step reaches beyond the given immediate aim and the socialist goal is implied as a tendency in the supposed advance.

That is certainly true about the present procedure of the German Social Democracy. It is true whenever a firm and conscious effort for conquest of political power impregnates the trade-union struggle and the work for social reforms. But if this effort is separated from the movement itself and social reforms are made an end in themselves, then such activity not only does not lead to the final goal of socialism but moves in a precisely opposite direction.

Konrad Schmidt simply falls back on the idea that an apparently mechanical movement, once started, cannot stop by itself, because "one's appetite grows with the eating," and the working class will not supposedly content itself with reforms till the final socialist transformation is realised.

Now the last mentioned condition is quite real. Its effectiveness is guaranteed by the very insufficiency of capitalist reforms. But the conclusion drawn from it could only be true if it were possible to construct an unbroken chain of augmented reforms leading from the capitalism of today to socialism. This is, of course, sheer fantasy. In accordance with the nature of things as they are the chain breaks quickly, and the paths that the supposed forward movement can take from the point on are many and varied.

What will be the immediate result should our party change its general procedure to suit a viewpoint that wants to emphasise the practical results of our struggle, that is social reforms? As soon as "immediate results" become the principal aim of our activity, the clear-cut, irreconcilable point of view, which has meaning only in so far as it proposes to win power, will be found more and more inconvenient. The direct consequence of this will be the adoption by the party of a "policy of compensation," a policy of political trading, and an attitude of diffident, diplomatic conciliation. But this attitude cannot be continued for a long time. Since the social reforms can only offer an empty promise, the logical consequence of such a program must necessarily be disillusionment.

It is not true that socialism will arise automatically from the daily struggle of the working class. Socialism will be the consequence of (1), the growing contradictions of capitalist economy and (2), of the comprehension by the working class of the unavailability of the suppression of these contradictions through a social transformation. When, in the manner of revisionism, the first condition is denied and the second rejected, the labour movement finds itself reduced to a simple co-operative and reformist movement. We move here in a straight line toward the total abandonment of the class viewpoint.

This consequence also becomes evident when we investigate the general character of revisionism. It is obvious that revisionism does not wish to concede that its standpoint is that of the capitalist apologist. It does not join the bourgeois economists in denying the existence of the contradictions of capitalism. But, on the other hand, what precisely constitutes the fundamental point of revisionism and distinguishes it from the attitude taken by the Social Democracy up to now, is that it does not base its theory on the belief that the contradictions of capitalism will be suppressed as a result of the logical inner development of the present economic system.

We may say that the theory of revisionism occupies an intermediate place between two extremes. Revisionism does not expect to see the contradictions of capitalism mature. It does not propose to suppress these contradictions through a revolutionary transformation. It wants to lessen, to attenuate, the capitalist contradictions. So that the antagonism existing between production and exchange is to be mollified by the cessation of crises and the formation of capitalist combines. The antagonism between Capital and Labour is to be adjusted by bettering the situation of the workers and by the conservation of the middle classes. And the contradiction between the class State and society is to be liquidated through increased State control and the progress of democracy.

It is true that the present procedure of the Social Democracy does not consist in waiting for the antagonisms of capitalism to develop and in passing on, only then, to the task of suppressing them. On the contrary, the essence of revolutionary procedure is to be guided by the direction of this development, once it is ascertained, and inferring from this direction what consequences are necessary for the political struggle. Thus the Social Democracy has combated tariff wars and militarism without waiting for their reactionary character to become fully evident. Bernstein's procedure is not guided by a consideration of the development of capitalism, by the prospect of the aggravation of its contradictions. It is guided by the prospect of the attenuation of these contradictions. He shows this when he speaks of the "adaptation" of capitalist economy.

Now when can such a conception be correct? If it is true that capitalism will continue to develop in the direction it takes at present, then its contradictions must necessarily become sharper and more aggravated instead of disappearing. The possibility of the attenuation of the contradictions of capitalism presupposes that the capitalist mode of production itself will stop its progress. In short, the general condition of Bernstein's theory is the cessation of capitalist development.

This way, however, his theory condemns itself in a twofold manner.

In the first place, it manifests its utopian character in its stand on the establishment of socialism. For it is clear that a defective capitalist development cannot lead to a socialist transformation.

In the second place, Bernstein's theory reveals its reactionary character when it refers to the rapid capitalist development that is taking place at present. Given the development of real capitalism, how can we explain, or rather state, Bernstein's position?

We have demonstrated in the first chapter the baselessness of the economic conditions on which Bernstein builds his analysis of existing social relationships. We have seen that neither the credit system nor cartels can be said to be "means of adaptation" of capitalist economy. We have seen that not even the temporary cessation of crises nor the survival of the middle class can be regarded as symptoms of capitalist adaptation. But even though we should fail to take into account the erroneous character of all these details of Bernstein's theory we cannot help but be stopped short by one feature common to all of them. Bernstein's theory does not seize these manifestations of contemporary economic life as they appear in their organic relationship with the whole of capitalist development, with the complete economic mechanism of capitalism. His theory pulls these details out of their living economic context. It treats them as *disjecta membra* (separate parts) of a lifeless machine.

Consider, for example, his conception of the adaptive effect of credit. If we recognise credit as a higher natural stage of the process of exchange and, therefore, of the contradictions inherent in capitalist exchange, we cannot at the same time see it as a mechanical means of adaptation existing outside of the process of exchange. It would be just as impossible to consider money, merchandise, and capital as "means of adaptation" of capitalism.

However, credit, like money, commodities and capital, is an organic link of capitalist economy at a certain stage of its development. Like them, it is an indispensable gear in the mechanism of capitalist economy, and at the same time, an instrument of destruction, since it aggravates the internal contradictions of capitalism.

The same thing is true about cartels and the new, perfected means of communication.

The same mechanical view is presented by Bernstein's attempt to describe the promise of the cessation of crises as a symptom of the "adaptation" of capitalist economy. For him, crises are simply derangements of the economic mechanism. With their cessation, he thinks, the mechanism could function well. But the fact is that crises are not "derangements" in the usual sense of the word. They are "derangements" without which capitalist economy could not develop at all. For if crises constitute the only method possible in capitalism — and therefore the normal method — of solving periodically the conflict existing between the unlimited extension of production and the narrow limits of the world market, then crises are an organic manifestation inseparable from capitalist economy.

In the "unhindered" advance of capitalist production lurks a threat to capitalism that is much greater than crises. It is the threat of the constant fall of the rate of profit, resulting not only from the contradiction between production and exchange, but from the growth of the productivity of labour itself. The fall in the rate of profit has the extremely dangerous tendency of rendering impossible any enterprise for small and middle-sized capitals. It thus limits the new formation and therefore the extension of placements of capital.

And it is precisely crises that constitute the other consequence of the same process. As a result of their periodic depreciation of capital, crises bring a fall in the prices of means of production, a paralysis of a part of the active capital, and in time the increase of profits. They thus create the possibilities of the renewed advance of production. Crises therefore appear to be the instruments of rekindling the fire of capitalist development. Their cessation — not temporary cessation, but their total disappearance in the world market — would not lead to the further development of capitalist economy. It would destroy capitalism.

True to the mechanical view of his theory of adaptation, Bernstein forgets the necessity of crises as well as the necessity of new placements of small and middle-sized capitals. And that is why the constant reappearance of small capital seems to him to be the sign of the cessation of capitalist development though it is, in fact, a symptom of normal capitalist development.

It is important to note that there is a viewpoint from which all the above-mentioned phenomena are seen exactly as they have been presented by the theory of "adaptation." It is the viewpoint of the isolated (single) capitalist who reflects in his mind the economic facts around him just as they appear when refracted by the laws of competition. The isolated capitalist sees each organic part of the whole of our economy as an independent entity. He sees them as they act on him, the single capitalist. He therefore considers these facts to be simple "derangements" of simple "means of adaptation." For the isolated capitalist, it is true, crises are really simple derangements; the cessation of crises accords him a longer existence. As far as he is concerned, credit is only a means of "adapting" his insufficient productive forces to the needs of the market. And it seems to him that the cartel of which he becomes a member really suppresses industrial anarchy.

Revisionism is nothing else than a theoretic generalisation made from the angle of the isolated capitalist. Where does this viewpoint belong theoretically if not in vulgar bourgeois economics?

All the errors of this school rest precisely on the conception that mistakes the phenomena of competition, as seen from the angle of the isolated capitalist, for the phenomena of the whole of capitalist economy. Just as Bernstein considers credit to be a means of "adaptation," to the needs of exchange. Vulgar economy, too, tries to find the antidote against the ills of capitalism in the phenomena of capitalism. Like Bernstein, it believes that it is possible to regulate capitalist economy. And in the manner of Bernstein, it arrives in time at the desire to palliate the contradictions of capitalism, that is, at the belief in the possibility of patching up the sores of capitalism. It ends up by subscribing to a program of reaction. It ends up in an utopia.

The theory of revisionism can therefore be defined in the following way. It is a theory of standing still in the socialist movement built, with the aid of vulgar economy, on a theory of capitalist standstill.

Chapter VI. Economic Development and Socialism

The greatest conquest of the developing proletarian movement has been the discovery of grounds of support for the realisation of socialism in the economic condition of capitalist society. As a result of this discovery, socialism was changed from an "ideal" dreamt of by humanity for thousands of years to a thing of historic necessity.

Bernstein denies the existence of the economic conditions for socialism in the society of today. On this count his reasoning has undergone an interesting evolution. At first, in the *Neue Zeit*, he simply contested the rapidity of the process of concentration taking place in industry. He based his position on a comparison of the occupational statistics of Germany in 1882 and 1895. In order to use these figures for his purpose, he was obliged to proceed in an entirely summary and mechanical fashion. In the most favourable case, he could not, even by demonstrating the persistence of middle-sized enterprises, weaken in any the Marxian analysis because the latter does not suppose as a condition for the realisation of socialism either a definite rate of concentration of industry — that is, a definite delay of the realisation of socialism — or, as we have already shown, the absolute disappearance of small capitals, usually described as the disappearance of the petit bourgeoisie.

In the course of the latest development of his ideas Bernstein furnishes us, in his book, a new assortment of proofs: the statistics of shareholding societies. These statistics are used in order to prove that the number of shareholders increases constantly and as a result the capitalist class does not become smaller but grows bigger. It is surprising that Bernstein has so little acquaintance with his material. And it is astonishing how poorly he utilises the existing data in his own behalf.

If he wanted to disprove the Marxian law of industrial development by referring to the condition of shareholding societies, he should have resorted to entirely different figures. Anybody who is acquainted with the history of shareholding societies in Germany knows that their average foundation capital has diminished almost constantly. Thus while before 1871 their average foundation capital reached the figure of 10.8 million marks, it was only 4.01 million marks in 1871, 3.8 million marks in 1873, less than a million from 1882 to 1887, 0.52 million in 1891 and only 0.62 million in 1892. After this date the figures oscillated around 1 million marks, falling to 1.78 in 1895 and to 1.19 in the course of the first half of 1897.

Those are surprising figures. Using them, Bernstein hoped to show the existence of a counter-Marxian tendency for retransformation of large enterprises into small ones. The obvious answer to his attempt is the following. If you are to prove anything at all by means of your statistics, you must first show that they refer to the same branches of industry. You must not show that small enterprises really replace large ones, that they do not. Instead, they appear only where small enterprises or even artisan industry were the rule before. This, however, you cannot show to be true. The statistical passage of immense shareholding societies to middle-size and small enterprises can be explained only by referring to the fact that the system of shareholding societies continues to penetrate new branches of production. Before, only a small number of large enterprises were organised as shareholding societies. Gradually shareholding organisation has won middle-size and even small enterprises. Today we can observe shareholding societies with a capital of below 1,000 marks.

Now, what is the economic significance of the extension of the system of shareholding societies? Economically, the spread of shareholding societies stands for the growing socialisation of production under the capitalist form — socialisation not only of large but also of middle-size and small production. The extension of shareholding does not, therefore, contradict Marxist theory but on the contrary, confirms it emphatically.

What does the economic phenomenon of a shareholding society actually amount to? It represents, on the one hand, the unification of a number of small fortunes into a large capital of production. It stands, on the other hand, for the separation of production from capitalist ownership. That is, it denotes that a double victory being won over the capitalist mode of production — but still on a capitalist base.

What is the meaning, therefore, of the statistics cited by Bernstein according to which an ever-greater number of shareholders participate in capitalist enterprises? These statistics go on to demonstrate precisely the following: at present a capitalist enterprise does not correspond, as before, to a single proprietor of capital but to a number of capitalists. Consequently, the economic notion of "capitalist" no longer signifies an isolated individual. The industrial capitalist of today is a collective person composed of hundreds and even of thousands of individuals. The category "capitalist" has itself become a social category. It has become "socialised" — within the frame-work of capitalist society.

In that case, how shall we explain Bernstein's belief that the phenomenon of share-holding societies stands for the dispersion and not the concentration of capital? Why does he see the extension of capitalist property where Marx saw its suppression?

That is a simple economic error. By "capitalist," Bernstein does not mean a category of production but the right to property. To him, "capitalist" is not an economic unit but a fiscal unit. And "capital" is for him not a factor of production but simply a certain quantity of money. That is why in his English sewing thread trust he does not see the fusion of 12,300 persons with money into a single capitalist unit but 12,300 different capitalists. That is why the engineer Schulze whose wife's dowry brought him a large number of shares from stockholder Mueller is also a capitalist for Bernstein. That is why for Bernstein the entire world seems to swarm with capitalists.

Here too, the theoretic base of his economic error is his "popularisation" of socialism. For this is what he does. By transporting the concept of capitalism from its productive relations to property relations, and by speaking of simple individuals instead of speaking of entrepreneurs, he moves the question of socialism from the domain of production into the domain of relations of fortune — that is, from the relation between Capital and Labour to the relation between poor and rich.

In this manner we are merrily led from Marx and Engels to the author of the Evangel of the Poor Fisherman. There is this difference, however. Weitling, with the sure instinct of the proletarian, saw in the opposition between the poor and the rich, the class antagonisms in their primitive form, and wanted to make of these antagonisms a lever of the movement for socialism. Bernstein, on the other hand, locates the realisation of socialism in the possibility of making the poor rich. That is, he locates it in the attenuation of class antagonisms and therefore in the petty bourgeoisie.

True, Bernstein does not limit himself to the statistics of incomes. He furnishes statistics of economic enterprises, especially those of the following countries: Germany, France, England, Switzerland, Austria and the United States. But these statistics are not the comparative figures of different periods in each country but of each period in different countries. We are not therefore offered (with the exception of Germany where he repeats the old contrast between 1895 and 1892), a comparison of the statistics of enterprises of a given country at different epochs but the absolute figures for different countries: England in 1891, France in 1894, United States in 1890, etc.

He reaches the following conclusion: "Though it is true that large exploitation is already supreme in industry today, it nevertheless, represents, including the enterprises dependent on large exploitation, even in a country as developed in Prussia, only half of the population occupied in production." This is also true about Germany, England, Belgium, etc.

What does he actually prove here? He proves not the existence of such or such a tendency of economic development but merely the absolute relation of forces of different forms of enterprise, or put in other words, the absolute relations of the various classes in our society.

Now if one wants to prove in this manner the impossibility of realising socialism one's reasoning must rest on the theory according to which the result of social efforts is decided by the relation of the numerical material forces of the elements in the struggle, that is, by the factor of violence. In other words, Bernstein, who always thunders against Blanquism, himself falls into the grossest Blanquist error. There is this difference, however. To the Blanquists, who represented a socialist and revolutionary tendency, the possibility of the economic realisation of socialism appeared quite natural. On this possibility they built the chances of a violent revolution—even by a small minority. Bernstein, on the contrary, infers from the numerical insufficiency of a socialist majority, the impossibility of the economic realisation of socialism. The Social-Democracy does not, however, expect to attain its aim either as a result of the victorious violence of a minority or through the numerical superiority of a majority. It sees socialism come as a result of economic necessity—and the comprehension of that necessity—leading to the suppression of capitalism by the working masses. And this necessity manifests itself above all in the anarchy of capitalism.

What is Bernstein's position on the decisive question of anarchy in capitalist economy? He denies only the great general crises. He does not deny partial and national crises. In other words, he refuses to see a great deal of the anarchy of capitalism; he sees only a little of it. He is—to use Marx's illustration—like the foolish virgin who had a child "who was only very small." But the misfortune is that in matters like economic anarchy little and much are equally bad. If Bernstein recognises the existence of a little of this anarchy, we may point out to him that by the mechanism of the market economy this bit of anarchy will be extended to unheard of proportions, to end in collapse. But if Bernstein hopes to transform gradually his bit of anarchy into order and harmony while maintaining the system of commodity production, he again falls into one of the fundamental errors of bourgeois political economy according to which the mode of exchange is independent of the mode of production.

This is not the place for a lengthy demonstration of Bernstein's surprising confusion concerning the most elementary principles of political economy. But there is one point—to which we are led by the fundamental questions of capitalist anarchy—that must be clarified immediately.

Bernstein declares that Marx's law of surplus value is a simple abstraction. In political economy a statement of this sort obviously constitutes an insult. But if surplus value is only a simple abstraction, if it is only a figment of the mind—then every normal citizen who has done military duty and pays his taxes on time has the same right as Karl Marx to fashion his individual absurdity, to make his own law of value. "Marx has as much right to neglect the qualities of commodities till they are no more than the incarnation of quantities of simple human labour as have the economists of the Böhm-Jevons school to make an abstraction of all the qualities of commodities outside of their utility."

That is, to Bernstein, Marx's social labour and Menger's abstract utility are quite similar—pure abstractions. Bernstein forgets completely that Marx's abstraction is not an invention. It is a discovery. It does not exist in Marx's head but in market economy. It has not an imaginary existence, but a real social existence, so real that it can be cut, hammered, weighed and put in the form of the money. The abstract human labour discovered by Marx is, in its developed form, no other than money. That is precisely one of the greatest of Marx's discoveries, while to all bourgeois political economists, from the first of the mercantilists to the last of the classicists, the essence of money has remained a mystic enigma.

The Boehm-Jevons abstract utility is, in fact, a conceit of the mind. Or stated more correctly, it is a representation of intellectual emptiness, a private absurdity, for which neither capitalism nor any other society can be made responsible, but only vulgar bourgeois economy itself. Hugging their brain-child, Bernstein, Böhm and Jevons, and the entire subjective fraternity, can remain twenty years or more before the mystery of money, without arriving at a solution that is different from the one reached by any cobbler, namely that money is also a "useful" thing.

Bernstein has lost all comprehension of Marx's law of value. Anybody with a small understanding of Marxian economics can see that without the law of value, Marx's doctrine is incomprehensible. Or to speak more concretely—for him who does not understand the nature of the commodity and its exchange the entire economy of capitalism, with all its concatenations, must of necessity remain an enigma.

What precisely was the key which enabled Marx to open the door to the secrets of capitalist phenomena and solve, as if in play, problems that were not even suspected by the greatest minds of classic bourgeois economy? It was his conception of capitalist economy as an historic phenomenon—not merely in the sense recognised in the best of cases by the classic economists, that is, when it concerns the feudal past of capitalism—but also in so far as it concerns the socialist future of the world. The secret of Marx's theory of value, of his analysis of the problem of money, of his theory of capital, of the theory of the rate of profit and consequently of the entire existing economic system is found in the transitory character of capitalist economy, the inevitability of its collapse leading—and this is only another aspect of the same phenomenon—to socialism. It is only because Marx looked at capitalism from the socialist's viewpoint, that is from the historic viewpoint, that he was enabled to decipher the hieroglyphics of capitalist economy. And it is precisely because he took the socialist viewpoint as a point of departure for his analysis of bourgeois society that he was in the position to give a scientific base to the socialist movement.

This is the measure by which we evaluate Bernstein's remarks. He complains of the "dualism" found everywhere in Marx's monumental Capital. "The work wishes to be a scientific study and prove, at the same time, a thesis that was completely elaborated a long time before the editing of the book; it is based on a schema that already contains the result to which he wants to lead. The return to the *Communist Manifesto* (that is the socialist goal!—R.L.), proves the existence of vestiges of utopianism in Marx's doctrine."

But what is Marx's "dualism" if not the dualism of the socialist future and the capitalist present? It is the dualism of Capitalism and Labour, the dualism of the bourgeoisie and the proletariat. It is the scientific reflection of the dualism existing in bourgeois society, the dualism of the class antagonism writhing inside the social order of capitalism.

Bernstein's recognition of this theoretic dualism in Marx as "a survival of utopianism" is really his naïve avowal that he denies the class antagonisms in capitalism. It is his confession that socialism has become for him only a "survival of utopianism." What is Bernstein's "monism"—Bernstein's unity—but the eternal unity of the capitalist regime, the unity of the former socialist who has renounced his aim and has decided to find in bourgeois society, one and immutable, the goal of human development?

Bernstein does not see in the economic structure of capitalism the development that leads to socialism. But in order to conserve his socialist program, at least in form, he is obliged to take refuge in an idealist construction placed outside of all economic development. He is obliged to transform socialism itself from a definite historical phase of social development into an abstract "principle."

That is why the "co-operative principle" — the meagre decantation of socialism by which Bernstein wishes to garnish capitalist economy — appears as a concession made not to the socialist future of society but to Bernstein's own socialist past.

Chapter VI. Co-operatives, Unions, Democracy

Bernstein's socialism offers to the workers the prospect of sharing in the wealth of society. The poor are to become rich. How will this socialism be brought about? His article in the *Neue Zeit* ('Problems of Socialism") contain only vague allusions to this question. Adequate information, however, can be found in his book.

Bernstein's socialism is to be realised with the aid of these two instruments: labour unions — or as Bernstein himself characterises them, economic democracy — and co-operatives. The first will suppress industrial profit; the second will do away with commercial profit.

Co-operatives — especially co-operatives in the field of production constitute a hybrid form in the midst of capitalism. They can be described as small units of socialised production within capitalist exchange.

But in capitalist economy exchanges dominate production. As a result of competition, the complete domination of the process of production by the interests of capital — that is, pitiless exploitation — becomes a condition for the survival of each enterprise. The domination of capital over the process of production expresses itself in the following ways. Labour is intensified. The work day is lengthened or shortened, according to the situation of the market. And, depending on the requirements of the market, labour is either employed or thrown back into the street. In other words, use is made of all methods that enable an enterprise to stand up against its competitors in the market. The workers forming a co-operative in the field of production are thus faced with the contradictory necessity of governing themselves with the utmost absolutism. They are obliged to take toward themselves the role of capitalist entrepreneur—a contradiction that accounts for the usual failure of production co-operatives which either become pure capitalist enterprises or, if the workers' interests continue to predominate, end by dissolving.

Bernstein has himself taken note of these facts. But it is evident that he has not understood them. For, together with Mrs. Potter-Webb, he explains the failure of production co-operatives in England by their lack of "discipline." But what is so superficially and flatly called here "discipline" is nothing else than the natural absolutist regime of capitalism, which it is plain, the workers cannot successfully use against themselves.

Producers' co-operatives can survive within capitalist economy only if they manage to suppress, by means of some detour, the capitalist controlled contradictions between the mode of production and the mode of exchange. And they can accomplish this only by removing themselves artificially from the influence of the laws of free competition. And they can succeed in doing the last only when they assure themselves beforehand of a constant circle of consumers, that is, when they assure themselves of a constant market.

It is the consumers' co-operative that can offer this service to its brother in the field of production. Here—and not in Oppenheimer's distinction between co-operatives that produce and co-operatives that sell—is the secret sought by Bernstein: the explanation for the invariable failure of producers' co-operatives functioning independently and their survival when they are backed by consumers' organisations.

If it is true that the possibilities of existence of producers' co-operatives within capitalism are bound up with the possibilities of existence of consumers' co-operatives, then the scope of the former is limited, in the most favourable of cases, to the small local market and to the manufacture of articles serving immediate needs, especially food products. Consumers' and therefore producers' co-operatives, are excluded from the most important branches of capital production—the textile, mining, metallurgical and petroleum industries, machine construction, locomotive and ship-building. For this reason alone (forgetting for the moment their hybrid character), co-operatives in the field of production cannot be seriously considered as the instrument of a general social transformation. The establishment of producers' co-operatives on a wide scale would suppose, first of all, the suppression of the world market, the breaking up of the present world economy into small local spheres of production and exchange. The highly developed, wide-spread capitalism of our time is expected to fall back to the merchant economy of the Middle Ages.

Within the framework of present society, producers' co-operatives are limited to the role of simple annexes to consumers' co-operatives. It appears, therefore, that the latter must be the beginning of the proposed social change. But this way the expected reform of society by means of co-operatives ceases to be an offensive against capitalist production. That is, it ceases to be an attack against the principal bases of capitalist economy. It becomes, instead, a struggle against commercial capital, especially small and middle-sized commercial capital. It becomes an attack made on the twigs of the capitalist tree.

According to Bernstein, trade unions too, are a means of attack against capitalism in the field of production. We have already shown that trade unions cannot give the workers a determining influence over production. Trade unions can determine neither the dimensions of production nor the technical progress of production.

This much may be said about the purely economic side of the "struggle of the rate of wages against the rate of profit," as Bernstein labels the activity of the trade union. It does not take place in the blue of the sky. It takes place within the well-defined framework of the law of wages. The law of wages is not shattered but applied by trade-union activity.

According to Bernstein, it is the trade unions that lead—in the general movement for the emancipation of the working class—the real attack against the rate of industrial profit. According to Bernstein, trade unions have the task of transforming the rate of industrial profit into "rates of wages." The fact is that trade unions are least able to execute an economic offensive against profit. Trade unions are nothing more than the organised defence of labour power against the attacks of profit. They express the resistance offered by the working class to the oppression of capitalist economy.

On the one hand, trade unions have the function of influencing the situation in the labour-power market. But this influence is being constantly overcome by the proletarianisation of the middle layers of our society, a process which continually brings new merchandise on the labour market. The second function of the trade unions is to ameliorate the condition of the workers. That is, they attempt to increase the share of the social wealth going to the working class. This share, however, is being reduced with the fatality of a natural process by the growth of the productivity of labour. One does not need to be a Marxist to notice this. It suffices to read Rodbertus' *In Explanation of the Social Question*.

In other words, the objective conditions of capitalist society transform the two economic functions of the trade unions into a sort of labour of Sisyphus, which is, nevertheless, indispensable. For as a result of the activity of his trade unions, the worker succeeds in obtaining for himself the rate of wages due to him in accordance with the situation of the labour-power market. As a result of trade union activity, the capitalist law of wages is applied and the effect of the depressing tendency of economic development is paralysed, or to be more exact, attenuated.

However, the transformation of the trade union into an instrument for the progressive reduction of profit in favour of wages presupposes the following social conditions; first, the cessation of the proletarianisation of the middle strata of our society; secondly, a stoppage of the growth of productivity of labour. We have in both cases a return to pre-capitalist conditions,

Co-operatives and trade unions are totally incapable of transforming the capitalist mode of production. This is really understood by Bernstein, though in a confused manner. For he refers to co-operatives and trade unions as a means of reducing the profit of the capitalists and thus enriching the workers. In this way, he renounces the struggle against the capitalist mode of production and attempts to direct the socialist movement to struggle against "capitalist distribution." Again and again, Bernstein refers to socialism as an effort towards a "just, juster and still more just" mode of distribution.

It cannot be denied that the direct cause leading the popular masses into the socialist movement is precisely the "unjust" mode of distribution characteristic of capitalism. When the Social-Democracy struggles for the socialisation of the entire economy, it aspires therewith also to a "just" distribution of the social wealth. But, guided by Marx's observation that the mode of distribution of a given epoch is a natural consequence of the mode of production of that epoch, the Social-Democracy does not struggle against distribution in the framework of capitalist production. It struggles instead for the suppression of the capitalist production itself. In a word, the Social-Democracy wants to establish the mode of socialist distribution by suppressing the capitalist mode of production. Bernstein's method, on the contrary, proposes to combat the capitalist mode of distribution in the hopes of gradually establishing, in this way, the socialist mode of production.

What, in that case, is the basis of Bernstein's program for the reform of society? Does it find support in definite tendencies of capitalist production? No. In the first place, he denies such tendencies. In the second place, the socialist transformation of production is for him the effect and not the cause of distribution. He cannot give his program a materialist base, because he has already overthrown the aims and the means of the movement for socialism, and therefore its economic conditions. As a result, he is obliged to construct himself an idealist base.

"Why represent socialism as the consequence of economic compulsion?" he complains. "Why degrade man's understanding, his feeling for justice, his will?" Bernstein's superlatively just distribution is to be attained thanks to man's free will; man's will acting not because of economic necessity, since this will is only an instrument, but because of man's comprehension of justice, because of man's idea of justice.

We thus quite happily return to the principle of justice, to the old war horse on which the reformers of the earth have rocked for ages, for the lack of surer means of historic transportation. We return to the lamentable Rosinate on which the Don Quixotes of history have galloped towards the great reform of the earth, always to come home with their eyes blackened.

The relation of the poor to the rich, taken as a base for socialism, the principle of co-operation as the content of socialism, the "most just distribution" as its aim, and the idea of justice as its only historic legitimisation—with how much more force, more with and more fire did Weitling defend that sort of socialism fifty years ago. However, that genius of a tailor did not know scientific socialism. If today, the conception tore into bits by Marx and Engels a half century ago is patched up and presented to the proletariat as the last world of social science, that too, is the art of a tailor but it has nothing of a genius about it.

Trade unions and co-operatives are the economic support for the theory of revisionism. Its principal political condition is the growth of democracy. The present manifestations of political reaction are to Bernstein only "displacement." He considers them accidental, momentary, and suggests that they are not to be considered in the elaboration of the general directives of the labour movement.

To Bernstein, democracy is an inevitable stage in the development of society. To him, as to the bourgeois theoreticians of liberalism, democracy is the great fundamental law of historic development, the realisation of which is served by all the forces of political life. However, Bernstein's thesis is completely false. Presented in this absolute force, it appears as a petty-bourgeois vulgarisation of results of a very short phase of bourgeois development, the last twenty-five or thirty years. We reach entirely different conclusions when we examine the historic development of democracy a little closer and consider, at the same time, the general political history of capitalism.

Democracy has been found in the most dissimilar social formations: in primitive communist groups, in the slave states of antiquity and in medieval communes. And similarly, absolutism and constitutional monarchy are to be found under the most varied economic orders. When capitalism began, with the first production of commodities, it resorted to a democratic constitution in the municipal-communes of the Middle Ages. Later, when it developed to manufacturing, capitalism found its corresponding political form in the absolute monarchy. Finally, as a developed industrial economy, it brought into being in France the democratic republic of 1793, the absolute monarchy of Napoleon I, the nobles' monarchy of the Restoration period (1850-1830), the bourgeois constitutional monarchy of Louis-Philippe, then again the democratic republic, and against the monarchy of Napoleon III, and finally, for the third time, the Republic.

In Germany, the only truly democratic institution—universal suffrage—is not a conquest won by bourgeois liberalism. Universal suffrage in Germany was an instrument for the fusion of the small States. It is only in this sense that it has any importance for the development of the German bourgeoisie, which is otherwise quite satisfied with semi-feudal constitutional monarchy. In Russia, capitalism prospered for a long time under the regime of oriental absolutism, without having the bourgeoisie manifest the least desire in the world to introduce democracy. In Austria, universal suffrage was above all a safety line thrown to a foundering and decomposing monarchy. In Belgium, the conquest of universal suffrage by the labour movement was undoubtedly due to the weakness of the local militarism, and consequently to the special geographic and political situation of the country. But we have here a "bit of democracy" that has been won not by the bourgeoisie but against it.

The uninterrupted victory of democracy, which to our revisionism as well as to bourgeois liberalism, appears as a great fundamental law of human history and, especially, modern history is shown upon closer examination to be a phantom. No absolute and general relation can be constructed between capitalist development and democracy. The political form of a given country is always the result of the composite of all the existing political factors, domestic as well as foreign. It admits within its limits all variations of the scale from absolute monarchy to the democratic republic.

We must abandon, therefore, all hope of establishing democracy as a general law of historical development even within the framework of modern society. Turning to the present phase of bourgeois society, we observe here, too, political factors which, instead of assuring the realisation of Bernstein's schema, led rather to the abandonment by bourgeois society of the democratic conquests won up to now.

Democratic institutions — and this is of the greatest significance — have completely exhausted their function as aids in the development of bourgeois society. In so far as they were necessary to bring about the fusion of small States and the creation of large modern States (Germany, Italy), they are no longer indispensable at present. Economic development has meanwhile effected an internal organic cicatrisation.

The same thing can be said concerning the transformation of the entire political and administrative State machinery from feudal or semi-feudal mechanism to capitalist mechanism. While this transformation has been historically inseparable from the development of democracy, it has been realised today to such an extent that the purely democratic "ingredients" of society, such as universal suffrage and the republican State form, may be suppressed without having the administration, the State finances, or the military organisation find it necessary to return to the forms they had before the March Revolution.

If liberalism as such is now absolutely useless to bourgeois society it has become, on the other hand, a direct impediment to capitalism from other standpoints. Two factors dominate completely the political life of contemporary States: world politics and the labour movement.

Each is only a different aspect of the present phase of capitalist development.

As a result of the development of the world economy and the aggravation and generalisation of competition on the world market, militarism and the policy of big navies have become, as instruments of world politics, a decisive factor in the interior as well as in the exterior life of the great States. If it is true that world politics and militarism represent a rising tendency in the present phase of capitalism, then bourgeois democracy must logically move in a descending line.

In Germany the era of great armament, began in 1893, and the policy of world politics inaugurated with the seizure of Kiao-Cheou were paid for immediately with the following sacrificial victim: the decomposition of liberalism, the deflation of the Centre Party, which passed from opposition to government. The recent elections to the Reichstag of 1907 unrolling under the sign of the German colonial policy were, at the same time, the historical burial of German liberalism.

If foreign politics push the bourgeoisie into the arms of reaction this is no less true about domestic politics — thanks to the rise of the working class. Bernstein shows that he recognises this when he makes the social-democratic "legend," which "wants to swallow everything" — in other words, the socialist efforts of the working class — responsible for the desertion of the liberal bourgeoisie. He advises the proletariat to disavow its socialist aim so that the mortally frightened liberals might come out of the mousehole of reaction. Making the suppression of the socialist labour movement an essential condition for the preservation of bourgeois democracy, he proves in a striking manner that this democracy is in complete contradiction with the inner tendency of development of the present society. He proves, at the same time, that the socialist movement is itself a direct product of this tendency.

But he proves, at the same time, still another thing. By making the denouncement of the socialist aim an essential condition of the resurrection of bourgeois democracy, he shows how inexact is the claim that bourgeois democracy is an indispensable condition of the socialist movement and the victory of socialism. Bernstein's reasoning exhausts itself in a vicious circle. His conclusion swallows his premises.

The solution is quite simple. In view of that fact that bourgeois liberalism has given up its ghost from fear of the growing labour movement and its final aim, we conclude that the socialist labour movement is today the only support for that which is not the goal of the socialist movement—democracy. We must conclude that democracy can have no support. We must conclude that the socialist movement is not bound to bourgeois democracy but that, on the contrary, the fate of democracy is bound up with the socialist movement. We must conclude from this that democracy does not acquire greater chances of survival, as the socialist movement becomes sufficiently strong to struggle against the reactionary consequences of world politics and the bourgeois desertion of democracy. He who would strengthen democracy should want to strengthen and not weaken the socialist movement. He who renounces the struggle for socialism renounces both the labour movement and democracy.

Chapter VI. Conquest of Political Power

The fate of democracy is bound up, we have seen, with the fate of the labour movement. But does the development of democracy render superfluous or impossible a proletarian revolution, that is, the conquest of political power by the workers?

Bernstein settles the question by weighing minutely the good and bad sides of social reform and social revolution. He does it almost in the same manner in which cinnamon or pepper is weighed out in a consumers' co-operative store. He sees the legislative course of historic development as the action of "intelligence," while the revolutionary course of historic development is for him the action of "feeling." Reformist activity, he recognises as a slow method of historic progress, revolution as a rapid method of progress. In legislation he sees a methodical force; in revolution, a spontaneous force.

We have known for a long time that the petty-bourgeoisie reformer finds "good" and "bad" sides in everything. He nibbles a bit at all grasses. But the real course of events is little affected by such combination. The carefully gathered little pile of the "good sides" of all things possible collapses at the first filip of history. Historically, legislative reform and the revolutionary method function in accordance with influences that are much more profound than the consideration of the advantages or inconveniences of one method or another.

In the history of bourgeois society, legislative reform served to strengthen progressively the rising class till the latter was sufficiently strong to seize political power, to suppress the existing juridical system and to construct itself a new one. Bernstein, thundering against the conquest of political power as a theory of Blanquist violence, has the misfortune of labelling as a Blanquist error that which has always been the pivot and the motive force of human history. From the first appearance of class societies having the class struggle as the essential content of their history, the conquest of political power has been the aim of all rising classes. Here is the starting point and end of every historic period. This can be seen in the long struggle of the Latin peasantry against the financiers and nobility of ancient Rome, in the struggle of the medieval nobility against the bishops and in the struggle of the artisans against the nobles, in the cities of the Middle Ages. In modern times, we see it in the struggle of the bourgeoisie against feudalism.

Legislative reform and revolution are not different methods of historic development that can be picked out at the pleasure from the counter of history, just as one chooses hot or cold sausages. Legislative reform and revolution are different factors in the development of class society. They condition and complement each other, and are at the same time reciprocally exclusive, as are the north and south poles, the bourgeoisie and proletariat.

Every legal constitution is the product of a revolution. In the history of classes, revolution is the act of political creation, while legislation is the political expression of the life of a society that has already come into being. Work for reform does not contain its own force independent from revolution. During every historic period, work for reforms is carried on only in the direction given to it by the impetus of the last revolution and continues as long as the impulsion from the last revolution continues to make itself felt. Or, to put it more concretely, in each historic period work for reforms is carried on only in the framework of the social form created by the last revolution. Here is the kernel of the problem.

It is contrary to history to represent work for reforms as a long-drawn out revolution and revolution as a condensed series of reforms. A social transformation and a legislative reform do not differ according to their duration but according to their content. The secret of historic change through the utilisation of political power resides precisely in the transformation of simple quantitative modification into a new quality, or to speak more concretely, in the passage of an historic period from one given form of society to another.

That is why people who pronounce themselves in favour of the method of legislative reform in place and in contradistinction to the conquest of political power and social revolution, do not really choose a more tranquil, calmer and slower road to the same goal, but a different goal. Instead of taking a stand for the establishment of a new society they take a stand for surface modifications of the old society. If we follow the political conceptions of revisionism, we arrive at the same conclusion that is reached when we follow the economic theories of revisionism. Our program becomes not the realisation of socialism, but the reform of capitalism; not the suppression of the wage labour system but the diminution of exploitation, that is, the suppression of the abuses of capitalism instead of suppression of capitalism itself.

Does the reciprocal role of legislative reform and revolution apply only to the class struggle of the past? It is possible that now, as a result of the development of the bourgeois juridical system, the function of moving society from one historic phase to another belongs to legislative reform and that the conquest of State power by the proletariat has really become "an empty phrase," as Bernstein puts it?

The very opposite is true. What distinguishes bourgeois society from other class societies—from ancient society and from the social order of the Middle Ages? Precisely the fact that class domination does not rest on "acquired rights" but on real economic relations—the fact that wage labour is not a juridical relation, but purely an economic relation. In our juridical system there is not a single legal formula for the class domination of today. The few remaining traces of such formulae of class domination are (as that concerning servants), survivals of feudal society.

How can wage slavery be suppressed the "legislative way," if wage slavery is not expressed the laws? Bernstein, who would do away with capitalism by means of legislative reforms, finds himself in the same situation s Uspensky's Russian policeman who said: "Quickly I seized the rascal by the collar! But what do I see? The confounded fellow has no collar!" And that is precisely Bernstein's difficulty.

"All previous societies were based on an antagonism between an oppressing class and an oppressed class" (*Communist Manifesto*). But in the preceding phases of modern society, this antagonism was expressed in distinctly determined juridical relations and could, especially because of that, accord, to a certain extent, a place to new relations within the framework of the old. "In the midst of serfdom, the serf raised himself to the rank of a member of the town community" (*Communist Manifest*). How was that made possible? It was made possible by the progressive of all feudal privileges in the environs of the city: the corvée, the right to special dress, the inheritance tax, the lord's claim to the best cattle, the personal levy, marriage under duress, the right to succession, etc., which all together constituted serfdom.

In the same way, the small bourgeoisie of the Middle Ages succeeded in raising itself, while it was still under the yoke of feudal absolutism, to the rank of bourgeoisie (*Communist Manifesto*). By what means? By means of the formal partial suppression or complete loosening of the corporative bonds, by the progressive transformation of the fiscal administration and of the army.

Consequently, when we consider the question from the abstract viewpoint, not from the historic viewpoint, we can imagine (in view of the former class relations) a legal passage, according to the reformist method, from feudal society to bourgeois society. But what do we see in reality? In reality, we see that legal reforms not only do not obviate the seizure of political power by the bourgeoisie but have, on the contrary, prepared for it and led to it. A formal social-political transformation was indispensable for the abolition of slavery as well as for the complete suppression of feudalism.

But the situation is entirely different now. No law obliges the proletariat to submit itself to the yoke of capitalism. Poverty, the lack of means of production, obliges the proletariat to submit itself to the yoke of capitalism. And no law in the world can give to the proletariat the means of production while it remains in the framework of bourgeois society, for not laws but economic development have torn the means of production from the producers' possession.

And neither is the exploitation inside the system of wage labour based on laws. The level of wages is not fixed by legislation but by economic factors. The phenomenon of capitalist exploitation does not rest on a legal disposition but on the purely economic fact that labour power plays in this exploitation the role of a merchandise possessing, among other characteristics, the agreeable quality of producing value—more than the value it consumes in the form of the labourer's means of subsistence. In short, the fundamental relations of the domination of the capitalist class cannot be transformed by means of legislative reforms, on the basis of capitalist society, because these relations have not been introduced by bourgeois laws, nor have they received the form of such laws. Apparently, Bernstein is not aware of this for he speaks of "socialist reforms." On the other hand, he seems to express implicit recognition of this when he writes, on page 10 of his book, "the economic motive acts freely today, while formerly it was masked by all kinds of relations of domination by all sorts of ideology."

It is one of the peculiarities of the capitalist order that within it all the elements of the future society first assume, in their development, a form not approaching socialism but, on the contrary, a form moving more and more away from socialism. Production takes on a progressively increasing social character. But under what form is the social character of capitalist production expressed? It is expressed in the form of the large enterprise, in the form of the shareholding concern, the cartel, within which the capitalist antagonisms, capitalist exploitation, the oppression of labour-power, are augmented to the extreme.

In the army, capitalist development leads to the extension of obligatory military service to the reduction of the time of service and consequently to a material approach to a popular militia. But all of this takes place under the form of modern militarism in which the domination of the people by the militarist State and the class character of the State manifest themselves most clearly.

In the field of political relations, the development of democracy brings—in the measure that it finds a favourable soil—the participation of all popular strata in political life and, consequently, some sort of "people's State." But this participation takes the form of bourgeois parliamentarism, in which class antagonisms and class domination are not done away with, but are, on the contrary, displayed in the open. Exactly because capitalist development moves through these contradictions, it is necessary to extract the kernel of socialist society from its capitalist shell. Exactly for this reason must the proletariat seize political power and suppress completely the capitalist system.

Of course, Bernstein draws other conclusions. If the development of democracy leads to the aggravation and not to the lessening of capitalist antagonisms, "the Social-Democracy," he answers us, "in order not to render its task more difficult, must by all means try to stop social reforms and the extension of democratic institutions," (page 71). Indeed, that would be the right thing to do if the Social-Democracy found to its taste, in the petty-bourgeois manner, the futile task of picking for itself all the good sides of history and rejecting the bad sides of history. However, in that case, it should at the same time "try to stop" capitalism in general, for there is not doubt that latter is the rascal placing all these obstacles in the way of socialism. But capitalism furnishes besides the obstacles also the only possibilities of realising the socialist programme. The same can be said about democracy.

If democracy has become superfluous or annoying to the bourgeoisie, it is on the contrary necessary and indispensable to the working class. It is necessary to the working class because it creates the political forms (autonomous administration, electoral rights, etc.) which will serve the proletariat as fulcrums in its task of transforming bourgeois society. Democracy is indispensable to the working class because only through the exercise of its democratic rights, in the struggle for democracy, can the proletariat become aware of its class interests and its historic task.

In a word, democracy is indispensable not because it renders superfluous the conquest of political power by the proletariat but because it renders this conquest of power both necessary and possible. When Engels, in his preface to the Class Struggles in France, revised the tactics of the modern labour movement and urged the legal struggle as opposed to the barricades, he did not have in mind — this comes out of every line of the preface — the question of a definite conquest of political power, but the contemporary daily struggle. He did not have in mind the attitude that the proletariat must take toward the capitalist State at the time of the seizure of power but the attitude of the proletariat while in the bounds of the capitalist State. Engels was giving directions to the proletariat oppressed, and not to the proletariat victorious.

On the other hand, Marx's well known sentence on the agrarian question in England (Bernstein leans on it heavily), in which he says: "We shall probably succeed easier by buying the estates of the landlords," does not refer to the stand of the proletariat before, but after its victory. For there evidently can be a question of buying the property of the old dominant class only when the workers are in power. The possibility envisaged by Marx is not of the pacific exercise of the dictatorship of the proletariat and not the replacement of the dictatorship with capitalist social reforms. There was no doubt for Marx and Engels about the necessity of having the proletariat conquer political power. It is left to Bernstein to consider the poultry-yard of bourgeois parliamentarism as the organ by means of which we are to realise the most formidable social transformation of history, the passage from capitalist society to socialism.

Bernstein introduces his theory by warning the proletariat against the danger of acquiring power too early. That is, according to Bernstein, the proletariat ought to leave the bourgeois society in its present condition and itself suffer a frightful defeat. If the proletariat came to power, it could draw from Bernstein's theory the following "practical" conclusion: to go to sleep. His theory condemns the proletariat at the most decisive moments of the struggle, to inactivity, to a passive betrayal of its own cause.

Our programme would be a miserable scrap of paper if it could not serve us in all eventualities, at all moments of the struggle and if it did not serve us by its application and not by its non-application. If our programme contains the formula of the historical development of society from capitalism to socialism, it must also formulate, in all its characteristic fundamentals, all the transitory phases of this development and it should, consequently, be able to indicate to the proletariat what ought to be its corresponding action at every moment on the road toward socialism. There can be no time for the proletariat when it will be obliged to abandon its programme or be abandoned by it.

Practically, this is manifested in the fact that there can be no time when the proletariat, placed in power by the force of events, is not in the condition or is not morally obliged to take certain measures for the realisation of its programme, that is, take transitory measures in the direction of socialism. Behind the belief that the socialist programme can collapse completely at any point of the dictatorship of the proletariat lurks the other belief that the socialist programme is generally and at all times, unrealisable.

And what if the transitory measures are premature? The question hides a great number of mistaken ideas concerning the real course of a social transformation.

In the first place, the seizure of political power by the proletariat, that is to say by a large popular class, is not produced artificially. It presupposes (with the exception of such cases as the Paris Commune, when the proletariat did not obtain power after a conscious struggle for its goal but fell into its hands like a good thing abandoned by everybody else) a definite degree of maturity of economic and political relations. Here we have the essential difference between coups d'etat along Blanqui's conception which are accomplished by an "active minority" and burst out like pistol shot, always inopportunely, and the conquest of political power by a great conscious popular mass which can only be the product of the decomposition of bourgeois society and therefore bears in itself the economic and political legitimisation of its opportune appearance.

If, therefore, considered from the angle of political effect the conquest of political power by the working class cannot materialise itself "too early" then from the angle of conservation of power, the premature revolution, the thought of which keeps Bernstein awake, menaces us like a sword of Damocles. Against that neither prayers nor supplication, neither scares nor any amount of anguish, are of any avail. And this for two very simple reasons.

In the first place, it is impossible to imagine that a transformation as formidable as the passage from capitalist society to socialist society can be realised in one happy act. To consider that as possible is, again, to lend colour to conceptions that are clearly Blanquist. The socialist transformation supposes a long and stubborn struggle, in the course of which, it is quite probable the proletariat will be repulsed more than once so that for the first time, from the viewpoint of the final outcome of the struggle, it will have necessarily come to power "too early."

In the second place, it will be impossible to avoid the "premature" conquest of State power by the proletariat precisely because these "premature" attacks of the proletariat constitute a factor and indeed a very important factor, creating the political conditions of the final victory. In the course of the political crisis accompanying its seizure of power, in the course of the long and stubborn struggles, the proletariat will acquire the degree of political maturity permitting it to obtain in time a definitive victory of the revolution. Thus these "premature" attacks of the proletariat against the State power are in themselves important historic factors helping to provoke and determine the point of the definite victory. Considered from this viewpoint, the idea of a "premature" conquest of political power by the labouring class appears to be a polemic absurdity derived from a mechanical conception of the development of society, and positing for the victory of the class struggle a point fixed outside and independent of the class struggle.

Since the proletariat is not in the position to seize power in any other way than "prematurely," since the proletariat is absolutely obliged to seize power once or several times "too early" before it can maintain itself in power for good, the objection to the "premature" conquest of power is at bottom nothing more than a general opposition to the aspiration of the proletariat to possess itself of State power. Just as all roads lead to Rome so too do we logically arrive at the conclusion that the revisionist proposal to slight the final aim of the socialist movement is really a recommendation to renounce the socialist movement itself.

Chapter IX. Collapse

Bernstein began his revision of the Social-Democracy by abandoning the theory of capitalist collapse. The latter, however, is the corner-stone of scientific socialism. By rejecting it Bernstein also rejects the whole doctrine of socialism. In the course of his discussion, he abandons one after another of the positions of socialism in order to be able to maintain his first affirmation.

Without the collapse of capitalism the expropriation of the capitalist class is impossible. Bernstein therefore renounces expropriation and chooses a progressive realisation of the "co-operative principle" as the aim of the labour movement.

But co-operation cannot be realised without capitalist production. Bernstein, therefore, renounces the socialisation of production and merely proposes to reform commerce and to develop consumers' co-operatives.

But the transformation of society through consumers' co-operatives, even by means of trade unions, is incompatible with the real material development of capitalist society. Therefore, Bernstein abandons the materialist conception of history.

But his conception of the march of economic development is incompatible with the Marxist theory of surplus-value. Therefore, Bernstein abandons the theory of value and surplus-value and, in this way, the whole economic system of Karl Marx.

But the struggle of the proletariat cannot be carried on without a given final aim and without an economic base found in the existing society. Bernstein, therefore, abandons the class struggle and speaks of reconciliation with bourgeois liberalism.

But in a class society, the class struggle is a natural and unavoidable phenomenon. Bernstein, therefore, contests even the existence of classes in society. The working class is for him a mass of individuals, divided politically and intellectually but also economically. And the bourgeoisie, according to him, does not group itself politically in accordance with its inner economic interest but only because of exterior pressure from above and below.

But if there is no economic base for the class struggle and, if consequently, there are no classes in our society, not only the future but even the past struggles of the proletariat against the bourgeoisie appear to be impossible and the Social-Democracy and its successes seem absolutely incomprehensible or they can be understood only as the results of political pressure by the government—that is, not as the natural consequence of historic development but as the fortuitous consequences of the policy of the Hohenzollern not as the legitimate offspring of capitalist society but as the legitimate offspring of capitalist society but as the bastard children of reaction. Rigorously logical, in this respect, Bernstein passes from the materialist conception of history to the outlook of the *Frankfurter Zeitung* and the *Vossische Zeitung*.

After rejecting the socialist criticism of capitalist society, it is easy for Bernstein to find the present state of affairs satisfactory—at least in a general way. Bernstein does not hesitate. He discovers that at the present time reaction is not very strong in Germany, that "we cannot speak of political reaction in the countries of western Europe," and that in all the countries of the West "the attitude of the bourgeois classes toward the socialist movement is at most an attitude of defence and not one of oppression." Far from becoming worse, the situation of the workers is getting better. Indeed, the bourgeoisie is politically progressive and morally sane. We cannot speak either of reaction or oppression. It is all for the best in the best of all possible worlds...

Bernstein thus travels in logical sequence from A to Z. He began by abandoning the final aim and supposedly keeping the movement. But as there can be no socialist movement without a socialist aim he ends by renouncing the movement.

And thus the Bernstein's conception of socialism collapses entirely. The proud and admirable symmetric construction of socialist thought becomes for him a pile of rubbish in which the debris of all systems, the pieces of thought of various great and small minds, find a common resting place. Marx and Proudhon, Leon von Buch and Franz Oppenheimer, Friedrich Albert Lange and Kant, Herr Prokopovich and R. Ritter von Neupauer, Herkner, and Schulze-Gävernitz, Lassalle and Professor Julius Wolff: all contribute something to Bernstein's system. From each he takes a little. There is nothing astonishing about that. For when he abandoned scientific socialism he lost the axis of intellectual crystallisation around which isolated facts group themselves in the organic whole of a coherent conception of the world.

His doctrine, composed of bits of all possible systems, seems upon first consideration to be completely free from prejudices. For Bernstein does not like talk of "party science," or to be more exact, of class science, any more than he likes to talk of class liberalism or class morality. He thinks he succeeds in expressing human, general, abstract science, abstract liberalism, abstract morality. But since the society of reality is made up of classes which have diametrically opposed interests, aspirations and conceptions, a general human science in social questions, an abstract liberalism, an abstract morality, are at present illusions, pure utopia. The science, the democracy, the morality, considered by Bernstein as general, human, are merely the dominant science, dominant democracy and dominant morality that is, bourgeois science, bourgeois democracy, bourgeois morality.

When Bernstein rejects the economic doctrine of Marx in order to swear by the teachings of Bretano, Böhm-Bawerk, Jevons, Say and Julius Wolff, he exchanges the scientific base of the emancipation of the working class for the apologetics of the bourgeoisie. When he speaks of the generally human character of liberalism and transforms socialism into a variety of liberalism, he deprives the socialist movement (generally) of its class character and consequently of its historic content, consequently of all content; and conversely, recognises the class representing liberalism in history, the bourgeoisie, as the champion of the general interests of humanity.

And when he wars against "raising of the material factors to the rank of an all-powerful force of development," when he protests against the so-called "contempt for the ideal" that is supposed to rule the Social-Democracy, when he presumes to talk for idealism, for morals, pronouncing himself at the same time against the only source of the moral rebirth of the proletariat, a revolutionary class struggle — he does no more than the following: preach to the working class the quintessence of the morality of the bourgeoisie, that is, reconciliation with the existing social order and the transfer of the hopes of the proletariat to the limbo of ethical simulacra.

When he directs his keenest arrows against our dialectic system, he is really attacking the specific mode of thought employed by the conscious proletariat in its struggle for liberation. It is an attempt to break the sword that has helped the proletariat to pierce the darkness of its future. It is an attempt to shatter the intellectual arm with the aid of which the proletariat, though materially under the yoke of the bourgeoisie, is yet enabled to triumph over the bourgeoisie. For it is our dialectical system that shows to the working class the transitory nature of this yoke, proving to workers the inevitability of their victory and is already realising a revolution in the domain of thought. Saying good-bye to our system of dialectics and resorting instead to the intellectual see-saw of the well known "on the one hand — on the other hand," "yes — but," "although — however," "more — less," etc., he quite logically lapses into a mode of thought that belongs historically to the bourgeoisie in decline, being the faithful intellectual reflection of the social existence and political activity of the bourgeoisie at that stage. The political "on the one hand — on the other hand," "yes — but" of the bourgeoisie today resembles, in a marked degree, Bernstein's manner of thinking which is the sharpest and surest proof of the bourgeois nature of his conception of the world.

But, as it us used by Bernstein, the word "bourgeois" itself is not a class expression but a general social notion. Logical to the end he has exchanged, together with his science, politics, morals and mode of thinking, the historic language of the proletariat for that of the bourgeoisie. When he uses, without distinction, the term "citizen" in reference to the bourgeois as well as to the proletarian intending, thereby, to refer to man in general, he identifies man in general with the bourgeois and human society with bourgeois society.

Chapter X. Opportunism and Theory in Practice

Bernstein's book is of great importance to the German and the international labour movement. It is the first attempt to give a theoretic base to the opportunist currents common in the Social-Democracy.

These currents may be said to have existed for a long time in our movement, if we take into consideration such sporadic manifestations of opportunism as the question of subsidisation of steamers. But it is only since about 1890, with the suppression of the anti-Socialist laws, that we have had a trend of opportunism of a clearly defined character. Vollmar's "State Socialism," the vote on the Bavarian budget, the "agrarian socialism" of south Germany, Heine's policy of compensation, Schippel's stand on tariffs and militarism, are the high points in the development of our opportunist practice.

What appears to characterise this practice above all? A certain hostility to "theory." This is quite natural, for our "theory," that is, the principles of scientific socialism, impose clearly marked limitations to practical activity — insofar as it concerns the aims of this activity, the means used in attaining these aims and the method employed in this activity. It is quite natural for people who run after immediate "practical" results to want to free themselves from such limitations and to render their practice independent of our "theory."

However, this outlook is refuted by every attempt to apply it in reality. State socialism, agrarian socialism, the policy of compensation, the question of the army, all constituted defeats to our opportunism. It is clear that, if this current is to maintain itself, it must try to destroy the principles of our theory and elaborate a theory of its own. Bernstein's book is precisely an effort in that direction. That is why at Stuttgart all the opportunist elements in our party immediately grouped themselves around Bernstein's banner. If the opportunist currents in the practical activity of our party are an entirely natural phenomenon which can be explained in the light of the special conditions of our activity and its development, Bernstein's theory is no less natural an attempt to group these currents into a general theoretic expression, an attempt to elaborate its own theoretic conditions and the break with scientific socialism. That is why the published expression of Bernstein's ideas should be recognised as a theoretic test for opportunism and as its first scientific legitimisation.

What was the result of this test? We have seen the result. Opportunism is not a position to elaborate a positive theory capable of withstanding criticism. All it can do is to attack various isolated theses of Marxist theory and, just because Marxist doctrine constitutes one solidly constructed edifice, hope by this means to shake the entire system from the top to its foundation.

This shows that opportunist practice is essentially irreconcilable with Marxism. But it also proves that opportunism is incompatible with socialism (the socialist movement) in general, that its internal tendency is to push the labour movement into bourgeois paths, that opportunism tends to paralyse completely the proletarian class struggle. The latter, considered historically, has evidently nothing to do with Marxist doctrine. For, before Marx and independently from him, there have been labour movements and various socialist doctrines, each of which, in its way, was the theoretic expression corresponding to the conditions of the time, of the struggle of the working class for emancipation. The theory that consists in basing socialism on the moral notion of justice, on a struggle against the mode of distribution, instead of basing it on a struggle against the mode of production, the conception of class antagonism as an antagonism between the poor and the rich, the effort to graft the "co-operative principle" on capitalist economy — all the nice notions found in Bernstein's doctrine — already existed before him. And these theories were, in their time, in spite of their insufficiency, effective theories of the proletarian class struggle. They were the children's seven-league boots thanks to which the proletariat learned to walk upon the scene of history.

But after the development of the class struggle and its reflex in its social conditions had led to the abandonment of these theories and to the elaboration of the principles of scientific socialism, there could be no socialism — at least in Germany — outside of Marxist socialism and there could be no socialist class struggle outside of the Social-Democracy. Form then on, socialism and Marxism, the proletarian struggle for emancipation and the Social-Democracy, were identical. That is why the return to pre-Marxist socialist theories no longer signifies today a return to the seven-league boots of the childhood of the proletariat, but a return to the puny worn-out slippers of the bourgeoisie.

Bernstein's theory was the first, and at the same time, the last attempt to give a theoretic base to opportunism. It is the last, because in Bernstein's system, opportunism has gone — negatively through its renunciation of scientific socialism, positively through its marshalling of every bit of theoretic confusion possible — as far as it can. In Bernstein's book, opportunism has crowned its theoretic development (just as it completed its practical development in the position taken by

Schippel on the question of militarism), and has reached its ultimate conclusion.

Marxist doctrine can not only refute opportunism theoretically. It alone can explain opportunism as an historic phenomenon in the development of the party. The forward march of the proletariat, on a world historic scale, to its final victory is not, indeed, "so simple a thing." The peculiar character of this movement resides precisely in the fact that here, for the first time in history, the popular masses themselves, in opposition to the ruling classes, are to impose their will but they must effect this outside of the present society, beyond the existing society. This will the masses can only form in a constant struggle against the existing order. The union of the broad popular masses with an aim reaching beyond the existing social order, the union of the daily struggle with the great world transformation, that is the task of the Social-Democratic movement, which must logically grope on its road of development between the following two rocks: abandoning the mass character of the party or abandoning its final aim falling into bourgeois reformism or into sectarianism, anarchism or opportunism.

In its theoretic arsenal, Marxist doctrine furnished, more than half a century ago, arms that are effective against both of these two extremes. But because our movement is a mass movement and because the dangers menacing it are not derived from the human brain but from social conditions, Marxist doctrine could not assure us, in advance and once for always, against the anarchist and opportunist tendencies. The latter can be overcome only as we pass from the domain of theory to the domain of practice but only with the help of the arms furnished us by Marx.

"Bourgeois revolutions," wrote Marx a half century ago, "like those of the eighteenth century, rush onward rapidly from success to success, their stage effects outbid one another, men and things seems to be set in flaming brilliants, ecstasy is the prevailing spirit; but they are short-lived, they reach their climax speedily and then society relapses into a long fit of nervous reaction before it learns how to appropriate the fruits of its period of feverish excitement. Proletarian revolutions, on the contrary, such as those of the nineteenth century, criticise themselves constantly; constantly interrupt themselves in their own course; come back to what seems to have been accomplished, in order to start anew; scorn with cruel thoroughness the half-measures, weakness and meanness of their first attempts;

seem to throw down their adversary only to enable him to draw fresh strength from the earth and again to rise up against them in more gigantic stature; constantly recoil in fear before the undefined monster magnitude of their own objects—until finally that situation is created which renders all retreats impossible and conditions themselves cry out: '*Hic Rhodus, hic salta!*' Here is the rose. And here we must dance!" (*Eighteenth Brumaire*)

This has remained true even after the elaboration of the doctrine of scientific socialism. The proletarian movement has not as yet, all at once, become social-democratic, even in Germany. But it is becoming more social-democratic, surmounting continuously the extreme deviations of anarchism and opportunism, both of which are only determining phases of the development of the Social-Democracy, considered as a process.

For these reasons, we must say that the surprising thing here is not the appearance of an opportunist current but rather its feebleness. As long as it showed itself in isolated cases of the practical activity of the party, one could suppose that it had a serious political base. But now that it has shown its face in Bernstein's book, one cannot help exclaim with astonishment: "What? Is that all you have to say?" Not the shadow of an original thought! Not a single idea that was not refuted, crushed, reduced into dust by Marxism several decades ago!

It was enough for opportunism to speak out to prove it had nothing to say. In the history of our party that is the only importance of Bernstein's book.

Thus saying good-bye to the mode of thought of the revolutionary proletariat, to dialectics and to the materialist conception of history, Bernstein can thank them for the attenuating circumstances they provide for his conversion. For only dialectics and the materialist conception of history, magnanimous as they are, could make Bernstein appear as an unconscious predestined instrument, by means of which the rising working class expresses its momentary weakness but which, upon closer inspection, it throws aside contemptuously and with pride.

The Socialist Crisis in France
(1901)

Part I

Jaurès and his adherents justified Millerand's entry into the Cabinet on three grounds: The Republic must be defended. It would be possible to put through social reforms of benefit to the working class. And, finally, the development of capitalist society into socialism must give birth to a transition period in which the political power is wielded in common by the bourgeoisie and the proletariat and finds its outward expression in the participation of socialists in the government.

After a time, the reference to the defense of the Republic became the chief argument.

The Republic is in danger! That is why it was necessary for a socialist to become the bourgeois Minister of Commerce. The Republic is in danger! That is why the socialist had to remain in the cabinet even after the massacre of the striking workers on the Island of Martinique and in Chalon. The Republic is in danger! As a result, inquiries into the massacres had to be blocked, the parliamentary investigations of the horrors perpetrated in the colonies had to be discarded, and the amnesty law accepted. All acts of the government, all positions and votes of the socialists are based upon a concern for the threatened Republic and its defense. It is time to analyze the situation calmly, undisturbed by the uproar of the daily struggle and its slogans. It is time to answer the question: just what do this danger and this defense consist of?

Despite violent class and party struggles, we do not hear of dangers threatening the republican form of government in the United States of America. This is entirely understandable, since the republic in America was won simultaneously with national independence. The Americans have never experienced monarchal rule as an independent nation. In France, on the contrary, the fears for the welfare of the Republic appear just as understandable, since it was twice established through violent struggle, only to be twice, after a short existence, overthrown by the monarchy. We, therefore, have these past experiences casting their ominous shadows on the present situation — shadows which conceal the vistas of historical development that lie between past and present.

Coup d'état : 1799 and 1851

Although the two Napoleonic coups d'état — the Eighteenth Brumaire of 1799 and December 2nd of 1851 — were produced by specific and immediate political situations, their roots went far below this surface. The First and the Second Empires alike were the direct products of preceding revolutions. They marked the extreme point of rest of the receding revolutionary wave and were supported in both cases by two powerful classes of bourgeois society, the big bourgeoisie and the peasantry.

In the Eighteenth Brumaire, we have a bourgeoisie in the period of the revolution's ascent, seeking to check it and lead it back to its starting point in order to strangle it, because it had been carried beyond the point they fixed for it — the creation of a constitutional bourgeois state — and was threatening the very foundations of this state. Hand in hand with this bourgeoisie went a peasantry, liberated and in possession of the land, fearing every new change as much as the return of the old regime, and anxious to consolidate its conquests through a government that was hostile to both the revolution and the legitimate monarchy. Facing these two classes across the barricades was a working class which during its short rule had frightened the petty bourgeoisie and driven it into the arms of reaction, but at the same time had shown that it did not yet possess an independent, practical program of action and had, therefore, been grinding itself to pieces in the revolutionary struggles. Finally, the threat offered by the anti-Jacobin coalition of feudal-reactionary Europe caused the internal contradictions and struggles to be pushed into the background and concentrated everything upon the necessity for a strong, external front.

In the coup d'état of December 2, 1851, we have a bourgeoisie in power, which, like the big landowners, is frightened by the revolutionary uprising of the proletariat and the petty bourgeoisie. It secures the help of the petty bourgeoisie to trample the proletariat underfoot in the June massacre, and then, in order to finish with the petty bourgeoisie, strengthens the state power more and more at the expense of popular representation. In doing this, it finally places its own neck in the noose, with the greater resignation since it, from the beginning, is monarchically minded, and only finds fault with the monarchy of Bonaparte because it would have preferred that of the house of Orleans or the Bourbons. Next to this bourgeoisie, we have a peasantry, which has been devoted to the Napoleon tradition since the First Empire. In the Second it sees a means of establishing order with the bayonets of the army, and of controlling the turbulent city population it hates and fears.

The pattern of the coup d'état is, therefore, the same in both cases: on the one hand, the positive economic and political interests of the dominant classes in society tied to the monarchy; on the other, the working class, by now rendered incapable of action, as the only real republican force. Finally, in both cases, the monarchy finds its foundation prepared in advance by the march of the counter-revolution, which has already created posts combining the supreme civil and military powers: the life-long consulships and the plebiscite-elected President. Whatever the coup d'état conquered, therefore, had already dropped into the lap of the Republic as a ripe fruit of the counter-revolution. The coup d'état did not establish a new state of affairs. It merely recognized the new situation and gave it its name.

The Bourgeois Republic

The events in France during the Dreyfus affair were fundamentally different. Those who interpreted the treason of certain generals and the rise of the Nationalists as omens of a third coup d'état modelled after the two previous ones, disregarded the entire social development of France in the last thirty years. The profound alterations in the social structure of France during this period may be summed up as follows. In 1799 and in 1851, the Republic was arrested and executed by the coup d'état before it had a chance to rid itself of its revolutionary baggage. The Third Republic, however, has been able to last long enough to enter a normal period of existence and prove to the bourgeoisie that it knows how to adapt itself to their interests, and much better than any monarchy in the world could possibly do.

The main body of the bourgeoisie achieved undivided political rule for the first time in the Third Republic and, has wielded it since the end of the 1870's almost continuously through the cabinets and parliamentary majorities of the opportunist petty-bourgeois parties. The French colonial policy and militarism, as well as the resulting gigantic state debt, have shown to the bourgeoisie that the Republic can compete with any monarchy in these most lucrative projects of the bourgeoisie. The Panama Canal and the South Railroad affairs have finally proved that Parliament and the Republican administration are tools no less adaptable to the lords of high finance than the political apparatus of the Orleanist monarchy.

The Third Republic, furthermore, has proved to be fertile soil for the petty bourgeoisie. A huge crop of small state creditors and state officials sprang up from the growing national debt and the continuously expanding bureaucracy. The entire existence of this army was dependent upon the peaceful stability of the Republic.

And finally, the Republic's oldest and most bitter enemies, the landowners — the small and even more the big — have been showered with golden fruits from the Republic's horn of plenty. If, at the time of the coup d'état of the second Napoleon, one section of the peasantry was already progressive enough to break with monarchal rule in a series of brutally suppressed revolts, it now had abundant opportunity to still further revise its views of the Republic. A whole series of important measures have been carried through in the last two decades that benefited most directly the wealthier peasants, the old support of Bonapartism. The reduction of land taxes alone since 1897 amounts to nearly 25 million francs. Despite the great increase of the government's net income, the tax burden of the landowners has decreased by one-sixth! The system of protective tariffs, particularly on cattle and grain, has above all added to the wealth of the landowners. Then there are the additional expenditures of hundreds of millions of francs for technical improvement, for the construction of roads, further reduction of freight rates on the products of the soil, etc.

In general, we note the nearly complete cessation of effective social reforms and the trend towards drawing the state income almost entirely from indirect taxes which bear most heavily on the masses. Between 1865 and 1897, while the population has remained constant, the income from the tariff has increased 183%, the proceeds of the tobacco monopoly by 49%, liquor taxes by 84%. All of this indicates a very obvious material gain for all the possessing classes, the costs of which are largely borne by the only non-possessing class—the proletariat.

It must be added that the Republic in its foreign affairs, was in its internal policies, gives ample proof of its usefulness by its alliance with Czarist Russia, the chieftain of European reaction. Once its greatest enemy, Russia today is the Republic's benevolent patron and ally.

The last thirty years have not passed over the stage of history without leaving their mark. They have transformed the Third Republic from the much-feared spectre of revolutionary upheaval into the normal form of existence of bourgeois society.

Today the Republic has the support of the main body of the bourgeoisie and of the peasantry—the suspicions of this one-time chief opponent having been disarmed by the Republic's proving itself a kindly protector. And the working class too, still loyal despite its being treated like a step-child, is no longer the same as in the days of the first and second coups d'état. Politically trained, clarified, organized, even if split into factions, the socialist proletariat of France, whose parties polled nearly a million votes in the last elections to the Chamber, commands respect today as firm bulwark of the Republic.

Grand Alliance in Bedlam

It is clear that in this milieu monarchism is reduced to a wholly different role than it formerly played. During the Dreyfus affair, everybody regarded the nationalist camp as the headquarters of the coup d'état purely because of the slogans of the daily struggle, even as every reactionary like Méline, Barthous, or Ribot was considered a monarchist without further thought. Closer and calmer examination, however, revealed that the Nationalists presented anything but an internally united and homogeneous political front. On the contrary, this camp was rather a rendezvous of heterogeneous elements with the most varied goals and interests.

In the center, we see the compromised top ranks of the army, the general staff, and its adherents. It is true that these, in their fear of being called to trial before the Republican civil authorities, were driven to rebel against this authority. But fundamentally, they have no serious interest in the reconstitution of the monarchy. On the contrary, it was just in the Third Republic that the army was glorified as never in the past, because of the spread of an idiotic chauvinist cult and through various reforms and special privileges. And the Dreyfus affair itself has best shown that the military heads have, from their own viewpoint, found the Republic to be a paradise. It can easily be demonstrated that a despotism and autocracy of the military chiefs such as existed under the wing of the opportunist Republic cannot be so easily conceived of under a monarchist regime. The military chiefs could not seriously feel a longing for the tight reins of the monarchy. Their anti-republicanism, in this case, was only the natural form of self-defense of swindlers who were unmasked and caught by the Republic.

Next we have the clergy, which has always been on guard under the Republic, watching for an opportunity to strangle it. No doubt the clerics exercized an enormous influence on public opinion, but they were incapable of any action, appearing only as the stage managers and prompters, and not as the actors.

Thirdly, we find a strong anti-Semitic tendency in the petty bourgeoisie, a natural development in France, the land of small enterprises and a Jewry active in the financial world. The agitation against the "Dreyfusards", as with every reactionary current, provided them with favorable grounds for a nationalist demagogy. But they had no need to declare their allegiance to a Caesarian coup d'état, nor, in fact, did they declare such an allegiance.

Finally, there are the real monarchists. Some represent the peasantry in the most backward regions of France. Others are aristocrats who were forced, during normal times, to conclude an open peace with the Third Republic as "monarchal republicans" — or at least to accomodate themselves quietly to the situation — but who now, taking heart from the crisis, appear on the political scene with their entourage of journalists and littérateurs.

It is to be expected that these elements, impotent by themselves, should, shoulder to shoulder with the papist hierarchy, at once group themselves around the hard-pressed generals, pushing them forward as the storming party and generally using the crisis for their own purposes. Nor is it to be wondered at that this circumstance, together with the rebellious attitude of the compromised general staff, should give the entire camp a tinge of Caesarism. The monarchist tendencies, injecting themselves into the Nationalist camp from without, really found no point of contact whatsoever. Not only was there no important movement in their direction from any class in society, but there was not even a focal point in the form of a seriously regarded pretender to the throne. The one, a First Lieutenant in the Russian Army, leads his obscure existence in a garrison of a provincial city of the Czar's Empire, and can no longer refer to Austerlitz and Jena as proof of his legitimacy, but must rely on Sedan and Metz. The other, a nonentity who idles about in foreign countries, has a following of a couple of hundred gray-haired men and women whose entire "agitation" consisted of gathering at an annual banquet as they lately did once more to give expression in hackneyed speeches to their hopes in the "course of events".

Under such circumstances, the united action of this camp had to content itself with whipping up a chauvinist delirium, with Jew-baiting, and with a glorification of the army it surpassed all previous performances. But nearly everything was missing for a serious political act, like the overthrow of the Republic. They lacked internal cohesiveness. organization, a program of action, and above all, an internal development of social conditions which, as in the previous cases, carried the monarchy in its womb and awaited but a coup d'état to give it birth. The Dreyfus affair provided an issue to rally around. It could supply the basis for a monarchist agitation, it could even furnish the political motive for the execution of a coup d'état, but it could not supply the positive forces which were lacking for an overthrow. Monarchism provided the outward coloration, not the content of the crisis.

The Independent role of the Army

The latter lay in a completely different direction. Even as the Third Republic was evolving into the final form of the political rule of the bourgeoisie, it was also simultaneously developing all its internal contradictions. One of these fundamental contradictions is that between a Republic based upon the rule of a bourgeois parliament and a big standing army adapted to the needs of colonial and world politics. In a strong monarchy, the army is reduced, as a matter of course, to an obedient tool in the hands of the executive power. However, in a parliamentary republic, with its momentarily changing government composed of civilians, with an elected chief-of-state whose post may go any one of the "rabble", whether formerly a tanner's apprentice or a slick-tongued lawyer, the army, with its outspoken caste-spirit, naturally shows the tendency to become an independent power, only loosely tied to the state apparatus as a whole.

The cultivation of "pressure group" politics on the part of the bourgeoisie of France has gone so far as to result their falling into separate groups, which, without any feeling of responsibility for the whole, have made the government and parliament a plaything of their special interests. This development has, on the other side, given rise to the army developing from an instrument of the state into an independent "pressure group" of its own, prepared to defend its interests without regard for the Republic, despite the Republic, and against the Republic.

The contradictions between the parliamentary Republic and the standing army can be solved only through the dissolution of the army into the civil population and the organization of the civil population into the army. This would mean changing the army from an instrument of conquest and colonial rule into an instrument of national defense In short, the solution must be found in replacing the standing army by a militia. As long as this is not done, the internal contradictions will continue to result in periodic crises, in clashes between the Republic and its own army, which the obvious results of the army's growing independence, its corruption and insubordination, become ever more prominent.

The mutiny of the military heads was one as of their attempt to assert their independence of the republican civil authorities. It by no means indicated a desire to lose this independence entirely through the establishment of monarchy. Hence the farcical character of the actions of the monarchists. A stormy pillow-fight in the press, an ear-splitting tumult by the anti-Semitic rowdies, the appearance of cheering crowds before the offices of the Nationalist press, and the noisy shattering of windows in the offices of the pro-Dreyfus papers, the insulting of innocent passers-by, the attempt to heat up the president at the race track ... but in the midst of this electrically-charged, nerve-wracking atmosphere — not a single serious political movement to carry through a coup d'état . The ferment came to a head in that great historical moment when the extravagant buffoon, Deroulede, grabbed General Roget's bridle as he was leading his troops into the barracks and, with an emphatic pose, sought to lead him against the President's palace in the Elysee, without having the slightest notion what General Roget was expected to do once he got there, nor what was to result from the whole adventure. The rogue in military uniform proved wiser than the fool in civilian clothes and a sword stroke across Deroulede's fingers was the answer to the beau geste of the anti Semitic leaders. Thus ended the sole attempt at a monarchist coup d'état.

Comedians — Monarchal and Socialist

Events in a word were considerably different than they appeared on the surface. Here, as ever, the security of the Republic did not depend on individual "saviors", above all not on a minister's seat, but upon the whole internal relationship of the economic and political conditions of the country. It is easy to understand how the danger of a coup d'etat in France could appear to be serious and great in the midst of the-tumult of the daily struggle, where an investigation of the social background of the phenomena is very difficult, virtually impossible for the participants, and where, as a matter of course, the events and facts assume exaggerated dimensions. An energetic action was natural on the part of the republicans to hold the nationalist mob and the General Staff in check — and an action outside of parliament was an even more crying need.

But to adhere to such views born in the daily struggle today, after the crisis is over and when it can be seen from a distance, and to celebrate in all seriousness the cabinet of Millerand as the true "saviors" of the French Republic, is nothing else but an example of that vulgar historical method, which, as a counterpart of vulgar economics, presents the events merely as they present themselves on the surface of political life and understands history to be the work of ministers and other "important" people, instead of understanding its true internal relationships. Millerand's salvation of the Republic is to be taken just as seriously as the monarchist threat presented by Deroulede.

Part II

If the existence of the republic had depended upon the Waldeck-Rousseau cabinet, it would have perished long ago. The buffoonery of the monarchist insurrection was matched by the buffoonery of the republican defense.

Seldom has a government taken the helm in a more serious moment and seldom has a government had greater hopes placed in it. It is time that the monarchist danger was more of a spectre than a reality. The really serious possibility, however, was that the guerilla war with the monarchist elements would reveal to the insubordinate army chiefs and mutiny-preaching clergy the impotence of the Republic and, thereby, make repetitions of similar crises inevitable in the future.

The eyes of the civilized world were turned to France. It was necessary to prove her ability to exist as an orderly state. It was necessary to show that bourgeois France still was powerful enough to isolate and neutralize the elements of disintegration that it had produced.

The measures to be taken were dictated by the situation itself. If the army has grown to an independent body and posed itself against the organism of the Republic, it is necessary to lay the axe to its independence and to draw it closer to civilian society through the abolition of the court-martial and the shortening of the period of military service. If the priests support the rebellious tendencies of the militarists and agitate against the Republic, it is necessary to destroy their power through the dissolution of the religious orders, confiscation of their property and separation of the school from the church and the church from the state.

And above all, if the corruption in the army and the legal lynching of Dreyfus — with its complex web of lies, falsifications, perjuries, and other crimes — if this has completely shattered the prestige of France, both internally and externally, it is necessary to reestablish the authority of republican justice by making an example of the guilty ones, by pardoning all those unjustly convicted, and by the full clarification of the issues.

The cabinet has been at the helm for nineteen months. It has twice outlived the average life-span of a French cabinet — the fatal nine months. What has it accomplished?

It is hard to imagine a more extreme contradiction between means and ends, between task and accomplishment, between the advance advertisement and the subsequent performance than is to be found in the expectations roused by the Waldeck-Rousseau cabinet and its achievements.

First—The Army

The whole program of reform of military justice has now been reduced to the promise of the Minister of War to take into account "mitigating circumstances" in the course of court-martial proceedings. The socialist, Pastre, speaking in the Chamber on December 27 of last year, proposed the introduction of the two year military term, a reform already introduced in semi-absolutist German). The Radical Minister of Republican Defense, General André, answered that he could take no position on this question. The socialist, Dejeante, demanded in the same session that the clergy be removed from the military academies, that the religious personnel of the military hospital be replaced by a secular personnel, and that the distribution of religious publications by the army be ended. The Minister of Republican Defense, whose task it was to secularize the army, answered with a blunt rejection of the proposals and a glorification of the spirituality of the army—amid the stormy applause of the Nationalists. In February, 1900, the socialists denounced a series of terrible abuses in the army, but the government rejected every proposal for a parliamentary investigation. The Radical, Vigne d'Octon made some gruesome revelations in the Chamber (session of December 7, 1900) on the conduct of the French military regime in the colonies, particularly in Madagascar and Indo-China. The government rejected the proposal for a parliamentary inquiry as being "dangerous and purposeless". Finally came the climax: the Minister of War mounted the tribune of the Chamber to tell of his heroic defense of—an officer of the Dragoons who was boycotted by his colleagues for having married a divorcée.

Next—The Church

A legal formula is devised which covers the monastic orders with the same provisions that apply in the case of open societies. Its application against the clergy will depend upon the good will and its application against the socialists upon the bad will of future ministers.

The Republic has in no way weakened the authorized orders. Then still have their property of almost 400 million francs, their state subsidized secular clergy headed by 87 Bishops, their 87 seminaries, their 42,000 priests, and their budget for publications of about 40 million francs. The chief strength of the clergy lies in its influence upon the education of two million French children who are at present being poisoned in the parochial schools and made into enemies of the Republic. The government bestirs itself and prohibits such instruction — by non-authorized religious orders. But almost the entire religious instruction is precisely in the hands of the authorized orders and the Radical reform results in 15,000 out of 2 million children being rescued from the holy water sprinklers. The capitulation of the government to the church was introduced with Waldeck-Rousseau's speech in which he paid his respects to the pope and was sealed with the vote of confidence in the government offered by the Nationalists.

Grand Climax: The Amnesty Laws

The "defense of the Republic" à la Waldeck-Rousseau reached its grand climax last December with the adoption of the Amnesty Law.

For two years France was in a turmoil. For two years the cry went up for truth, light, and justice. For two years a judicial murder weighed upon its conscience. Society was being literally suffocated in the poisoned atmosphere of lies, perjuries, and falsifications.

At last the government of Republican Defense arrived on the scene. All the world held its breath. The "great sun of justice" was about to rise.

And it rose. On December 19 the government had the Chamber adopt a law which guaranteed immunity to all charged with crime, which denied legal satisfaction to those falsely accused, and quashed all trials already in process. Those who were yesterday declared the most dangerous enemies of the Republic are today again taken to its bosom as prodigal sons returned home. In order to defend the Republic, a general pardon is extended to all its attackers. In order to rehabilitate Republican justice, all victims of the judicial frame-ups are denied the opportunity for vindication.

Petty-bourgeois radicalism ran true to type. In 1893 the bourgeois radicals took the helm through the Cabinet of Ribot to liquidate the crisis caused by the Panama scandal. But because the Republic was declared in danger, the accused deputies were not prosecuted and the whole affair was allowed to dissolve into thin air. Waldeck-Rousseau, commissioned to handle the Dreyfus Affair, dissolves it in a complete fiasco "in order to close the door to the monarchist danger".

The pattern is an old one:

"The shattering overture that announces the battle loses itself in a timid growl as soon as the action is to start. The actors cease to take themselves seriously, and the performance falls flat like an inflated balloon that is pricked with a needle." (Marx, *The Eighteenth Brumaire*.)

Was it to realize these grotesque, piddling, laughable measures—I speak not from the viewpoint of socialism, or even of a half-way capable radical party, but merely in comparison to the republican measures of the opportunists in the '80s, like Gambetta, Jules Ferry, Constant, and Tirard—was it for this that a socialist, the representative of working-class power, had to be taken into the cabinet?

The opportunist Gambetta, with his moderate Republicans, demanded in 1879 the removal of all monarchists from government service and, through this agitation, drove MacMahon from the presidency. In 1880 these same "respectable" Republicans carried through the expulsion of the Jesuits, and a system of compulsory, free education. The opportunist Jules Ferry drove over six hundred monarchist judges from the bench in his judicial reforms in 1883 and dealt a hard blow at the clergy with his law on divorce The opportunists Constant and Tirard, in order to cut the ground from under Boulangism, reduced the term of military service from five to three years.

The radical cabinet of Waldeck-Rousseau failed to even rise to the stature of these most modest republican measures of the opportunists. In a series of equivocal manoeuvres in the course of nineteen months it accomplished nothing, absolutely nothing. It did not carry out the least reorganization of military justice. It did not bring about the slightest reduction in the period of military service. It did not take one decisive step to drive the monarchists out of the army, judiciary, and administration. It did not undertake a single thorough measure against the clericals. The one thing it did do was to maintain its pose of fearlessness, firmness, inflexibility—the classic pose of petty-bourgeois politicians when they get into hot water. Finally, after much ado, it declared that the Republic is not in a position to do anything about the band of military rogues and simply must let them go. Was it for this that the collaboration of a socialist was necessary in the Cabinet?

How "Necessary" Was Millerand?

It has been said that Millerand was personally indispensable for the building of the Waldeck-Rousseau cabinet. As far as is generally known, France is not suffering from a lack of men who are covetous of a cabinet portfolio. If Waldeck-Rousseau could find two useful Generals in the ranks of the rebellious army to serve as Ministers of War, he could have found a half-dozen men in his own party who were eager for the post of Minister of Commerce. But after one has come to know the record of the cabinet, one must in any case admit that Waldeck-Rousseau could have calmly taken any agreeable Radical as a co-worker and the comedy of the "defense of the republic" would not have come out one hair worse. The Radicals have always understood how to compromise themselves without outside assistance.

We have seen that the monarchist danger, which scared everyone so much during the Dreyfus crisis, was more of a phantom than reality. The "defense" of Waldeck-Rousseau, therefore, was not necessary to save the Republic from a coup d'état. Those, however, who still today defend the entry of Millerand into the government as they did two years ago, and point to the monarchist danger as both the motive for the entry and for remaining, are playing a dangerous game. The more serious one paints the picture, the more pitiful appear the actions of the cabinet, and the more questionable the role of the socialists who participated.

If the monarchist danger was very slight, as we sought to establish, then the rescuing efforts of the government begun with pomp and circumstance and ended in fiasco, were a farce. If, on the other hand, the danger was great and serious, then the sham actions of the cabinet were a betrayal of the Republic and of the parties that placed their confidence in it.

In either case, the working class has not, in sending Millerand into the cabinet, taken over that "large share of responsibility" which Jaurès and his friends speak of so proudly. It has merely fallen heir to a part of the shameful "republican" disgrace of petty-bourgeois radicalism.

The contradiction between the hopes confided in the cabinet of Waldeck-Rousseau and its actual achievements has confronted the Jaurès-Millerand section of French socialism with but one alternative. It could confess its disillusionment, admit the uselessness of Millerand's participation in the government, and demand his resignation. Or it could declare itself satisfied with the politics of the government, pronounce the realities to be just what it had expected, and gradually tone down its expectations and demands to correspond with the gradual evaporation of the government's will-to-action.

As long as the cabinet avoided the main question and remained in the stage of preliminary skirmishes—and this stage lasted an entire eighteen months—all political tendencies that followed its policies, including the socialists, could still drift along with it. However, the first decisive step of the government—the Amnesty Law—pushed matters out of their twilight zone into the clear light of day.

"The Whole Truth!"

The outcome of the Dreyfus Affair was of decisive importance for the Jaurès group, whether they liked it or not. To play on this card, and this card only, had been their tactic for two full years. The Dreyfus Affair was the axis of all their politics. They described it as "one of the greatest battles of the century, one of the greatest of human history!". To shrink from this great task of the working class would mean "the worst abdication, the worst humiliation". *"Toute la verité! La pleine lumiére!"* The whole truth, full light, that was the goal of the socialist campaign. Nothing could stop Jaurès and his friends—neither difficulties nor nationalist manoeuvres nor the protests of the socialist group led by Guesde and Vaillant.

"We battle onward, (Jaurès called out with noble pride) and if the judges of Rennes, deceived by the detestable manoeuvres of the reactionaries, should again victimize the innocent in order to save the criminal army chiefs, we will again stand up on the morrow, despite all proclamations of expulsion, despite all mealy-mouthed references to the falsification, distortion, and belittling of the class struggle, despite all dangers, and call out to the generals and the judges: You are hangmen and criminals!"

During the trial at Rennes, Jaurès wrote confidently:

"Be it as it may, justice will triumph! The hour is drawing nigh for the freeing of the martyrs and for the punishment of the criminals!"

As late as November of last year, shortly before the passage of the Amnesty Law, Jaurès declared at Lille:

"For my part I was prepared to go further. I wanted to continue until the poisonous beasts would be forced to spit out their poison. Yes, it was necessary to prosecute all forgers, all liars, all criminals, all traitors; it is necessary to pursue them to the extreme summits of the truth, as on the extreme point of a knife, until they were forced to admit their crimes and the ignominy of their crimes before the entire world."

And Jaurès was right. The Dreyfus Affair had awakened all the latent forces of reaction in France. The old enemy of the working class, militarism, stood completely exposed, and it was necessary to direct all spears against its body. The working class was called upon for the first time to fight out a great political battle. Jaurès and his friends led the workers into the struggle and thereby opened up a new epoch in the history of French socialism.

Jaurès Crosses the Rubicon

As the Amnesty Law was presented to the Chamber, the right-wing socialists suddenly found themselves facing a Rubicon. It was now clear that the government that had been formed to liquidate the Dreyfus crisis, instead of "turning on the spotlight", instead of establishing the "entire truth", and instead of forcing the military despots to their knees, had extinguished truth and light and bowed its own knee to the military despots. This was a betrayal of the hopes Jaurès and his friends had placed on the government. This ministerial post revealed itself to be a useless tool for socialist politics and the defense of the Republic. The tool had turned against the master. If the Jaurès group wanted to remain true to their position in the Dreyfus campaign and to the task of republican defense, they immediately had to turn their weapons and use every means to defeat the Amnesty Law. The government had laid their cards on the table. It was necessary to trump them.

But to decide on the Amnesty proposal was also to decide on the existence of the cabinet. Since the Nationalists declared themselves against the Amnesty, and made the question one of a vote of confidence in the government, it was easy for a majority to be formed against the proposal and lead to the downfall of the cabinet.

Jaurès and his friends now had to make a choice: either fight through to the finish their two-year campaign on the Dreyfus issue, or to support the Waldeck-Rousseau cabinet, either for the "full truth" or the cabinet, either for the defense of the Republic or the ministerial post of Millerand. The question balanced in the scales for only a few minutes. Waldeck-Millerand outweighed Dreyfus. The cabinet's ultimatum accomplished what the Guesde-Vaillant manifestoes of excommunication had failed to accomplish: in order to save the cabinet, Jaurès and his group voted for the amnesty and thereby gave up the Dreyfus campaign.

The die had been cast. With the acceptance of the Amnesty Law, the right-wing socialists made as the guide for their conduct, not their own political interests, but the maintenance at the helm of the Waldeck-Rousseau cabinet. The vote for the Amnesty Law was the Waterloo of their Dreyfus campaign. In the twinkling of an eye, Jaurès had brought to naught all he accomplished in the course of two years.

The Retreat Becomes a Rout

After surrendering their chief political stock, the Jaurès group sped merrily on their sportive way. To save the government, they gave up — reluctantly and with internal Katzenjammer over the costly price — the goal of two years of gigantic struggles: the "whole truth" and "complete light". But to justify their own adherence to a government of political fiascos, they had to deny the fiascos. Their next step was to justify the capitulation of the government.

The government pigeon-holed the Dreyfus Affair instead of fighting it through to the end? But that was necessary "in order to put an end to the now useless and boring trials and avoid sickening the people with too much publicity, which would now soon obscure the truth."

It is true that two years ago the whole of "loyal and honest France" had been called upon to pledge: "I swear that Dreyfus is innocent, that the innocent shall be vindicated and the guilty shall be punished".

But today "all these judicial trials would be an absurdity. They would only tire the country without clarifying it and hurt the cause we are trying to serve ... The true justification of the Dreyfus Affair lies today in the work for the Republic as a whole".

Yet another step and the former heroes of the Dreyfus Campaign appear to the Jaurès group as troublesome ghosts of the past with whom one cannot finish quickly enough.

Zola, the "great defender of justice", "the pride of France and of humanity", the man of the thundering *J'Accuse!*, issues a protest against the Amnesty Law. He insists now, as previously, on "the whole truth and the full light". He accuses once more. What confusion! Does he not see, asks Jaurès, that there is already "enough light" to penetrate all intellects? Zola should forget his failure to be vindicated before a court of law and remember that he is glorified in the eyes of "that great judge, the whole of humanity", and please, be so kind as not to bother us with his eternal *J'Accuse*! "Only no accusations, no empty reiterations!" The work for the Republic as a whole, that is the main thing.

The heroic Picquart, "the honor and pride of the French army", "the pure knight of truth and justice", rejects as an insult his prospective recall to the army under the Amnesty Law—what arrogance! Does not the government offer him, with its intended recall to the army, "the most brilliant vindication"? True enough, Picquart has a right to have the truth spread on the records of the courts. But our good friend Picquart should not forget that the truth is not only a concern of Col. Picquart, but of the whole of humanity. And in comparison to humanity as a whole, Picquart's concern for vindication plays a little role indeed. "In fact, we must not permit ourselves, in, our insistence upon justice, to be limited to individual cases." The work for the Republic as a whole, that is the main thing.

Dreyfus, this "example of human suffering in its deepest agony", this "incarnation of humanity itself upon the summits of misfortune and desperation"—Dreyfus defended himself, bewildered, against the Amnesty Law, which cut off his last hope for legal rehabilitation— what rapacity! Do not his tormentors suffer enough already? Esterhazy drags himself through the streets of London, "hungry and broken in spirit". Boisdeffre was forced to flee from the general staff. Gonse is out of the top ranks and goes about dejected. DePellieux died in disgrace. Henry committed suicide by cutting his throat. Du Paty de Clam is out of the service. What more can one ask for? Are not the pangs of their conscience enough punishment for the criminals? And if Dreyfus is not content with this favorable outcome of events and insists upon punishment by human courts—just let him be patient. "There will come a time when punishment will overtake the wretches." "There will come a time" but right now the good Dreyfus must realize that there are more important problems in the world than these "useless and boring trials". "We have better things to gain from the Dreyfus affair than all this agitation and acts of revenge." The work for the Republic as a whole, that is the main thing.

One more step and the Jaurès group regard all criticism of the government's policies, to which the Dreyfus campaign was offered as a sacrificial lamb, as frivolous playing with the "government of Republican Defense".

Sobering voices are gradually raised in Jaurès' own camp to question the action of the cabinet in the "democratization of the army" and the "secularization of the Republic" — what light-mindedness! How terrible "systematically and with nervous impatience (after eighteen months — R.L.) to discredit the first achievements of our common efforts ... Why discourage the proletariat?" The proposals of the government on the religious orders was a capitulation to the church? Only a "dilettante and mealy-mouthed performer" could say that. As a matter of fact, "it is the greatest struggle between the church and bourgeois society since the laws on the secularization of the schools"

And if, in general, the government flounders from one fiasco to another, does not the "assurance of future victories" remain? Is not a matter of single laws — the work for the Republic as a whole, that is the main thing.

Just what, after all of this procrastination, is the "work for the Republic as a whole"? It is no longer the liquidation of the Dreyfus Affair, nor the reorganization of the army, nor the subordination of the church. As soon as the existence of the cabinet is threatened, everything else is given up. It suffices for the government, in order to pass its favorite measures, to pose it as a vote of confidence and Jaurès and his friends are safely put into the harness

Yesterday, the cabinet must take defensive action it order to save the Republic. Today, the defense of the Republic must be given up in order to save the cabinet. "The work for the Republic as a whole" means, today, the mobilization of all Republican forces to keep the cabinet of Waldeck-Millerand at the helm.

Part III

The present attitude of the Jaurès group towards the policies of the government is, in one sense, in direct contradiction to its position during the Dreyfus Affair. But, in another sense, it is nothing but a direct continuation of the previous policy. The same principle — unity with the bourgeois democrats — served as the basis of socialist policy in both cases. It served during two years of unyielding struggle for a solution of the Dreyfus Affair, and, today, because the bourgeois democrats have deserted the fight, it leads the socialists to also liquidate the Dreyfus Affair and to give up all attempts at a fundamental reformation of the army and a change in the relations between Republic and Church.

Instead of making the independent political struggle of the Socialist party the permanent. fundamental element and unity with bourgeois radicals the varying and incidental element, this principle caused Jaurès to adopt the opposite tactic: the alliance with the bourgeois democrats became the constant, and the independent political struggles the incidental element.

Already in the Dreyfus campaign, the Jaurès socialists failed to understand the line of demarcation between the bourgeois and the proletarian camps: If the question presented itself to the friends of Dreyfus as an attack upon the by-products of militarism—as the cleansing of the army and the suppression of corruption—a socialist had to view it as a struggle against the root of the evil—against the standing army itself. And if the bourgeois radicals considered justice for Dreyfus and punishment for the guilty ones as the single central point of the campaign, a socialist had to view the Dreyfus Affair as the basis for an agitation in favor of the militia system. Only thus would the Dreyfus Affair and the admirable efforts of Jaurès and his friends have been a great agitational service to socialism. Actually, however, the agitation of the socialist camp, on the whole, ran in the same shallow channels as the agitation of the bourgeois radicals with a few individual exceptions in which the deeper significance of the Dreyfus Affair was touched upon. It was exactly in this sphere that the socialists, despite their greater efforts, perseverance, and brilliance, failed to be the vanguard, and acted as the co-workers and camp followers of the bourgeois radicals. With the entry of Millerand into the radical cabinet, the socialists stood entirely upon the same ground as their bourgeois allies.

The circumstance which divides socialist politics from bourgeois politics is that the socialists are opponents of the entire existing order and must function in a bourgeois parliament fundamentally as an opposition. The most important aim of socialist activity in a parliament, the education of the working class, is achieved by a systematic criticism of the ruling party and its politics. The socialists are too far removed from the bourgeois order to be able to achieve practical and thorough-going reforms of a progressive character. Therefore, principled opposition to the ruling party becomes, for every minority party and above all for the socialists, the only feasible method with which to achieve practical results.

Not having the possibility of carrying their own policies with a parliamentary majority, the Socialists are forced to wring concessions from the bourgeois majority by constant struggle. They achieve this through their critical opposition in three ways.

1.Their demands are the most advanced, so that when they compete with the bourgeois parties at the polls, they bring to bear the pressure of the voting masses.

2.They constantly expose the government before the people and arouse public opinion.

3.Their agitation in and out of parliament attracts ever greater masses about them and they thus grow to become a power with which the government and the entire bourgeoisie must reckon.

The French socialists grouped about Jaurès have closed all three roads to the masses by the entry of Millerand into the government.

Above all, an uncompromising criticism of the government's policies has become impossible for the Jaurès socialists. If they wanted to chastise the cabinet for its weaknesses, its half-measures, its treachery, the blows would beat down upon their own backs. If the efforts of the government at Republican defense are a fiasco, the question immediately arises, what is the role of a socialist in such a government? In order not to compromise the ministerial post of Millerand, Jaurès and his friends must remain silent in the face of all the acts of the government that could be used to open the eyes of the working class. It is a fact that since the organization of the Waldeck-Rousseau Cabinet, all criticism of the government has vanished from the organ of the right wing of the socialist movement, Pétite République and every attempt at such criticism is immediately denounced by Jaurès as "nervousness," "pessimism," and "extremism." The first consequence of socialist participation in a coalition cabinet is, therefore, the renunciation of the most important task of all socialist activity and, above all, of parliamentary activity: the political education and clarification of the masses.

Furthermore, in those instances where they have been critical, the followers of Millerand have robbed their criticism of all practical significance. Their conduct in the matter of the amnesty proposals showed that no sacrifice is too great for them in order to keep the government in power. It revealed that they arc prepared is advance to cast their votes for the government in every instance when the government levels a pistol, in the form of a vote of confidence, at their breast.

It is true that the socialists in a country governed by a parliament are not as free in their conduct as, for instance, in the German

Reichstag where they can take a position of opposition without regard for the consequences and at all times express themselves unmistakably on it. Out of regard for the "lesser evil," the French socialists on the contrary, see themselves constantly forced to defend a bourgeois government with their votes. But, on the other hand, it is specifically through the parliamentary régime that the socialists gain a sharp weapon which they can hold over the head of the government like a Sword of Damocles and with which they can give their demands and their criticisms added emphasis. But in making themselves dependent upon the government through the cabinet post of Millerand, Jaurès and his friends remade the government independent of them. Instead of being able to use the spectre of a cabinet crisis to force concessions from the government, the socialists, on the contrary, placed the government in a position where it could use the cabinet crisis as a Damocles sword over the head of the socialists to be used at any time to force them into line.

The Jaurès group has become a second Prometheus hound. A striking example is the recent debate on the law regulating the right of association. Jaurès' friend, Vivian, tore to pieces the government's proposals on the religious orders in a brilliant speech in the Chamber and counterposed the real solution to the problems. When, however, Jaurès, on the following day, after overwhelming praise for the speech, puts into the mouth of the government the answers to Viviani's criticism, and when, without even waiting for the debate to open and before all attempts to improve the government's proposals, Jaurès advises the socialists and the Radicals to guarantee. the acceptance of the government's measures at any price, the entire political effect of Viviani's speech is destroyed.

The ministerial position of Millerand transforms—this is its second consequence—the socialist criticism of his friends in the Chamber into empty holiday speeches, without any influence whatsoever upon the practical politics the government.

Finally, the tactic of pushing the bourgeois parties forward through the pressure of the socialists reveals itself this instance, as an empty dream.

In order to safeguard the future existence of the government, the supporters of Millerand think they must maintain the closest cooperation with the other groups of the Left. The Jaurès group is swallowed up entirely by general "republican" swamp of the Left, of which Jaurès is the leading brain.

In the service of Millerand, his socialist friends play present, the role usually played by the bourgeois Radicals.

Yes, contrary to general practice, the Radicals play the role of the most thorough-going oppositionists within present Republican majority and the socialists play the role of the right wing, the moderate governmental elements.

D'Octon and Pelletan, both Radicals, were the ones forcefully demanded an inquiry into the horrible colonial administration, while two socialist deputies of the right wing found it possible to vote against the inquiry. It was the Radical Vazeille who opposed the strangling of Dreyfus Affair by means of the Amnesty Law, while the socialists finally voted against Vazeille.

Finally, it is the socialistic Radical, Pelletan, who gives the following advice to the Socialists.

The question comes down to this; does a government exist to serve the ideas of the party that supports it or to lead that party to a betrayal of its ideas? O, the men whom we maintain at the helm don't fool us! With the exception of two or three Ministers, they all rule about in the same manner as a Cabinet headed by Méline would. And those parties that should warn the Cabinet and chastise it, crawl upon their stomachs before it. I, for my part, belong to those who view as excellent strategy the attempt of the Socialist party to place one of its people in power, instead of isolating itself as a result of a systematic struggle against government. Yes, I hold this strategy to be first rate. But to what purpose? So that the progressive policies in the Cabinet receive added support, and not so that the worst omissions by the Cabinet find the socialists as hostages.... Today, Waldeck-Rousseau is no longer an ally, as we would like to believe, but the guide of the conscience of the progressive parties. And he guides them, it appears to me, a little too far. It suffices to have him pull out of his pocket the bogey-man of the Cabinet crisis to make himself obeyed. Beware! The politics of the country will lose something when out of us and out of you there will be formed a new category of sub-opportunists.

Socialists who attempt to win away petty-bourgeois Democrats from their position of opposition to the government, and petty-bourgeois Democrats who accuse the Socialists of crawling on their stomachs before the government and of betraying their own ideas — that is the lowest level to which socialism has yet sunk, and at the same time the final consequence of socialist Ministerialism.

Thus the tactic of Jaurès, which through the sacrifice of the socialist principle of opposition sought to achieve practical results, has revealed itself to be the most impractible in the world.

Instead of increasing the influence of the socialists upon the government and the bourgeois parliament, the tactics of Jaurès has made them into involuntary tools of the government and passive appendages of the petty-bourgeois radicals.

Instead of giving the progressive policies of the Chamber a new impetus, the withdrawal of the socialist opposition killed the last chance of bringing the Chamber to act in a decisive and courageous manner.

And this is their greatest failure. The fiasco of the Waldeck-Millerand-inspired actions of republican defense was not accidental but the logical result of the impotence from which the bourgeois radicals in the Chamber suffered from the very beginning and to which the socialists condemned themselves through their participation in the bourgeois radical government.

If the miserable "actions" of the Waldeck-Rousseau government signified the sad end of its republican mission to an impartial observer, they signified to Jaurès, despite weaknesses which he could not deny when pointed out from his own ranks, the happy beginning of a great era of democratic renaissance in France, based upon the firm alliance of socialism with petty bourgeois democracy.

"That is why (writes Jaurès), the building of an ever so timid left majority for the support of an ever so indecisive and weak a government of the left, is, in my view, a fact of the greatest importance. I regard it as an embryonic, but necessary foundation of the legislative and administrative organism which will lead society into the path toward the realization of the highest equality for which we strive."

It is this distant vision of the coming epoch when the socialist proletariat and the radical petty bourgeoisie will rule together that makes it necessary to maintain the government of Waldeck-Rousseau at the price of principled political aims! This it is that makes it necessary to maintain the alliance with the bourgeois left at the expense of independent Socialist opposition! Jaurès has only left out of sight, in this grandiose political cloud-castle, the fact that petty bourgeois radicalism, which he wants to place in power with the support of the socialists, has already collapsed long ago as the result of a tactic which has sad similarities to that of Jaurès.

The Republican program has been the foundation for the political role of the French petty bourgeoisie since the Great Revolution. As long as the big bourgeoisie entrenched themselves behind the monarchy, the petty bourgeoisie could appear as the leader of the masses. The contradiction between the working class and the bourgeoisie, in large measure, took the form of a difference between the Republic and the Monarchy and constituted a firm backbone for the petty-bourgeois opposition.

These circumstances have changed with the development of the Third Republic. With the transformation of the big bourgeoisie from an enemy into the very backbone of the Republic and the realization of the petty-bourgeois program—republican form of government, "sovereignty of the people" through a parliamentary regime, freedom of press, organization, and conscience—the ground was pulled from under the feet of petty-bourgeois politics and its spear directed against the bourgeoisie was broken. Only the outer decorations of a bourgeois republic remain as the aim of the petty-bourgeois "radical" program, like a progressive tax system, reform of public education, and the struggle with clericalism.

While the political differences between the petty bourgeoisie and the big bourgeoisie disappeared, the social differences between the bourgeoisie and the working class developed still more deeply. Together with the soul of program, the petty-bourgeois radicals lost many of their supporters. The proletariat appeared on the scene as at independent party in the sharpest conflict with the Radicals as well as with the Moderates. Within the Radical camp itself a differentiation took place. While one section was impelled by material interests to draw close to the bourgeoisie, another section found itself forced to adopt a socialist coloration.

"Pure" middle class radicalism, reduced to the role of weak buffer party, could only choose one of two courses to carry through its program. It could either limit itself to the role of an opposition in the Chamber and use the extra parliamentary pressure of the masses to support it, or it could limit itself to parliamentary combinations for the purpose of participating in the government of the big bourgeoisie.

The first course, to win the support of the masses in competition with a socialist working class party, had now become doubly impossible for the Radicals. Not only could they offer the working class little, but due to the prominence and stability of small industry in France, the petty bourgeoisie was frightened away by the social aspirations of the proletariat. And since it persisted with its paltry program there was no other way left open but parliamentary cooperation with the bourgeoisie. And this was the beginning of its collapse.

In ordinary times, petty-bourgeois radicalism was assigned the role of being a passive accomplice of the opportunistic bourgeoisie in the joint cabinets. But from time to time it had the opportunity to prove that it was absolutely indispensable. This occurred whenever the bourgeoisie had compromised itself by some scandal and threw the Republic into a crisis. In such a situation, radicalism finds the opportunity to again pull out its old tattered program of "defense of the Republic" and to temporarily take over the helm Regularly at this point, the fact that the Radicals lack parliamentary majority to carry through their program is "discovered," though this is always a known fact from which the proper conclusions can be drawn in advance.

In order to keep itself at the helm and to rule, Radicalism is forced to desert its own program and either hide behind pretenses designed to conceal its inactivity or to take to the road of openly opportunistic politics. In either case it reveals to the Chamber its superfluity and to the country its unreliability and thus becomes ever more an impotent tail to the bourgeois kite.

The record of the Waldeck-Rousseau Cabinet is a faithful picture of such Radical politics. If one regards the "united left," upon which Jaurès wants to build the entire present-day politics of the Socialist party, as a compact political group that has come together for the cleansing and reforming of the Republic, one makes the same mistake of overestimation as made in that view according to which the nationalist camp is a compact mass with serious monarchist longings.

Quite the contrary, we see in the "united left" the most varied elements, with all shades from socialism to reaction represented. The extreme right wing, the Progressives of the Isembére group, rub elbows with the storm troops of Méline. The "united left", internally divided, has only come together out of a common necessity for the reconstitution of law and order. When this objective has been achieved—and it appears as if the Amnesty Law is its classic solution—the binding interests recede into the background, the left disintegrates, and the "government of Republican defense" is left suspended in mid-air. The fact that the Méline Cabinet had a majority in this very same Chamber indicates that the present majority is only a temporary one. And the recent election of Deschanels to the presidency of the Chamber, which could only take place due to the betrayal of their own candidate, Brisson, by a section of the Left, shows that the collapse of the "united left" is only a matter of time.

And this situation gives a logical explanation of the conduct of the Waldeck-Rousseau Cabinet. Not having the possibility to undertake any sort of thoroughgoing action, it feels itself compelled to blunt the edges of the contradictions that had been sharpened by the crisis through a series of capitulations. Thus it emerges true to the traditions of petty-bourgeois radicalism. Taking over the helm without the power to carry out its own program, it ends up by betraying it.

The government of Waldeck-Millerand is, therefore, not the beginning of an era of democratic rule based upon the socialist-radical alliance, as Jaurès sees it. It is much more the continuation of the previous history of the petty-bourgeois radicals who feel themselves called upon, not to realize their own democratic program, but to periodically clean away the political dirt piled up by the big bourgeoisie so that bourgeois reaction can continue a normal existence in its republican form. The new era begun with the Cabinet of Waldeck-Rousseau, unfortunately, consists of the fact that for the first time the socialists have participated in this historic mission of the petty bourgeoisie. The socialists, under the illusion that they were serving the program of socialism, were in reality serving as shock troops for the petty-bourgeois radicals in the same manner that the latter, under the illusion that they were serving the program of democracy, were in reality serving as the shock troops of the big bourgeoisie.

The tactic of Jaurès is, therefore, built on sand. The rise of petty-bourgeois democracy, which was to be facilitated by Millerand's entry into the government and by the surrender of their position as parliamentary opposition by the socialists, reveals itself to be a phantom. Contrary to his aim, Jaurès has crippled the only force in France that could have defended democracy and the Republic, by chaining the socialist proletariat to the corpse of petty bourgeois radicalism.

From
Marxist Theory and the Proletariat
(1903)

In his article on Feuerbach, Engels formulated the essence of philosophy as its attempt to answer the eternal quest of the relationship between thinking and being, the problem of human consciousness in an objective material world. If we transfer these concepts of being and thinking from the abstract world of nature and individual speculation, i.e., from spheres where philosophers by profession operate, into the sphere of social life, then the same thing can in a certain sense be said about socialism that Engels said about philosophy. From ancient times socialism has been the search, the groping for ways and means to harmonize being with thinking, that is to say, to harmonize historical forms of life with social consciousness.

Marx together with his friend Engels was destined to discover the solution to this problem over which men had racked their brains for centuries. Marx discovered that history of all previous societies was in the last analysis the history of the relations of production and distribution in these societies, and that the development of these relations under the rule of private property manifests itself in the sphere of political and social institutions in the form of the class struggle; and by this discovery Marx laid bare the most important motive force in history. At the same time an explanation was discovered for the necessary disharmony in all societies existing up to now between consciousness and existence, between the desires of mankind and the social reality, between intentions and results.

Thus, thanks to the ideas of Karl Marx, men learned the first time the secret of their own social progress. Over and above this, the discovery of the laws of capitalist development likewise pointed out the road along which society is moving—from the spontaneous and unconscious stages during which men made history in the same manner as bees construct their hives, to the conscious, creative and genuinely human historical stage, that stage when the will of society and social reality shall for the first time be harmoniously correlated with each other, when the actions of the social man will for the first time produce precisely the results he will desire.

In Engels' words, this final "leap from the animal kingdom into the domain of human freedom" will be achieved for society as a whole only with the accomplishment of the socialist overturn; but this is already being accomplished within framework of the existing order through the social-democratic policies. With the Ariadne thread of Marx's teachings in its hands, the workers' party is today the only party which, from the historical point of view, is conscious of what it is doing; and by virtue of this is doing precisely that which it desires. This is the whole secret of the power of social-democracy (revolutionary Marxism was known by this name in Rosa's time— Editor).

The bourgeois world has long been astonished by the extraordinary, insuperable and constant growth of the social-democracy. Now and then, isolated senile or infantile naive minds are to be found, who, being blinded by the extraordinary moral successes of our politics, advise the bourgeoisie to take us as an "example" and to drink deeply of the mysterious wisdom and idealism of the social-democracy. They are incapable of understanding that what is a source of life and vigor, a fountain of youth, for the developing working class is for the bourgeois parties—mortal poison.

And indeed what is it that gives us moral strength, courageously and laughingly to undergo and free ourselves from the cruellest repressions, such as the current twenty-year law against the socialists? Is it perhaps the stubbornness of paupers seeking petty improvements in their material conditions? The modern proletariat is not a shopkeeper, not a petty bourgeois ready to become a hero for the sake of miserable day-to-day comforts. The lack of idealism, the sober narrowness of the English trade unions demonstrates how little capable of creating a high moral upsurge among the proletariat is the mere calculation for petty material boons.

Is it perhaps the ascetic stoicism of a sect like that among the early Christians — a stoicism which flares all the more brightly the more it is persecuted? The modern proletariat, as the heir and foster-child of bourgeois society, is far too much a born materialist, far too much an individual of flesh and blood and healthy instincts to draw its strength and devotion to ideas, in accordance with the morale of slaves, from sufferings alone.

Or, finally, is it perhaps the "justice" of the cause for which we are fighting that makes us unconquerable? The cause of the Chartists and of the followers of Weitling, the cause of the utopian socialist doctrines was no less "just" than our cause. Nevertheless all these doctrines were shattered against the obstacles of modern society.

If, contrary to all the efforts of our enemies, the modern labor movement marches triumphantly forward, its head raised high, then it owes this first and foremost to its calm understanding of the lawfulness of objective historical development, its understanding that "capitalist society with the inevitability of a natural process creates its own negation, namely, the expropriation of the expropriators, the socialist overturn." In this, its understanding, the labor movement sees a reliable guarantee of its final victory. And from this same source it draws not only its ability to surge forward but also its patience; not only strength for action, but also the courage to stand firm and to endure.

The National Question
(1909)

1. The Right of Nations to Self-Determination

Among other problems, the 1905 Revolution in Russia has brought into focus the nationality question. Until now, this problem has been urgent only in Austria-Hungary. At present, however, it has become crucial also in Russia, because the revolutionary development made all classes and all political parties acutely aware of the need to solve the nationality question as a matter of practical politics. All the newly formed or forming parties in Russia, be they radical, liberal or reactionary, have been forced to include in their programs some sort of a position on the nationality question, which is closely connected with the entire complex of the state's internal and external policies. For a workers' party, nationality is a question both of program and of class organization. The position a workers' party assumes on the nationality question, as on every other question, must differ in method and basic approach from the positions of even the most radical bourgeois parties, and from the positions of the Pseudo-socialistic, petit bourgeois parties. Social Democracy, whose political program is based on the scientific method of historical materialism and the class struggle, cannot make an exception with respect to the nationality question. Moreover, it is only by approaching the problem from the standpoint of scientific socialism that the politics of Social Democracy will offer a solution which is essentially uniform, even though the program must take into account the wide variety of forms of the nationality question arising from the social, historical, and ethnic diversity of the Russian empire.

In the program of the Social Democratic Labor Party (RSDLP) of Russia, such a formula, containing a general solution of the nationality question in all its particular manifestations, is provided by the ninth point; this says that the party demands a democratic republic whose constitution would insure, among other things, "that all nationalities forming the state have the right to self-determination."

This program includes two more extremely important propositions on the same matter. These are the seventh point, which demands the abolition of classes and the full legal equality of all citizens without distinction of sex, religion, race or nationality, and the eighth point, which says that the several ethnic groups of the state should have the right to schools conducted in their respective national languages at state expense, and the right to use their languages at assemblies and on an equal level with the state language in all state and public functions. Closely connected to the nationality question is the third point of the program, which formulates the demand for wide self-government on the local and provincial level in areas which are characterized by special living conditions and by the special composition of their populations. Obviously, however, the authors of the program felt that the equality of all citizens before the law, linguistic rights, and local self-government were not enough to solve the nationality problem, since they found it necessary to add a special paragraph granting each nationality the "right to self-determination."

What is especially striking about this formula is the fact that it doesn't represent anything specifically connected with socialism nor with the politics of the working class. "The right of nations to self-determination" is at first glance a paraphrase of the old slogan of bourgeois nationalism put forth in all countries at all times: "the right of nations to freedom and independence." In Poland, the "innate right of nations" to freedom has been the classic formula of nationalists from the Democratic Society to Limanowski's Pobudka, and from the national socialist Pobudka to the anti-socialist National League before it renounced its program of independence. Similarly, a resolution on the "equal rights of all nations" to freedom was the only tangible result of the famous pan-Slav congress held in Prague, which was broken up in 1848 by the pan-Slavic bayonets of Windischgraetz. On the other hand, its generality and wide scope, despite the principle of "the right of nations to self-determination" which obviously can be applied not only to the peoples living in Russia but also to the nationalities living in Germany and Austria, Switzerland and Sweden, America—strangely enough is not to be found in any of the programs of today's socialist parties. This principle is not even included in the program of Austrian Social Democracy, which exists in a state with an extremely mixed population, where the nationality question is of crucial importance.

The Austrian party would solve the nationality question not by a metaphysical formula which leaves the determination of the nationality question up to each of the nationalities according to their whims, but only by means of a well-defined plan. Austrian Social Democracy demands the elimination of the existing state structure of Austria, which is a collection of "kingdoms and princely states" patched together during the Middle Ages by the dynastic politics of the Hapsburgs, and includes various nationalities mixed together territorially in a hodgepodge manner. The party rather demands that these kingdoms and states should be divided into territories on the basis of nationality, and that these national territories be joined into a state union. But because the nationalities are to some extent jumbled together through almost the entire area of Austria, the program of Social Democracy makes provision for a special law to protect the smaller minorities in the newly created national territories.

Everyone is free to have a different opinion on this plan. Karl Kautsky, one of the most knowledgeable experts on Austrian conditions and one of the spiritual fathers of Austrian Social Democracy, shows in his latest pamphlet, *Nationality and Internationalism*, that such a plan, even if it could be put into effect, would by no means completely eliminate the conflicts and difficulties among the nationalities. Nonetheless, it does represent an attempt to provide a practical solution of these difficulties by the party of the proletariat, and because of the importance of the nationality question in Austria, we shall quote it in full.

The nationality program of the Austrian party, adopted at the Brünn Congress in 1899, says:

"Because national conflicts in Austria are obstructing all political progress and the cultural development of the nationalities, because these conflicts result primarily from the backwardness of our public institutions and because the prolongation of these conflicts is one of the methods by which the ruling classes insure their domination and prevent measures in the true interests of the people, the congress declares that:

"The final settlement of the nationality and language question in Austria in the spirit of equality and reason is primarily a cultural demand, and therefore is one of the vital interests of the proletariat.

"This is possible only under a truly democratic regime based on universal, equal, and direct elections, a regime in which all feudal privileges in the state and the principalities will have been abrogated. Only under such a regime will the working classes, the elements which really support the state and society, be able to express their demands.

"The nurturing and development of the national peculiarities of all peoples in Austria are possible only on the basis of equal rights and the removal of oppression. Therefore, state-bureaucratic centralism and the feudal privileges of the principalities must be opposed.

"Only under such conditions will it be possible to create harmony among the nationalities in Austria in place of the quarrelling that takes place now, namely, through the recognition of the following guiding principles:

"Austria is to be transformed into a democratic federation of nationalities (*Nationalitätenbundesstaat*).

"The historic Crown lands are to be replaced by nationally homogeneous self-ruling bodies, whose legislation and administration shall be in the hands of national chambers, elected on the basis of universal, equal, and direct franchise.

"All self-governing regions of one and the same nation are to form together a nationally distinct union, which shall take care of this union's affairs autonomously. (That is, linguistic and cultural, according to the explanation given in the draft by the party's leadership.)

"A special law should be adopted by the parliament to safeguard the rights of national minorities.

"We do not recognize any national privilege; therefore we reject the demand for a state language. Whether a common language is needed, a federal parliament can decide.

"The party congress, as the organ of international social democracy in Austria, expresses its conviction that on the basis of these guiding principles, understanding among peoples is possible.

"It solemnly declares that it recognizes the right of each nationality to national existence and national development.

"Peoples can advance their culture only in close solidarity with one another, not in petty quarrels; particularly the working class of all nations must, in the interest of the individual nationalities and in the general interest, maintain international cooperation and fraternity in its struggle and must conduct its political and economic struggle in closely united ranks."

In the ranks of international socialism, the Russian Workers' Party is the only one whose program includes the demand that "nationalities be granted the right to self-determination."

Apart from Russian Social Democracy, we find this formula only in the program of the Russian Social Revolutionaries, where it goes hand in hand with the principle of state federalism. The relevant section of the political declaration of the Social Revolutionary Party states that "the wide application of the principle of federalism in the relations between individual nationalities is possible," and stresses the "recognition of their unlimited right to self-determination."

It is true that the above formula exists in another connection with international socialism: namely, it is a paraphrase of one section of the resolution on the nationality problem adopted in 1896 by the International Socialist Congress in London. However, the circumstances which led to the adoption of that resolution, and the way in which the resolution was formulated, show clearly that if the ninth paragraph in the program of the Russian party is taken as an application of the London Resolution, it is based on a misunderstanding.

The London resolution was not at all the result of the intention or need to make a statement at an international congress on the nationality question in general, nor was it presented or adopted by the Congress as a formula for the practical resolution of that question by the workers' parties of the various countries. Indeed, just the opposite was true. The London Resolution was adopted on the basis of a motion presented to the Congress by the social-patriotic faction of the Polish movement, or the Polish Socialist Party (PPS), a motion which demanded that the reconstruction of an independent Poland be recognized as one of the most urgent demands of international socialism. Influenced by the criticism raised at the Congress by Polish Social Democracy and the discussion concerning this in the socialist press, as well as by the first mass demonstration of the workers' movement in Russia, the memorable strike of forty thousand textile workers in Petersburg in May 1896, the International Congress did not consider the Polish motion, which was directed in its arguments and in its entire character against the Russian revolutionary movement. Instead, it adopted the London Resolution already mentioned, which signified a rejection of the motion for the reconstruction of Poland.

"The Congress" — the resolution states — "declares itself in favor of the complete right of all nations to self-determination, and expresses its sympathy for the workers of every country now suffering under the yoke of military, national, or other despotism; the Congress calls on the workers of all these countries to join the ranks of the class-conscious workers of the whole world in order to fight together with them for the defeat of international capitalism and for the achievement of the aims of international Social Democracy."

As we can see, in its content, the London Resolution replaces the exclusive consideration of the Polish question by the generalization of the question of all suppressed nationalities, transferring the question from a national basis onto an inter-national one, and instead of a definite, completely concrete demand of practical politics, which the motion of the PPS demanded — the reconstruction of independent Poland — the resolution expresses a general socialist principle: sympathy for the proletariat of all suppressed nationalities and the recognition of their right to self-determination. There can be no doubt that this principle was not formulated by the Congress in order to give the international workers' movement a practical solution to the nationality problem. On the contrary, a practical guideline for socialist politics is contained not in the first part of the London Resolution quoted above, but in the second part, which "calls upon the workers of all countries suffering national oppression to enter the ranks of international Social Democracy and to work for the realization of its principles and goals." It is an unambiguous way of emphasizing that the principle formulated in the first part — the right of nations to self-determination can be put into effect only in one way: viz., by first realizing the principles of international socialism and by attaining its ultimate goals.

Indeed, none of the socialist parties took the London Resolution to be a practical solution of the nationality question, and they did not include it in their programs. Even Austrian Social Democracy, for which the solution of the nationality problem was a question involving its very existence, did not do this; instead, in 1899, it created for itself independently the practical "nationality program" quoted above. What is most characteristic, even the PPS did not do this, because, despite its efforts to spread the tale that the London Resolution was a formula in "the spirit" of socialism, it was obvious that this Resolution meant rather a rejection of its motion for the reconstruction of Poland, or at the very least, a dilution of it into a general formula without any practical character. In point of fact, the political programs of the modern workers' parties do not aim at stating abstract principles of a social ideal, but only at the formulation of those practical social and political reforms which the class-conscious proletariat needs and demands in the framework of bourgeois society to facilitate the class struggle and their ultimate victory. The elements of a political program are formulated with definite aims in mind: to provide a direct, practical, and feasible solution to the crucial problems of political and social life, which are in the area of the class struggle of the proletariat; to serve as a guideline for everyday politics and its needs; to initiate the political action of the workers' party and to lead it in the right direction; and finally, to separate the revolutionary politics of the proletariat from the politics of the bourgeois and petit bourgeois parties.

The formula, "the right of nations to self-determination," of course doesn't have such a character at all. It gives no practical guidelines for the day to day politics of the proletariat, nor any practical solution of nationality problems. For example, this formula does not indicate to the Russian proletariat in what way it should demand a solution of the Polish national problem, the Finnish question, the Caucasian question, the Jewish, etc. It offers instead only an unlimited authorization to all interested "nations" to settle their national problems in any way they like. The only practical conclusion for the day to day politics of the working class which can be drawn from the above formula is the guideline that it is the duty of that class to struggle against all manifestations of national oppression. If we recognize the right of each nation to self-determination, it is obviously a logical conclusion that we must condemn every attempt to place one nation over another, or for one nation to force upon another any form of national existence. However, the duty of the class party of the proletariat to protest and resist national oppression arises not from any special "right of nations," just as, for example, its striving for the social and political equality of sexes does not at all result from any special "rights of women" which the movement of bourgeois emancipationists refers to. This duty arises solely from the general opposition to the class regime and to every form of social inequality and social domination, in a word, from the basic position of socialism. But leaving this point aside, the only guideline given for practical politics is of a purely negative character. The duty to resist all forms of national oppression does not include any explanation of what conditions and political forms the class-conscious proletariat in Russia at the present time should recommend as a solution for the nationality problems of Poland, Latvia, the Jews, etc., or what program it should present to match the various programs of the bourgeois, nationalist, and pseudo-socialist parties in the present class struggle. In a word, the formula, "the right of nations to self-determination," is essentially not a political and problematic guideline in the nationality question, but only a means of avoiding that question.

II

The general and cliché-like character of the ninth point in the program of the Social Democratic Labor Party of Russia shows that this way of solving the question is foreign to the position of Marxian socialism. A "right of nations" which is valid for all countries and all times is nothing more than a metaphysical cliché of the type of "rights of man" and "rights of the citizen." Dialectic materialism, which is the basis of scientific socialism, has broken once and for all with this type of "eternal" formula. For the historical dialectic has shown that there are no "eternal" truths and that there are no "rights." ... In the words of Engels, "What is good in the here and now, is an evil somewhere else, and vice versa" — or, what is right and reasonable under some circumstances becomes nonsense and absurdity under others. Historical materialism has taught us that the real content of these "eternal" truths, rights, and formulae is determined only by the material social conditions of the environment in a given historical epoch.

On this basis, scientific socialism has revised the entire store of democratic clichés and ideological metaphysics inherited from the bourgeoisie. Present-day Social Democracy long since stopped regarding such phrases as "democracy," "national freedom," "equality," and other such beautiful things as eternal truths and laws transcending particular nations and times. On the contrary, Marxism regards and treats them only as expressions of certain definite historical conditions, as categories which, in terms of their material content and therefore their political value, are subject to constant change, which is the only "eternal" truth.

When Napoleon or any other despot of his ilk uses a plebiscite, the extreme form of political democracy, for the goals of Caesarism, taking advantage of the political ignorance and economic subjection of the masses, we do not hesitate for a moment to come out wholeheartedly against that "democracy," and are not put off for a moment by the majesty or the omnipotence of the people, which, for the metaphysicians of bourgeois democracy, is something like a sacrosanct idol.

When a German like Tassendorf or a tsarist gendarme, or a "truly Polish" National Democrat defends the "personal freedom" of strikebreakers, protecting them against the moral and material pressure of organized labor, we don't hesitate a minute to support the latter, granting them the fullest moral and historical right to force the unenlightened rivals into solidarity, although from the point of view of formal liberalism, those "willing to work" have on their side the right of "a free individual" to do what reason, or unreason, tells them.

When, finally, liberals of the Manchester School demand that the wage worker be left completely to his fate in the struggle with capital in the name of "the equality of citizens," we unmask that metaphysical cliché which conceals the most glaring economic inequality, and we demand, point-blank, the legal protection of the class of wage workers, thereby clearly breaking with formal "equality before the law."

The nationality question cannot be an exception among all the political, social, and moral questions examined in this way by modern socialism. It cannot be settled by the use of some vague cliché, even such a fine-sounding formula as "the right of all nations to self-determination." For such a formula expresses either absolutely nothing, so that it is an empty, noncommittal phrase, or else it expresses the unconditional duty of socialists to support all national aspirations, in which case it is simply false.

On the basis of the general assumptions of historical materialism, the position of socialists with respect to nationality problems depends primarily on the concrete circumstances of each case, which differ significantly among countries, and also change in the course of time in each country. Even a superficial knowledge of the facts enables one to see that the question of the nationality struggles under the Ottoman Porte in the Balkans has a completely different aspect, a different economic and historical basis, a different degree of international importance, and different prospects for the future, from the question of the struggle of the Irish against the domination of England. Similarly, the complications in the relations among the nationalities which make up Austria are completely different from the conditions which influence the Polish question. Moreover, the nationality question in each country changes its character with time, and this means that new and different evaluations must be made about it. Even our three national movements, beginning from the time of the Kosciuszko Insurrection, could be seen as a triple, stereotyped repetition of the same historical play (that is, "the struggle of a subjugated nationality for independence") only in the eyes of either a metaphysician of the upper-class Catholic ideology such as Szujski, who believed that Poland had historical mission to be the "Christ of nations," or in the eyes of an ignoramus of the present-day social-patriotic "school." Whoever cuts deeper with the scalpel of the researcher—more precisely, of the historical-materialist researcher—will see beneath the surface of our three national uprisings three completely different socio-political movements, which took on an identical form of struggle with the invader in each case only because of external circumstances. To measure the Kosciuszko Insurrection and the November and January insurrections by one and the same yardstick—by the sacred laws of the "subjugated nation"—actually reveals a lack of all judgment and the complete absence of any historical and political discrimination.

A glaring example of how the change of historical conditions influences the evaluation and the position of socialists with respect to the nationality question is the so-called Eastern question. During the Crimean war in 1855, the sympathies of all democratic and socialist Europe were on the side of the Turks and against the South Slavs who were seeking their liberty. The "right" of all nations to freedom did not prevent Marx, Engels, and Liebknecht from speaking against the Balkan Slavs and from resolutely supporting the integrity of the Turks. For they judged the national movements of the Slavic peoples in the Turkish empire not from the standpoint of the "eternal" sentimental formulae of liberalism, but from the standpoint of the material conditions which determined the content of these national movements, according to their views of the time. Marx and Engels saw in the freedom movement of the socially backward South Slavs only the machinations of Russian tsardom trying to irritate the Turks, and thus, without any second thoughts, they subordinated the question of the national freedom of the Slavs to the interests of European democracy, insisting on the integrity of Turkey as a bulwark of defense against Russian reaction. This political position was maintained in German Social Democracy as late as the second half of the 1890s, when the gray-haired Wilhelm Liebknecht, on the occasion of the struggle of the Ormian Turks, still spoke in that spirit. But by this time the position of German and international Social Democracy on the Eastern question had changed. Social Democracy began to support openly the aspirations of the suppressed nationalities in Turkey to a separate cultural existence, and abandoned all concern for the artificial preservation of Turkey as a whole. And at this time it was guided not by a feeling of duty toward the Ormians or the Macedonians as subjugated nationalities, but by the analysis of the material base of conditions in the East in the second half of the last century. By this analysis, the Social Democrats became convinced that the political disintegration of Turkey would result from its economic-political development in the second half of the nineteenth century, and that the temporary preservation of Turkey would serve the interests of the reactionary diplomacy of Russian absolutism. Here, as in all other questions, Social Democracy was not contrary to the current of objective development, but with it, and, profiting from its conclusions, it defended the interests of European civilization by supporting the national movements within Turkey. It also supported all attempts to renew and reform Turkey from within, however weak the social basis for such a movement may have been.

A second example of the same thing is provided by the diametrically opposite attitudes of Marx and Engels during the revolution of 1848 with respect to the national aspirations of the Czechs and the Poles. There is no doubt that from the point of view of the "right of nations to self-determination" the Czechs deserved the support of the European socialists and democrats no less than the Poles. Marx, however, did not pay any attention to that abstract formula, and hurled thunderbolts at the heads of the Czechs and their aspirations for freedom, aspirations which he regarded as a harmful complication of the revolutionary situation, all the more deserving of severe condemnation, since, to Marx, the Czechs were a dying nationality, doomed to disappear soon. The creators of *The Communist Manifesto* put forth these views at the same time that they were defending the nationalist movement of the Poles with all their strength, calling upon all revolutionary and progressive forces to help our patriots.

The sober realism, alien to all sentimentalism, with which Marx examined the national problems during the revolution itself, is shown by the way he treated the Polish and Czech questions:

"The Revolution of 1848," wrote Marx in his articles on the revolution which appeared in February 1852 in the American paper, *Daily Tribune*, "calling forth at once the claim of all oppressed nations to an independent existence, and to the right to settle their own affairs for themselves, it was quite natural that the Poles should at once demand the restoration of their country within the frontiers of the old Polish Republic before 1772. It is true, this frontier, even at that time, had become obsolete, if taken as the delimitation of German and Polish nationality; it had become more so every year since by the progress of Germanization; but then, the Germans had proclaimed such an enthusiasm for the restoration of Poland, that they must expect to be asked, as a first proof of the reality of their sympathies, to give up their share of the plunder. On the other hand, should whole tracts of land, inhabited chiefly by Germans, should large towns, entirely German, be given up to a people that as yet had never given any proofs of its capability of progressing beyond a state of feudalism based upon agricultural serfdom? The question was intricate enough. The only possible solution was in a war with Russia. The question of delimitation between the different revolutionized nations would have been made a secondary one to that of first establishing a safe frontier against the common enemy. The Poles, by receiving extended territories in the east, would have become more tractable and reasonable in the west; and Riga and Milan would have been deemed, after all, quite as important to them as Danzig and Elbing. Thus the advanced party in Germany, deeming a war with Russia necessary to keep up the Continental movement, and considering that the national reestablishment even of a part of Poland would inevitably lead to such a war, supported the Poles; while the reigning, middle-class party clearly foresaw its downfall from any national war against Russia, which would have called more active and energetic men to the helm, and, therefore, with a feigned enthusiasm for the extension of German nationality, they declared Prussian Poland, the chief seat of Polish revolutionary agitation, to be part and parcel of the German Empire that was to be."

Marx treated the Czech question with no less political realism:

"The question of nationality gave rise to another struggle in Bohemia. This country, inhabited by two millions of Germans, and three millions of Slavonians of the Czechian tongue, had great historical recollections, almost all connected with the former supremacy of the Czechs. But then the force of this branch of the Slavonic family had been broken ever since the wars of the Hussites in the fifteenth century. The province speaking the Czechian tongue was divided, one part forming the kingdom of Bohemia, another the principality of Moravia, a third the Carpathian hill country of the Slovaks, being part of Hungary. The Moravians and Slovaks had long since lost every vestige of national feeling, and vitality, although mostly preserving their language. Bohemia was surrounded by thoroughly German countries on three sides out of four. The German element had made great progress on her own territory; even in the capital, in Prague, the two nationalities were pretty equally matched; and everywhere capital, trade, industry, and mental culture were in the hands of the Germans. The chief champion of the Czechian nationality, Professor Palacky, is himself nothing but a learned German run mad, who even now cannot speak the Czechian language correctly and without foreign accent. But, as it often happens, dying Czechian nationality, dying according to every fact known in history for the last four hundred years, made in 1848 a last effort to regain its former vitality an effort whose failure, independently of all revolutionary considerations, was to prove that Bohemia could only exist, henceforth, as a portion of Germany, although part of her inhabitants might yet, for some centuries, continue to speak a non□German language." *(Revolution and Konterrevolution in Deutschland, pp.57-62)*

We quote the above passages in order to stress the methods which Marx and Engels used with respect to the nationality question, methods not dealing in abstract formulae, but only in the real issues of each individual case. That method did not, though, keep them from making a faulty evaluation of the situation, or from taking a wrong position in certain cases. The present state of affairs shows how deeply Marx was in error in predicting, sixty years ago, the disappearance of the Czech nationality, whose vitality the Austrians today find so troublesome. Conversely, he overestimated the international importance of Polish nationalism: this was doomed to decay by the internal development of Poland, a decay which had already set in at that time. But these historical errors do not detract an ounce from the value of Marx's method, for there are in general no methods of research which are, a priori, protected against a wrong application in individual cases. Marx never claimed to be infallible, and nothing, in the last resort, is so contrary to the spirit of his science as "infallible" historical judgments. It was possible for Marx to be mistaken in his position with respect to certain national movements, and the author of the present work tried to show in 1896 and 1897 that Marx's views on the Polish question, as on the Eastern question, were outdated and mistaken. But it is this former position of Marx and Engels on the question of Turkey and the South Slavs, as well as on the national movement of the Czechs and Poles, that shows emphatically how far the founders of scientific socialism were from solving all nationality questions in one manner only, on the basis of one slogan adopted a priori. It also shows how little they were concerned with the "metaphysical" rights of nations when it was a matter of the tangible material problems of European development.

Finally, an even more striking example of how the creators of modern socialist politics treated the national question is their evaluation of the freedom movement of the Swiss in the fourteenth century. This is part of history, therefore free from the influence of all the expectations and passions of day to day politics. The uprising of the Swiss cantons against the bloody oppression of the Hapsburg despotism (which, in the form of the historical myth of William Tell, is the object of absolute worship by the liberal-bourgeois romantic idealist) was appraised by Friedrich Engels in 1847 in the following way:

"The struggle of the early Swiss against Austria, the famous oath at Rytli, the heroic shot of Tell, the immortal victory at Morgarten — all this represented the struggle of restless shepherds against the thrust of historical development, a struggle of hidebound, conservative, local interests against the interests of the entire nation, a struggle of primitivism against enlightenment, barbarism against civilization. They won their victory over the civilization of that period, but as punishment they were cut off from the whole later progress of civilization."

To this evaluation Kautsky adds the following commentary:

"A question mark could be added to the above concerning the civilizing mission which the Hapsburgs were carrying out in Switzerland in the fourteenth century. On the other hand it is correct that the preservation of the independence of the cantons was an event which was conservative to the nth degree, and in no way revolutionary, and that thenceforth the freedom of those cantons served as a means of preserving an element of blackest reaction in the center of Europe. It was those forest cantons which defeated Zwingli and his army in 1531 at the battle of Kappel, and thereby put a stop to the spread of Protestantism in Switzerland. They provided armies to all the despots of Europe, and it was the Swiss of the forest cantons who were the staunchest supporters of Louis XVI against the revolution. For this the republic raised a magnificent monument to them in Lucerne." (*Die Neue Zeit*, 1904-1905, Vol.II, p.146.)

From the point of view of the "right of nations to self-determination," the Swiss uprising obviously deserves the sympathy of socialists on all scores. There is no doubt that the aspirations of the Swiss to free themselves from the Hapsburg yoke were an essential expression of the will of the "people" or a huge majority of them. The national movement of the Swiss had a purely defensive character, and was not informed by the desire to oppress other nationalities. It was intended only to throw off the oppression of a foreign and purely dynastic invader. Finally, this national movement formally bore all the external characteristics of democratism, and even revolutionism, since the people were rebelling against absolute rule under the slogan of a popular republic.

In complete contrast to this movement is the national uprising in Hungary in 1848. It is easy to see what would have been the historical outcome of the victory of the Hungarians because the social and national conditions of that country insured the absolute domination of the Magyar minority over the mixed majority of the other, subjugated nationalities. A comparison of these two struggles for national independence — the Hungarian in 1848 and the Swiss five centuries earlier — is all the more significant since both were directed against the same enemy: the absolutism of the Austrian Hapsburgs. The method and the viewpoint on national politics of Marx and Engels are brought into high relief by this comparison. Despite all the external evidences of revolutionism in the Swiss movement, and despite the indisputable two-edged character of the Magyar movement, obvious in the flunkeyism with which the Hungarian revolutionaries helped the Vienna government to suppress the Italian revolution, the creators of scientific socialism sharply criticized the Swiss uprising as a reactionary event, while they supported fervently the Hungarian uprising in 1848. In both cases they were guided not by the formula of "the right of nations to self-determination," which obviously was much more applicable to the Swiss than to the Magyars, but only by a realistic analysis of the movements from a historical and political standpoint. The uprising of the fragmented peasant cantons, with their regionalism against the centralist power of the Hapsburgs, was, in the eyes of Engels, a sign of historical reaction, just as the absolutism of the princely power, moving toward centralism, was at that time an element of historical progress. From a similar standpoint, we note in passing, Lassalle regarded the peasant wars, and the parallel rebellion of the minor knights of the nobility in Germany in the sixteenth century against the rising princely power, as signs of reaction. On the other hand, in 1848, Hapsburg absolutism was already a reactionary relic of the Middle Ages, and the national uprising of the Hungarians—a natural ally of the internal German revolution—directed against the Hapsburgs naturally had to be regarded as an element of historical progress.

III

What is more, in taking such a stand Marx and Engels were not at all indulging in party or class egoism, and were not sacrificing entire nations to the needs and perspectives of Western European democracy, as it might have appeared.

It is true that it sounds much more generous, and is more flattering to the overactive imagination of the young "intellectual," when the socialists announce a general and universal introduction of freedom for all existing suppressed nations. But the tendency to grant all peoples, countries, groups, and all human creatures the right to freedom, equality, and other such joys by one sweeping stroke of the pen, is characteristic only of the youthful period of the socialist movement, and most of all of the phraseological bravado of anarchism.

The socialism of the modern working class, that is, scientific socialism, takes no delight in the radical and wonderful-sounding solutions of social and national questions, but examines primarily the real issues involved in these problems.

The solutions of the problems of Social Democracy are not in general characterized by "magnanimity," and in this respect they are always outdone by socialist parties which are not hampered by scientific "doctrines," and which therefore always have their pockets full of the most beautiful gifts for everyone. Thus, for example, in Russia, the Social Revolutionary Party leaves Social Democracy far behind in the agricultural question; it has for the peasants a recipe for the immediate partial introduction of socialism in the village, without the need of a boring period of waiting for the conditions of such a transformation in the sphere of industrial development. In comparison with such parties, Social Democracy is and always will be a poor party, just as Marx in his time was poor in comparison with the expansive and magnanimous Bakunin, just as Marx and Engels were both poor in comparison with the representatives of "real" or rather "philosophical" socialism. But the secret of the magnanimity of all socialists with an anarchist coloration and of the poverty of Social Democracy, is that anarchistic revolutionism measures "strength by intentions, not intentions according to strength"; that is, it measures its aspirations only by what its speculative reason, fumbling with an empty utopia, regards as "good" and "necessary" for the salvation of humanity. Social Democracy, on the other hand, stands firmly on historical ground in its aspirations, and therefore reckons with historical possibilities. Marxian socialism differs from all the other brands of socialism because, among other things, it has no pretensions to keeping patches in its pocket to mend all the holes made by historical development.

Actually, even if as socialists we recognized the immediate right of all nations to independence, the fates of nations would not change an iota because of this. The "right" of a nation to freedom as well as the "right" of the worker to economic independence are, under existing social conditions, only worth as much as the "right" of each man to eat off gold plates, which, as Nicolaus Chernyshevski wrote, he would be ready to sell at any moment for a ruble. In the 1840s the "right to work" was a favorite postulate of the Utopian Socialists in France, and appeared as an immediate and radical way of solving the social question. However, in the Revolution of 1848 that "right" ended, after a very short attempt to put it into effect, in a terrible fiasco, which could not have been avoided even if the famous "national work-shops" had been organized differently. An analysis of the real conditions of the contemporary economy, as given by Marx in his *Capital*, must lead to the conviction that even if present-day governments were forced to declare a universal "right to work," it would remain only a fine-sounding phrase, and not one member of the rank and file of the reserve army of labor waiting on the sidewalk would be able to make a bowl of soup for his hungry children from that right.

Today, Social Democracy understands that the "right to work" will stop being an empty sound only when the capitalist regime is abolished, for in that regime the chronic unemployment of a certain part of the industrial proletariat is a necessary condition of production. Thus, Social Democracy does not demand a declaration of that imaginary "right" on the basis of the existing system, but rather strives for the abolition of the system itself by the class struggle, regarding labor organizations, unemployment insurance, etc., only as temporary means of help.

In the same way, hopes of solving all nationality questions within the capitalist framework by insuring to all nations, races, and ethnic groups the possibility of "self-determination" is a complete utopia. And it is a utopia from the point of view that the objective system of political and class forces condemns many a demand in the political program of Social Democracy to be unfeasible in practice. For example, important voices in the ranks of the international workers' movement have expressed the conviction that a demand for the universal introduction of the eight-hour day by legal enactment has no chance of being realized in bourgeois society because of the growing social reaction of the ruling classes, the general stagnation of social reforms, the rise of powerful organizations of businessmen, etc. Nonetheless, no one would dare call the demand for the eight-hour day a utopia, because it is in complete accordance with the progressive development of bourgeois society.

However, to resume: the actual possibility of "self-determination" for all ethnic groups or otherwise defined nationalities is a utopia precisely because of the trend of historical development of contemporary societies. Without examining those distant times at the dawn of history when the nationalities of modern states were constantly moving about geographically, when they were joining, merging, fragmenting, and trampling one another, the fact is that all the ancient states without exception are, as a result of that long history of political and ethnic upheavals, extremely mixed with respect to nationalities. Today, in each state, ethnic relics bear witness to the upheavals and intermixtures which characterized the march of historical development in the past. Even in his time, Marx maintained that these national survivals had no other function but to serve as bastions of the counter-revolution, until they should be completely swept from the face of the earth by the great hurricane of revolution or world war. "There is no country in Europe," he wrote in the *Neue Rheinische Zeitung*: "which doesn't have in some corner one or more of these ruins of nations, the remains of an ancient people displaced and conquered by a nation which later became a standard-bearer of historical development. These remains of nationalities, mercilessly trampled on by history—as Hegel says—these national left-overs will all become and will remain until their final extermination or denationalization fanatic partisans of the counter-revolution, since their entire existence is in general a protest against the great historical revolution. For ex-ample, in Scotland the Gaels were the mainstays of the Stuarts from 1640 to 1745; in France, it was the Bretons who were the mainstays of the Bourbons from 1792 to 1800; while in Spain, the Basques were the supporters of Don Carlos. In Austria, to take another example, the pan-Slavic South Slavs are nothing more than the national left-overs of a highly confused thousand-year-long development." (*Aus dem literarischen Nachlass von Karl Marx, Friedrich Engels und Ferdinand Lasalle*, Vol. III, p.241)

In another article, treating the pan-Slavs' strivings for the independence of all Slavic nations, Marx writes, "The Germans and Hungarians, during the times when great monarchies were a historical necessity in Europe, forged all those petty, crippled, powerless little nations into one big state, thereby allowing them to participate in the development of history which, if left to themselves, they would have completely missed. Today, because of the huge progress of industry, trade, and communications, political centralization has become an even more pressing need than it was in the fifteenth and sixteenth centuries. What is not yet centralized is being centralized." (Ibid., p.255.)

We abandoned Marx's views on the South Slavs a long time ago: but the general fact is that historical development, especially the modern development of capitalism, does not tend to return to each nationality its independent existence, but moves rather in the opposite direction, and this is as well known today as during the time of the *Neue Rheinische Zeitung*.

In his most recent paper, *Nationality and Internationalism*, Karl Kautsky makes the following sketch of the historical fates of nationalities:

"We have seen that language is the most important means of social intercourse. As that intercourse grows with economic development, so the circle of people using the same language must grow as well. From this arises the tendency of unified nations to expand, to swallow up other nations, which lose their language and adopt the language of the dominant nation or a mixture."

According to Kautsky, three great cultural communities of humanity developed simultaneously: the Christian, the Muslim, and the Buddhist.

"Each of these three cultural groupings includes the most variegated languages and nationalities. Within each one most of the culture is not national but international. But universal communication has further effects. It expands even more and everywhere establishes the domination of the same capitalist production ... Whenever a closely knit community of communication and culture exists for a fairly long time among a large number of nations, then one or a few nations gain ascendancy over the government, the military, the scientific and artistic heights. Their language becomes indispensable for every merchant and educated man in that international cultural community. Their culture — in economy, art, and literature — lends its character to the whole civilization. Such a role was played in the Mediterranean basin until the end of ancient times by Greek and Latin. In the Mohammedan world it is played by Arabic; in the Christian, including Jews and atheists, German, English, and French have become universal languages ... Perhaps economic and political development will add Russian to these three languages. But it is equally possible that one of them, English, will become the only common language ... The joining of nations to the international cultural community will be reflected in the growth of universal languages among merchants and educated people. And this union was never as closely knit as it is now; never was a purely national culture less possible. Therefore it strikes us as very strange when people talk always of only a national culture and when a goal of socialism is considered to be the endowing of the masses with a national culture ... When socialist society provides the masses with an education, it also gives them the ability to speak several languages, the universal languages, and therefore to take part in the entire international civilization and not only in the separate culture of a certain linguistic community. When we have got to the point where the masses in our civilized states can master one or more of the universal languages besides their native language, this will be a basis for the gradual withdrawal and ultimately the complete disappearance of the languages of the smaller nations, and for the union of all civilized humanity into one language and one nationality, just as the peoples in the eastern basin of the Mediterranean were united in Hellenism after Alexander the Great, and the peoples of the western area later merged into the Roman nationality.

"The variety of languages within our circle of civilization makes understanding among members of the various nations difficult and is an obstacle to their civilized progress. But only socialism will overcome that obstacle, and much work will be needed before it can succeed in educating entire masses of people to obtain visible results. And we must keep in mind already today that our internationalism is not a special type of nationalism differs from bourgeois nationalism only in that it does not behave aggressively—that it leaves to each nation the same right which it demands for its own nation, and thereby recognizes the complete sovereignty (Soveränität) of each nation. Such a view, which transforms the position of anarchism concerning individuals onto nations, does not correspond to the close cultural community existing between nations of contemporary civilisation."

These last, in fact, in regard to economy and civilization, form one single social body whose welfare depends on the harmony of the cooperation of the parts, possible only by the subordination of all the parts to the whole. The Socialist International is not a conglomerate of autocratic nations, each doing what it likes, as long as it does not interfere with the equality of rights of the others; but rather an organism wherein the better it works, the easier it is for its parts to come to agreement and the more they work together according to a common plan.

Such is the historical scheme as described by Kautsky. To be sure, he presents the matter from a different point of view than Marx does, emphasizing mainly the side of cultural, peaceful development, whereas Marx accents its political side, an external armed conquest. Both, however, characterize the fate of nationalities in the course of events, not as tending to separate themselves and become independent, but completely vice-versa. Kautsky formulates—as far

as we know, for the first time in socialistic literature of recent times –
"the historical tendency to remove completely all national distinctions
within the socialist system and to fuse all of civilized humanity into
one nationality". (K. Kautsky, *Nationalität und Internationaliät*, pp.12-
17 & p.23.)

"However"' – that theoretician believes – "at the present time
capitalist development gives rise to phenomena which seem to work
in the opposite direction: the awakening and intensification of
national consciousness as well as the need for a national state" which
is the state form "best corresponding to modern conditions, the form
in which it can most easily fulfill its tasks." (ibid.)

The "best national state" is only an abstraction which can be easily
described and defined theoretically, but which doesn't correspond to
reality. Historical development toward a universal community of
civilization will, like all social development, take place in the midst of
a contradiction, but this contradiction, with respect to the
consolidating growth of international civilization, lies in another area
than where Kautsky seeks it, not in the tendency toward the idea of a
"national state," but rather where Marx indicates it to be, in the
deadly struggle among nations, in the tendency to create – alongside
the great areas of civilization and despite them – great capitalist
states. The development of world powers, a characteristic feature of
our times growing in importance along with the progress of
capitalism, from the very outset condemns all small nations to
political impotence. Apart from a few of the most powerful nations,
the leaders in capitalist development, which possess the spiritual and
material resources necessary to maintain their political and economic
independence, "self-determination," the independent existence of
smaller and petty nations, is an illusion, and will become even more
so. The return of all, or even the majority of the nations which are
today oppressed, to independence would only be possible if the
existence of small states in the era of capitalism had any chances or
hopes for the future. Besides, the big-power economy and politics – a
condition of survival for the capitalist states – turn the politically
independent, formally equal, small European states into mutes on the
European stage and more often into scapegoats. Can one speak with
any seriousness of the "self-determination" of peoples which are
formally independent, such as Montenegrins, Bulgarians, Rumanians,
the Serbs, the Greeks, and, as far as that goes, even the Swiss, whose
very independence is the product of the political struggles and

diplomatic game of the "Concert of Europe"? From this point of view, the idea of insuring all "nations" the possibility of self-determination is equivalent to reverting from Great-Capitalist development to the small medieval states, far earlier than the fifteenth and sixteenth centuries.

The other principal feature of modern development, which stamps such an idea as utopian, is capitalist imperialism. The example of England and Holland indicates that under certain conditions a capitalist country can even completely skip the transition phase of "national state" and create at once, in its manufacturing phase, a colony-holding state. The example of England and Holland, which, at the beginning of the seventeenth century, had begun to acquire colonies, was followed in the eighteenth and nineteenth centuries by all the great capitalist states. The fruit of that trend is the continuous destruction of the independence of more and more new countries and peoples, of entire continents.

The very development of international trade in the capitalist period brings with it the inevitable, though at times slow ruin of all the more primitive societies, destroys their historically existing means of "self-determination," and makes them dependent on the crushing wheel of capitalist development and world politics. Only complete formalist blindness could lead one to maintain that, for example, the Chinese nation (whether we regard the people of that state as one or several nations) is today really "determining itself." The destructive action of world trade is followed by outright partition or by the political dependence of colonial countries in various degrees and forms. And if Social Democracy struggles with all its strength against colonial policy in all its manifestations, trying to hinder its progress, then it will at the same time realize that this development, as well as the roots of colonial politics, lies at the very foundations of capitalist production, that colonialism will inevitably accompany the future progress of capitalism, and that only the innocuous bourgeois apostles of "peace" can believe in the possibility of today's states avoiding that path. The struggle to stay in the world market, to play international politics, and to have overseas territories is both a necessity and a condition of development for capitalist world powers. The form that best serves the interests of exploitation in the contemporary world is not the "national" state, as Kautsky thinks, but a state bent on conquest. When we compare the different states from the point of view of the degree to which they approach this ideal, we see that it is not the French state which best fits the model, at least not in its European part which is homogeneous with respect to nationality. Still less does the Spanish state fit the model; since it lost its colonies, it has shed its imperialist character and is purely "national" in composition. Rather do we look to the British and German states as models, for they are based on national oppression in Europe and the world at large — and to the United States of America, a state which keeps in its bosom like a gaping wound the oppression of the Negro people, and seeks to conquer the Asiatic peoples.

The following table illustrates the imperialist tendency of national conquest. The figures refer to the number of oppressed people in colonies belonging to each country.

The huge figures quoted, which include around five hundred million people, should be increased by the colossal addition of the countries which do not figure as colonies, but are actually completely dependent on European states, and then we should break these totals down into countless nationalities and ethnic groups to convey an idea of the effects to date of capitalist imperialism on the fates of nations and their ability to "determine themselves."

	Asia	Africa	America	Australasia
Great Britain	361,445,000	40,028,000	7,557,300	5,811,000
France	18,073,000	31,500,000	428,819	89,000
Germany	120,041	11,447,000	—	448,000
Holland	37,734,000	—	142,000	—
Belgium	—	19,000,000	—	—
Denmark	—	—	42,422	—
Spain	—	291,000	—	—
Portugal	810,000	6,460,000	—	—
USA	7,635,426	—	953,243	13,000

Of course, the history of the colonial expansion of capitalism displays to some extent the contradictory tendency of the legal, and then political gaining of independence of the colonial countries. The history of the breaking away of the United States from England at the end of the eighteenth century, of the countries of South America from Spain and Portugal in the twenties and thirties of the last century, as well as the winning of autonomy by the Australian states from England, are the most obvious illustrations of this tendency. However, a more careful examination of these events will point at once to the special conditions of their origins. Both South and North America, until the nineteenth century, were the victims of a still primitive system of colonial administration, based more on the plundering of the country and its natural resources for the benefit of the treasures of European states than on a rational exploitation for the benefit of capitalist production. In these cases, it was a matter of an entire country, which possessed all the conditions for the independent development of capitalism, making its own way by breaking the rotting fetters of political dependence. The force of that capitalist thrust was stronger in North America, which was dependent on England, while South America, until then predominantly agricultural, met a much weaker resistance from Spain and Portugal, which were economically backward. Obviously, such an exceptional wealth of natural resources is not the rule in all colonies. On the other hand, the contemporary system of colonization has created a dependence which is much less superficial than the previous one. But the winning of independence by the American colonies did not remove national dependence, it only transferred it to another nationality — only changed its role. Take first the United States: the element freeing itself from the scepter of England was not a foreign nation but only the same English emigrants who had settled in America on the ruins and corpses of the redskin natives — which is true also of the Australian colonies of England, in which the English constitute 90 percent of the population. The United States is today in the vanguard of those nations practicing imperialist conquest. In the same way, Brazil, Argentina, and the other former colonies whose leading element is immigrants — Portuguese and Spanish — won independence from the European states primarily in order to exercise control over the trade in Negroes and their use on the plantations, and to annex all the weaker colonies in the area. Most likely the same conditions prevail in India, where lately there has appeared a rather serious "national" movement against England. The very existence in India of a huge number of nationalities at different degrees of social and civilized development, as well as their mutual dependence, should warn against too hasty evaluation of the Indian movement under the simple heading of "the rights of the nation."

Apparent exceptions only confirm on closer analysis the conclusion that the modern development of capitalism cannot reconciled with the true independence of all nationalities.

It is true the problem appears much simpler if, when discussing nationality, we exclude the question of colonial partitions. Such a technique is often applied, consciously or unconsciously, by the defenders of the "rights of nations"; it also corresponds to the position with respect to colonial politics taken, for example, by Eduard David in the German Social Democracy or van Kol in the Dutch. This point of view considers colonialism in general as the expression of the civilizing mission of European peoples, inevitable even in a socialist regime. This view can be briefly described as the "European" application of the philosophical principle of Fichte in the well known paraphrase of Ludwig Brone: *"Ich bin ich — was ausser mir ist Lebensmittel"* ("I am myself — what is outside of me is the means of life"). If only the European peoples are regarded as nations proper, while colonial peoples are looked on as "supply depots," then we may use the term "nation-state" in Europe for countries like France, Denmark, or Italy, and the problem of nationality can be limited to intra-European dimensions. But in this case, "the right of nations to self-determination" becomes a theory of the ruling races and betrays clearly its origin in the ideologies of bourgeois liberalism together with its "European" cretinism. In the approach of socialists, such a right must, by the nature of things, have a universal character. The awareness of this necessity is enough to indicate that the hope of realizing this "right" on the basis of the existing setup is a utopia; it is in direct contradiction to the tendency of capitalist development on which Social Democracy has based its existence. A general attempt to divide all existing states into national units and to re-tailor them on the model of national states and statelets is a completely hopeless, and historically speaking, reactionary undertaking.

IV

The formula of the "right of nations" is inadequate to justify the position of socialists on the nationality question, not only because it fails to take into account the wide range of historical conditions (place and time) existing in each given case and does not reckon with the general current of the development of global conditions, but also because it ignores completely the fundamental theory of modern socialists — the theory of social classes.

When we speak of the "right of nations to self-determination, " we are using the concept of the "nation" as a homogeneous social and political entity. But actually, such a concept of the "nation" is one of those categories of bourgeois ideology which Marxist theory submitted to a radical re-vision, showing how that misty veil, like the concepts of the "freedom of citizens," "equality before the law," etc., conceals in every case a definite historical content.

In a class society, "the nation" as a homogeneous socio-political entity does not exist. Rather, there exist within each nation, classes with antagonistic interests and "rights." There literally is not one social area, from the coarsest material relationships to the most subtle moral ones, in which the possessing class and the class-conscious proletariat hold the same attitude, and in which they appear as a consolidated "national" entity. In the sphere of economic relations, the bourgeois classes represent the interests of exploitation—the proletariat the interests of work. In the sphere of legal relations, the cornerstone of bourgeois society is private property; the interest of the proletariat demands the emancipation of the propertyless man from the domination of property. In the area of the judiciary, bourgeois society represents class "justice," the justice of the well-fed and the rulers; the proletariat defends the principle of taking into account social influences on the individual, of humaneness. In international relations, the bourgeoisie represent the politics of war and partition, and at the present stage, a system of trade war; the proletariat demands a politics of universal peace and free trade. In the sphere of the social sciences and philosophy, bourgeois schools of thought and the school representing the proletariat stand in diametric opposition to each other. The possessing classes have their world view; it is represented by idealism, metaphysics, mysticism, eclecticism; the modern proletariat has its theory—dialectic materialism. Even in the sphere of so-called "universal" conditions—in ethics, views on art, on behavior—the interests, world view, and ideals of the bourgeoisie and those of the enlightened proletariat represent two camps, separated from each other by an abyss. And whenever the formal strivings and the interests of the proletariat and those of the bourgeoisie (as a whole or in its most progressive part) seem identical—for example, in the field of democratic aspirations—there, under the identity of forms and slogans, is hidden the most complete divergence of contents and essential politics.

There can be no talk of a collective and uniform will, of the self-determination of the "nation" in a society formed in such a manner. If we find in the history of modern societies "national" movements, and struggles for "national interests," these are usually class movements of the ruling strata of the bourgeoisie, which can in any given case represent the interest of the other strata of the population only insofar as under the form of "national interests" it defends progressive forms of historical development, and insofar as the working class has not yet distinguished itself from the mass of the "nation" (led by the bourgeoisie) into an independent, enlightened political class.

In this sense, the French bourgeoisie had the right to come forth as the third estate in the Great Revolution in the name of the French people, and even the German bourgeoisie in 1848 could still regard themselves, to a certain degree, as the representatives of the German "nation" – although *The Communist Manifesto* and, in part, the *Neue Rheinische Zeitung* were already the indicators of a distinct class politics of the proletariat in Germany. In both cases this meant only that the revolutionary class concern of the bourgeoisie was, at that stage of social development, the concern of the class of people who still formed, with the bourgeoisie, a politically uniform mass in relation to reigning feudalism.

This circumstance shows that the "rights of nations" cannot be a yardstick for the position of the Socialist Party on the nationality question. The very existence of such a party is proof that the bourgeoisie has stopped being the representative of the entire mass of the people, that the class of the proletariat is no longer hidden in the skirts of the bourgeoisie, but has separated itself off as an independent class with its own social and political aspirations. Because the concepts of "nations," of "rights," and the "will of the people" as a uniform whole are, as we have said, remnants from the times of immature and unconscious antagonism between the proletariat and the bourgeoisie, the application of that idea by the class-conscious and independently organized proletariat would be a striking contradiction – not a contradiction against academic logic, but a historical contradiction.

With respect to the nationality question in contemporary society, a socialist party must take class antagonism into account. The Czech nationality question has one form for the young Czech petite bourgeoisie and another for the Czech proletariat. Nor can we seek a single solution of the Polish national question for Koscielski and his stable boy in Miroslawie, for the Warsaw and Lodz bourgeoisie and for class-conscious Polish workers all at the same time; while the Jewish question is formulated in one way in the minds of the Jewish bourgeoisie, and in another for the enlightened Jewish proletariat. For Social Democracy, the nationality question is, like all other social and political questions, primarily a question of class interests.

In the Germany of the 1840s there existed a kind of mystical-sentimental socialism, that of the "true socialists" Karl Grün and Moses Hess; this kind of socialism was represented later in Poland by Limanowski. After the 1840s there appeared in Poland a Spartan edition of the same—see the *Lud Polski* (Polish People) in the early 1870s and *Pobudka* (Reveille) at the end of that decade. This socialism strove for everything good and beautiful. And on that basis, Limanowski, later the leader of the PPS, tried to weld together Polish socialism and the task of reconstructing Poland, with the observation that socialism is an idea that is obviously beautiful, and patriotism is a no less beautiful idea, and so "Why shouldn't two such beautiful ideas be joined together?"

The only healthy thing in this sentimental socialism is that it is a utopian parody of the correct idea that a socialist regime has, as the final goal of the proletariat's aspirations, taken the pledge that by abolishing the domination of classes, for the first time in history it will guarantee the realization of the highest ideals of humanity.

And this is really the content and the essential meaning of the principle presented to the International Congress at London in 1896 in the resolution quoted. "The right of Nations to self-determination" stops being a cliché only in a social regime where the "right to work" has stopped being an empty phrase. A socialist regime, which eliminates not only the domination of one class over another, but also the very existence of social classes and their opposition, the very division of society into classes with different interests and desires, will bring about a society which is the sum total individuals tied together by the harmony and solidarity their interests, a uniform whole with a common, organized will and the ability to satisfy it. The socialist regime will realize directly the "nation" as a uniform will— insofar as the nations within that regime in general will constitute separate social organisms or, as Kautsky states, will join into one— and the material conditions for its free self-determination. In a word, society will win the ability to freely determine its national existence when it has the ability to determine its political being and the conditions of its creation. "Nations" will control their historical existence when human society controls its social processes.

Therefore, the analogy which is drawn by partisans of the "right of nations to self-determination" between that "right" and all democratic demands, like the right of free speech, free press, freedom of association and of assembly, is completely incongruous. These people point out that we support the freedom of association because we are the party of political freedom; but we still fight against hostile bourgeois parties. Similarly, they say, we have the democratic duty to support the self-determination of nations, but this fact does not commit us to support every individual tactic of those who fight for self-determination.

The above view completely overlooks the fact that these "rights," which have a certain superficial similarity, lie on completely different historical levels. The rights of association and assembly, free speech, the free press. etc., are the legal forms of existence of a mature bourgeois society. But "the right of nations to self-determination" is only a metaphysical formulation of an idea which in bourgeois society is completely non-existent and can be realized only on the basis of a socialist regime.

However, as it is practiced today, socialism is not at all a collection of all these mystical "noble" and "beautiful" desires, but only a political expression of well-defined conditions, that is, the fight of the class of the modern proletariat against the domination of the bourgeoisie. Socialism means the striving of the proletariat to bring about the dictatorship of its class in order to get rid of the present form of production. This task is the main and guiding one for the Socialist Party as the party of the proletariat: it determines the position of that party with respect to all the several problems of social life.

Social Democracy is the class party of the proletariat. Its historical task is to express the class interests of the proletariat and also the revolutionary interests of the development of capitalist society toward realizing socialism. Thus, Social Democracy is called upon to realize not the right of nations to self-determination but only the right of the working class, which is exploited and oppressed, of the proletariat, to self-determination. From that position Social Democracy examines all social and political questions without exception, and from that standpoint it formulates its programmatic demands. Neither in the question of the political forms which we demand in the state, nor in the question of the state's internal or external policies, nor in the questions of law or education, of taxes or the military, does Social Democracy allow the "nation" to decide its fate according to its own vision of self-determination. All of these questions affect the class interests of the proletariat in a way that questions of national-political and national-cultural existence do not. But between those questions and the national-political and national-cultural questions, exist usually the closest ties of mutual dependence and causality. As a result, Social Democracy cannot here escape the necessity of formulating these demands individually, and demanding actively the forms of national-political and national-cultural existence which best correspond to the interests of the proletariat and its class struggle at a given time and place, as well as to the interests of the revolutionary development of society. Social Democracy cannot leave these questions to be solved by "nations."

This becomes perfectly obvious as soon as we bring the question down from the clouds of abstraction to the firm ground of concrete conditions.

The "nation" should have the "right" to self-determination. But who is that "nation" and who has the authority and the "right" to speak for the "nation" and express its will? How can we find out what the "nation" actually wants? Does there exist even one political party which would not claim that it alone, among all others, truly expresses the will of the "nation," whereas all other parties give only perverted and false expressions of the national will? All the bourgeois, liberal parties consider themselves the incarnation of the will of the people and claim the exclusive monopoly to represent the "nation." But conservative and reactionary parties refer no less to the will and interests of the nation, and within certain limits, have no less of a right to do so. The Great French Revolution was indubitably an expression of the will of the French nation, but Napoleon, who juggled away the work of the Revolution in his coup of the 18th Brumaire, based his entire state reform on the principle of "la volonté generale" (the general will).

In 1848, the will of the "nation" produced first the republic and the provisional government, then the National Assembly, and finally Louis Bonaparte, who cashiered the Republic, the provisional government, and the national assembly. During the 1905 Revolution in Russia, liberalism demanded in the name of the people a "cadet" ministry; absolutism, in the name of the same people, arranged the pogroms of the Jews, while the revolutionary peasants expressed their national will by sending the estates of the gentry up in smoke. In Poland, the party of the Black Hundreds, National Democracy, had a claim to be the will of the people, and in the name of "the self-determination of the nation" incited "national" workers to assassinate socialist workers.

Thus the same thing happens to the "true" will of the nation as to the true ring in Lessing's story of Nathan the Wise: it has been lost and it seems almost impossible to find it and to tell it from the false and counterfeit ones. On the surface, the principle of democracy provides a way of distinguishing the true will of the people by determining the opinion of the majority.

The nation wants what the majority of the people want. But woe to the Social Democratic Party which would ever take that principle as its own yardstick: that would condemn to death Social Democracy itself as the revolutionary party. Social Democracy by its very nature is a party representing the interests of a huge majority of the nation. But it is also for the time being in bourgeois society, insofar as it is a matter of expressing the conscious will of the nation, the party of a minority which only seeks to become the majority. In its aspirations and its political program it seeks to reflect not the will of a majority of the nation, but on the contrary, the embodiment of the conscious will of the proletariat alone. And even within that class, Social Democracy is not and does not claim to be the embodiment of the will of the majority. It expresses only the will and the consciousness of the most advanced and most revolutionary section of the urban-industrial proletariat. It tries to expand that will and to clear a way for a majority of the workers by making them conscious of their own interests. "The will of the nation" or its majority is not therefore an idol for Social Democracy before which it humbly prostrates itself. On the contrary, the historical mission of Social Democracy is based above all on revolutionizing and forming the will of the "nation"; that is, its working-class majority. For the traditional forms of consciousness which the majority of the nation, and therefore the working classes, display in bourgeois society are the usual forms of bourgeois consciousness, hostile to the ideals and aspirations of socialism. Even in Germany, where Social Democracy is the most powerful political party, it is still today, with its three and a quarter million voters, a minority compared to the eight million voters for bourgeois parties and the thirty million who have the right to vote. The statistics on parliamentary electors give, admittedly, only a rough idea of the relation of forces in times of peace. The German nation then "determines itself" by electing a majority of conservatives, clerics, and freethinkers, and puts its political fate in their hands. And the same thing is happening, to an even greater degree, in all other countries.

V

Let us take a concrete example in an attempt to apply the principle that the "nation" should "determine itself."

With respect to Poland at the present stage of the revolution, one of the Russian Social Democrats belonging to the editorial committee of the now defunct paper, *Iskra*, in 1906 explained the concept of the indispensable Warsaw constituent assembly in the following way: "if we start from the assumption that the political organization of Russia is the decisive factor determining the current oppression of the nationalities, then we must conclude that the proletariat of the oppressed nationalities and the annexed countries should be extremely active in the organization of an all-Russian constituent assembly.

"This assembly could, if it wished, carry out its revolutionary mission, and break the fetters of force with which tsardom binds to itself the oppressed nationalities.

"And there is no other satisfactory, that is, revolutionary way of solving that question than by implementing the rights of the nationalities to determine their own fate. The task of a united proletarian party of all nationalities in the assembly will be to bring about such a solution of the nationality question, and this task can be realized by the Party only insofar as it is based on the movement of the masses, on the pressure they put on the constituent assembly."

"But in what concrete form should the admitted right to self-determination be realized?

"Where the nationality question can be more or less identified with the existence of a legal state — as is the case in Poland — then the organ which can realize the nation's right to self-determination can and should be a national constituent assembly whose special task is to determine the relation of a given "borderland country" to the state as a whole, to decide whether it should belong to the state or break away from it, to decide its internal set-up and its future connection with the state as a whole.

"And therefore the constituent assembly of Poland should decide whether Poland will become part of a new Russia and what its constitution should be. And the Polish proletariat should use all its strength to insure that its class makes its mark on the decision of that organ of national self-government.

"If we should ask the all-Russian assembly to hand the solution of the Polish national question over to the Warsaw sejm, I do not believe that there is any need to put off calling that sejm until the Petersburg constituents should take up the nationality question.

"On the contrary, I think that the slogan of a constituent assembly in Warsaw should be put forth now, at the same time as the slogan for an all-Russian constituent assembly. The government which finally calls a constituent assembly for all Russia should also call (or sanction the calling of) a special constituent sejm for Poland. The job of the all-Russian assembly will be to sanction the work of the Warsaw sejm, and in the light of the different social forces involved in the Petersburg constituent assembly, the more this is given on the basis of the real principles of democracy the more decisively and clearly will the Polish nation express its national will. It will do this most clearly in the elections to the sejm especially called to decide the future fate of Poland. On the basis of this sejm's decisions, the representatives of the Polish and Russian proletariat in the all-Russian assembly will be able to energetically defend the real recognition of the right to self-determination.

"Thus, the simultaneous calling of all-Russian and all-Polish constituent assemblies: this should be our slogan.

"The presentation by the proletariat of the demand for a constituent assembly for Poland should not be taken to mean that the Polish nation would be represented in the all-Russian assembly by any delegation of the Warsaw sejm.

"I think that such representation in the all-Russian assembly would not correspond to the interests of revolutionary development. It would join the proletariat and bourgeois elements of the Polish sejm by bonds of mutual solidarity and responsibility, in contradiction to the real mutual relations of their interests.

"In the all-Russian assembly, the proletariat and bourgeoisie of Poland should not be represented by one delegation. But this would occur even if a delegation were sent from the sejm to an assembly which included representatives of all the parties of the sejm proportionally to their numbers. In this case, the direct and independent representation of the Polish proletariat in the assembly would disappear, and the very creation of real political parties in Poland would be made difficult. Then the elections to the Polish sejm, whose main task is to define the political relations between Poland and Russia, would not show the political and social faces of the leading parties, as elections to an all-Russian assembly could do; for the latter type of elections would advance, besides the local, partial, historically temporary and specifically national questions, the general questions of politics and socialism, which really divide contemporary societies. (Here as everywhere I speak of a definite manner of solving the nationality question for Poland, not touching those changes which may prove themselves indispensable while resolving this question for other nations. — Note of the author of the cited article.)" (The above article appeared in Robotnik, the organ of the PPS, no.75, February 7, 1906.- Note of the editorial board of *Przeglad Sozial-demokratyczny*)

This article gives a moral sanction on the part of the opportunist wing of Russian Social Democracy to the slogan put forth by the PPS in the first period of the revolution: that is, to the Warsaw constituent assembly. However, it had no practical result. After the dissolution of the PPS, the so-called left wing of that party, having publicly rejected the program of rebuilding Poland, found itself forced to abandon its partial program of nationalism in the form of the slogan of a Warsaw constituent assembly. But the article remains a characteristic attempt to give practical effect to the principle of "the right of nations to self-determination."

In the above argument, which we quoted in full in order to be able to examine it from all aspects, several points strike the reader. Above all, according to the author, on the one hand "a constituent assembly of Poland should decide whether Poland should enter the formation of a new Russia and what kind of constitution it should have." On the other, "the Polish proletariat should use its strength to insure that its class will make the greatest mark on the decisions of that organ of national self-government. " Here the class will of the Polish proletariat is expressly opposed to the passive will of the Polish "nation." The class will of the proletariat can obviously leave "its mark" on the decisions of the Warsaw constituent assembly only if it is clearly and expressly formulated; in other words, the class party of the Polish proletariat, the Socialist Party, must have a well-defined program with respect to the national question, which it can introduce in the Warsaw constituent assembly a program which corresponds not to the will of "the nation" but only to the will and interests of the Polish proletariat. Then, in the constituent assembly, in the national question, one will, or "the self-determination of the proletariat" will come out against the will or "the self-determination of the nation." For Polish Socialists, the "nation's right to self-determination" as an obligatory principle in fact disappears, and is replaced by a clearly defined political program on the national question.

The result is rather strange. The Russian Social Democratic Labor Party leaves the solution of the Polish question up to the Polish "nation." The Polish Socialists should not pick it up but try, as hard as they can, to solve this question according to the interests and will of the proletariat. However, the party of the Polish proletariat is organizationally tied to the all-state party, for instance, the Social Democracy of the Kingdom of Poland and Lithuania is a part of the Russian Social Democratic Labor Party. Thus, Social Democracy of all of Russia, united both in ideas and factually, has two different positions. As a whole, it stands for the "nations in its constituent parts, it stands for the separate proletariat of each nation. But these positions can be quite different and may even be completely opposed to each other. The sharpened class antagonism in all of Russia makes it a general rule that in the national-political question, as in questions of internal politics, the proletarian parties take completely different positions from the bourgeois and petit bourgeois parties of the separate nationalities. What position should the Labor Party of Russia then take in the case of such a collision?

Let us suppose for the sake of argument, that in the federal constituent assembly, two contradictory programs are put forth from Poland: the autonomous program of National Democracy and the autonomous program of Polish Social Democracy, which are quite at odds with respect to internal tendency as well as to political formulation. What will the position of Russian Social Democracy be with regard to them? Which of the programs will it recognize as an expression of the will and "self-determination" of the Polish "nation"? Polish Social Democracy never had any pretensions to be speaking in the name of the "nation." National Democracy comes forth as the expresser of the "national" will. Let us also assume for a moment that this party wins a majority at the elections to the constituent assembly by taking advantage of the ignorance of the petit bourgeois elements as well as certain sections of the proletariat. In this case, will the representatives of the all-Russian proletariat, complying with the requirements of the formula of their program, come out in favor of the proposals of National Democracy and go against their own comrades from Poland? Or will they associate themselves with the program of the Polish proletariat, leaving the "right of nations" to one side as a phrase which binds them to nothing? Or will the Polish

Social Democrats be forced, in order to reconcile these contradictions in their program, to come out in the Warsaw constituent assembly, as well as in their own agitation in Poland, in favor of their own autonomous program, but to the federal constituent assembly, as members well aware of the discipline of the Social Democratic Party of Russia, for the program of National Democracy, that is, against their own program?

Let us take yet another example. Examining the question in a purely abstract form, since the author has put the problem on that basis, let us suppose, to illustrate the principle, that in the national assembly of the Jewish population of Russia for why should the right to create separate constituent assemblies be limited to Poland, as the author wants? — the Zionist Party somehow wins a majority and demands that the all-Russian constituent assembly vote funds for the emigration of the entire Jewish community. On the other hand, the class representatives of the Jewish proletariat firmly resist the position of the Zionists as a harmful and reactionary utopia. What position will Russian Social Democracy take in this conflict?

It will have two choices. The "right of nations to self-determination" might be essentially identical with the determination of the national question by the proletariat in question that is, with the nationality program of the concerned Social Democratic parties. In such a case, however, the formula of the "right of nations" in the program of the Russian party is only a mystifying paraphrase of the class position. Or, alternatively, the Russian proletariat as such could recognize and honor only the will of the national majorities of the nationalities under Russian subjugation, even though the proletariat of the respective "nations" should come out against this majority with their own class program. And in this case, it is a political dualism of a special type; it gives dramatic expression to the discord between the "national" and class positions: it points up the conflict between the position of the federal workers' party and that of the parties of the particular nationalities which make it up.

A special Polish constituent assembly is to be the organ of realizing the right of the nation to self-determination. But that right is, in reality, severely limited by the author, and in two directions. First, the competence of the Warsaw constituent assembly is reduced to the special question of the relation of Poland to Russia and to the constitution for Poland. Then, even within this domain, the decisions of the "Polish nation" are subordinated to the sanction of an all-

Russian constituent assembly. The assembly, however—if this reservation is to have any meaning at all—can either grant or deny these sanctions. Under such conditions the unlimited "right of the nation to self-determination" becomes rather problematic. The national partisans of the slogan of a separate Warsaw constituent assembly would not at all agree to the reduction of their competence to the narrow area of relations between Poland and Russia. They wanted to give the assembly the power over all the internal and external relations of the social life of Poland. And from the standpoint of the "right of nations to self-determination," they would undoubtedly have right and logic on their side. For there seems to be no reason why "self-determination" should mean only the solution of the external fate of the nation and of its constitution, and not of all social and political matters. Besides, the separation of the relation of Poland to Russia and the constitution of Poland from the "general problems of politics and socialism" is a construction which is artificial to the highest degree. If the "constitution of Poland" is to determine—as it evidently must—the electoral law, the law of unions and meetings, the law of the press, etc., etc., for Poland, then it is not clear what political questions remain for the federal constituent assembly to solve with respect to Poland. From this point of view, only one of two points of view is possible: either the Warsaw constituent assembly is to be the essential organ for the self-determination of the Polish nation, and in this case it can be only an organ on the same level as the Petersburg constituent assembly; or, the constituent assembly of Warsaw plays only the role of a national sejm in a position of dependence on and subordination to the federal constituent assembly, and in this case, "the right of the nation to self-determination," dependent on the sanction of the Russian "nation," reminds one of the German concept: "*Die Republik mit dem Grossherzog an der Spitze*" ("The Republic with the Grand Duke at the Head") .

The author himself helps us to guess how, in his understanding, the "right of the nation," proclaimed in the introduction so charmingly in the form of a Warsaw constituent assembly, is finally canceled out by the competence and right of sanction of the Petersburg constituent assembly.

In this matter, the Menshevik journalist adopts the view that the Warsaw constituent assembly will be the organ of national interests, whereas the federal assembly will be the organ of the class and general social interests, the terrain of the class struggle between the proletariat and the bourgeoisie. Thus, the author shows so much mistrust of the Warsaw organ of the "national will" that he opposes the representation of that national sejm in the Petersburg constituent assembly, for which he demands direct elections from Poland to insure the best representation of the interests of the Polish proletariat. The defender of two constituent assemblies feels instinctively that even with universal and equal elections to the Warsaw assembly, its very individual nature would weaken the position of the Polish proletariat, while the combined entry of the Polish proletariat with the proletariat of the entire state in a general constituent assembly would strengthen the class position and its defense. Hence arises his vacillation between one and the other position and his desire to subordinate the organ of the "national" will to the organ of the class struggle. This is, then, again an equivocal political position, in which the collision between the "national" point of view and the class point of view takes the form of the opposition between the Warsaw and the Petersburg constituent assemblies. Only one question remains: since the representation in a federal constituent assembly is more useful for the defense of the Polish proletariat, then why cannot that body resolve the Polish national question, in order to insure the preponderance of the will and interests of the Polish proletariat? So many hesitations and contradictions show how desirable it would be for the "nation" and the working class to develop a common position.

Apart from this, we must add that the entire construction of the Warsaw constituent assembly as the organ of national "self-determination" is only a house of cards: the dependence or independence of nation-states is determined not by the vote of majorities in parliamentary representations, but only by socio-economic development, by material class interests, and as regards the external political affairs, by armed struggle, war, or insurrection. The Warsaw assembly could only really determine the fate of Poland if Poland had first, by means of a successful uprising, won factual independence from Russia. In other words, the Polish people can realize its "right" to self-determination only when it has the actual ability, the necessary force for this, and then it will realize it not on the basis of its "rights" but on the basis of its power. The present revolution did not call forth an independence movement in Poland; it did not show the least tendency to separate Poland from Russia. On the contrary, it buried the remains of these tendencies by forcing the national party (National Democracy) to renounce the program of the reconstruction of Poland, while the other party (the PPS) was smashed to bits and also, midway in the struggle, was forced to renounce this program explicitly. Thus, the "right" of the Polish nation to self-determination remains – the right to eat off gold plates.

The demand for a Warsaw constituent assembly is therefore obviously deprived of all political or theoretical importance and represents only a momentary tentative improvisation of deteriorated Polish nationalism, like a soap bubble which bursts immediately after appearing. This demand is useful only as an illustration of the application of "the right of a nation to self-determination" in practice. This illustration is a new proof that by recognizing the "right of nations to self-determination" in the framework of the present regime, Social Democracy is offering the "nations" either the cheap blessing to do what they (the "nations") are in a position to do by virtue of their strength, or else an empty phrase with no force at all. On the other hand, this position brings Social Democracy into conflict with its true calling, the protection of the class interests of the proletariat and the revolutionary development of society, which the creators of scientific socialism used as the basis of their view on the nationality question.

The preservation of that metaphysical phrase in the program of the Social Democratic Party of Russia would be a betrayal of the strictly class position which the party has tried to observe in all points of its program. The ninth paragraph should be replaced by a concrete formula, however general, which would provide a solution of the nationality question in accordance with the interests of the proletariat of the particular nationalities. That does not in the least mean that the program of the Social Democratic organization of the respective nationalities should become, eo ipso, the program of the all-Russian party. A fundamental critical appraisal of each of these programs by the whole of the workers' party of the state is necessary, but this appraisal should be made from the point of view of the actual social conditions, from the point of view of a scientific analysis of the general tendencies of capitalist development, as well as the interests of the class struggle of the proletariat. This alone can indicate a uniform and consistent position of the party as a whole and in its constituent parts.

2. The Nation-State and the Proletariat

The question of nationality cannot be solved merely by presuming that socialists must approach it from the point of view of the class interests of the proletariat. The influence of theoretical socialism has been felt indirectly by the workers' movement as a whole, to such an extent that at present there is not a socialist or workers' party which does not use at least the Marxist terminology, if not the entire Marxist way of thinking. A famous example of this is the present Social Revolutionary Party of Russia, in whose theory—as far as one can speak of such—there are at least as many elements borrowed from the Marxist School as there are elements inherited from the Narodniki and the People's Will. In like manner, all socialist groups of the petit bourgeois and nationalistic type in Russia have their own fancies which are solely "in the interest of the proletariat and socialism." The Polish Social Democracy, now in decline, had especially distinguished itself in comparison with the naive, patriarchal—let us say—national socialism of Mr. Limanowski, particularly in that the "good-hearted" Mr. Limanowski never even used the name of Karl Marx, while social patriotism, from the beginning, sought to legitimize its program with Marxist terminology as a "class interest of the proletariat."

But it is obvious that the class character of any particular demand is not established by merely incorporating it mechanically into the program of a socialist party. What this or any other party considers a "class interest" of the proletariat can only be an imputed interest, concocted by subjective reasoning. It is very easy, for instance, to state that the workers' class interest demands the establishment of a minimum-wage law. Such a law would protect the workers against the pressures of competition, which might come from a less developed locality. It would assure them of a certain minimum standard of living, etc. Such demands have been presented repeatedly by socialist circles; however, the principle has not yet been accepted by the socialist parties in general, for the valid reason that the universal regulation of wages by means of legislation is but a utopian dream under today's anarchistic conditions of private economy. This is because workers' wages, like the prices of any kind of commodity, are set up in the capitalistic system under the operation of "free competition" and the spontaneous movement of capital. Therefore, the legal regulation of wages can be achieved only in exceptional, clearly defined areas, e.g., in small communities. And since the general establishment of a minimum-wage law clashes with the current conditions of capitalism, we must admit that it is not a true proletarian interest, but rather a fabricated or imputed one, in spite of the fact that it can be supported by a completely logical argument.

Likewise, one can, in a purely abstract way, figure out various "class interests" for the proletariat, which, however, would have to remain as mere clichés in the socialist program. This is especially so, as, the more that other social elements attach themselves to the workers' movement, the stronger is the tendency to suggest various sincere but unrealistic demands of these foreign elements as class interests of the proletariat. The other social elements referred to here include those members of society who have been deprived of political shelter by the failure of the bourgeois parties; in this category are the bourgeois and petit bourgeois intelligentsia. If the socialist parties had no objective criterion by which to establish just what fits the class interests of the proletariat, but were only directed by what certain people might think would be good or useful for the workers, then socialist programs would be a motley collection of subjective, and often completely utopian, desires.

Basing itself on historical foundations — on the foundations of the development of capitalist society — today's Social Democracy derives its immediate interests (the demands of today's proletariat) as well as its long-range goals, not merely from subjective reasoning about what would be "good" or "useful" for the proletariat, but from examining the objective development of society for a verification of its actual interests, as well as for material means for their realization. It is from this standpoint that the main alternatives for a practical solution to the question of nationality should be examined — those which are suggested by historical examples as well as those which correspond to the slogans popular in socialist circles.

We should first consider the idea of a nation-state. In order to evaluate this concept accurately, it is first necessary to search for historical substance in the idea, to see what is actually hiding behind the mask.

In his article on the struggles of nationalities and the social-democratic program in Austria, published over ten years ago, Kautsky enumerates three factors, which, according to him, make up the "roots of the modern national idea," as found in the rise of the modern state in all of Europe. These factors are: "the desire of the bourgeoisie to assure for itself an internal or domestic market for its own commodity production; second, the desire for political freedom — democracy; and finally, expansion of the national literature and culture to the populace."

In Kautsky's theory one can see, above all, his basic position, his own view of nationality as a historical category. According to his reasoning, the idea of the nation is intimately connected with a definite era of modern development. The market interests of the bourgeoisie, democratic currents, culture of the people—these are typical aspects of a bourgeois society.

Naturally, we are not speaking here of a nationality as a specific ethnic or cultural group. Such nationality is, of course, separate and distinct from the bourgeois aspect; national peculiarities had already existed for centuries. But here we are concerned with national movements as an element of political life, with the aspirations of establishing a so-called nation-state; then the connection between those movements and the bourgeois era is unquestionable. The history of the national unification of Germany is a typical example of this connection, as the nucleus around which the later German Reich crystallized was the German Zollverein and Zollparlament. Their sponsor, Friedrich List, with his trivial theory of "national economy," can be more justifiably considered the real messiah of the national unity of Germany than the idealist Fichte, mentioned usually as the first apostle of German national rebirth. This "national" movement, which captured the imagination of the German "people and princes" during Fichte's time, and which the pseudo-revolutionary Burschenschaften loudly ushered in (in spite of Fichte's ardent sympathy for the Great French Revolution), basically represented only a medieval reaction against the seeds of the Revolution, which were brought to Germany by Napoleon, and against the elements of the modern bourgeois system. The sultry, romantic wind of "national rebirth" finally died out after the victorious return of Germany to feudal subdivision and to pre-March reaction. By contrast, the gospel of that vulgar agent of German industry, List, in the thirties and forties based the "national rebirth" on the elements of bourgeois development, on industry and trade, on the theory of the "domestic market." The material basis for this patriotic movement, which in the thirties and forties of the nineteenth century aroused such strong political, educational, philosophical, and literary currents in Germany, was above all, the need to unify all the German territories (which were divided into several dozen feudal statelets and were criss-crossed by customs and tax barriers) into one great, integrated, capitalistic "fatherland," establishing a broad foundation for mechanized manufacturing and big industry.

The history of the industrial and commercial unification of Germany is so completely intertwined with the fate of Germany's political unification, that the history of the Customs Union (*Zollverein*), which reflected all the political developments and happenings in Germany, passes over, with perfect continuity, into the history of the birth of the present German Reich. In 1834, the Customs Union was born, grouping seventeen minor states around Prussia; and gradually, one after another, the remaining states also joined this Union. However, Austria remained altogether separate from the Union, and the Schleswig-Holstein War finally decided the matter in favor of Prussia. In 1867, the last renewal of the Customs Union became superfluous in the presence of the new national union; and the North German Union, after the Franco-Prussian War, transferred its customs rights and duties by inheritance to the newly formed Reich. In the place of the Zollbundesrat and the Zollparlament there were now the Bundesrat and Reichstag. In this example from modern history, Germany excellently demonstrates the true economic foundation of modern nation-states.

Although the bourgeois appetite for markets for "its own" commodities is so elastic and extensive that it always has the natural tendency to include the entire globe, the very essence of the modern bourgeois "national idea" is based on the premise that in the eyes of the bourgeoisie of every country, its own nation — their "fatherland" — is called and destined by nature to serve the bourgeoisie as a field for the sale of products. It is as if this were an exclusive patrimony determined by the god Mercury. At least this is how the national question appears where the development of capitalism takes place "normally," without abrupt fluctuations, i.e., where production for the domestic market exceeds production for export. This is exactly what happened in Germany and in Italy.

However, it would be wrong to take Kautsky's formulation literally; we cannot assume that the material foundation of modern national movements is only the vaguely understood appetite of the industrial bourgeoisie for a "native" market for its commodities. Moreover, a capitalistic bourgeoisie needs many other conditions for its proper development: a strong military, as a guarantee of the inviolability of this "fatherland," as well as a tool to clear a path for itself in the world market; furthermore, it needs a suitable customs policy, suitable forms of administration in regard to communications, jurisdiction, school systems, and financial policy. In a word, capitalism demands for its proper development not only markets, but also the whole apparatus of a modern capitalistic state. The bourgeoisie needs for its normal existence not only strictly economic conditions for production, but also, in equal measure, political conditions for its class rule.

From all this it follows that the specific form of national aspirations, the true class interest of the bourgeoisie, is state independence. The nation-state is also simultaneously that indispensable historical form in which the bourgeoisie passes over from the national defensive to an offensive position, from protection and concentration of its own nationality to political conquest and domination over other nationalities. Without exception, all of today's "nation-states" fit this description, annexing neighbors or colonies, and completely oppressing the conquered nationalities.

This phenomenon becomes understandable only when one takes into consideration the fact that, according to the bourgeois way of thinking, it is possible to have a national movement for unification and defense of one's own nationality, and at the same time, to oppress another nationality (which is, of course, contrary to the very ideology of the "nation-state"). The German bourgeoisie in 1848 presents a striking example of this phenomenon in its attitude toward the Polish question. As is known, during the revolution of 1848, when German national patriotism was most evident, Karl Marx and his circle advocated Polish independence; however, he proved to be but a prophet crying in the wilderness. The German "nation-state," from its first stages of development, did not conform at all with the accepted understanding of a nation-state in regard to nationalities. The borders of the Reich actually split the German nation, dividing it between Austria and the new "national" state of Germany, and putting together the Germans and the racially distinct peoples in territories annexed from Poland, Denmark, and France.

An even more striking example is Hungary, whose struggle for national independence was so much admired in its time. Even our own Polish revolutionary leaders—Bem, Wysocki, and Dembicki— had "tilted their lances" to assist them. But when examined from the viewpoint of nationality, this struggle was nothing more than an attempt to assure class rule of the Magyar minority over a country of nine nationalities, with the Magyars oppressing the other nationalities. The national "independence" of the Hungarians was bought by severing the Carpathian Slovaks from their brothers, the

Sudeten Czechs; separating the Germans of Bratislava, Temesvar, and Transylvania from the Austrian Germans; and the Croats and Dalmatian Serbs from Croatia and the Slovenians.

The aspirations of the Czechs are characterized by the same dichotomy. These aspirations arouse distrust among the Germans because, among other things, they are directed clearly at separating the German population of Sudetenland from the Germans of the Alpine countries. The primary objective of the Czechs was to force the Germans, as minority group under the crown of Wenceslaus (Vaclav), into complete dependence on the Czechs in matters of culture and administration. As if this were not enough, the division of the Czech lands created a nationality division for the Czechs themselves by uniting five and one-third million Czechs with three million Germans and nearly two hundred thousand Poles. Still separated from this "national" Czech state were two million Carpathian Slovaks, a group closely related to the Czechs and left at the mercy of the Magyars. Therefore, these Slovaks are also loudly advocating their cause, which has been completely neglected by the Czech nationalists.

Finally, and we do not have to go far for an example, Polish bourgeois nationalism is directed as much against the Ruthenians as against the Lithuanians. The very nationality which had to endure the bitter policy of extermination by the partitioning powers — Prussia and Russia — now refuses the right of independent existence to other nationalities. According to the Stanczyk policy in Galicia, the Poles oppressed the Ruthenians, whose struggle for nationality runs like a red thread through the political history of the development of Galicia in the second half of the last century. The recent movement for national rebirth of the Lithuanians was met with similar hostility in Polish nationalistic circles.

This strange double-edged character of bourgeois patriotism, which is essentially based on the conflicting interests of various nationalities rather than on harmony becomes understandable only when one takes into consideration the fact that the historical basis of the modern national movements of the bourgeoisie is nothing more than its aspirations to class rule, and a specific social form in whose aspirations this expression is found: the modern capitalistic state — "national," in the sense of the dominance of the bourgeoisie of a certain nationality over the entire mixed population of the state. A democratic organization, together with general education of the people — these distinctly ideological elements of the nation mentioned by Kautsky—are merely details of a modern bourgeois state, easily attainable by the bourgeoisie within the framework and spirit of the state. Therefore, independence and state unification constitute the real axis around which the national movements of the bourgeoisie rotate.

This matter appears quite different from the point of view of the interests of the proletariat. The contemporary proletariat, as a social class, is the offspring of the capitalist economy and the bourgeois state. The capitalist society and bourgeois state—taking them not as an abstract idea, but in tangible form as history has created them in each country—were already, from the very beginning, a frame of activity for the proletariat. A bourgeois state—national or not national—is just that foundation, together with capitalistic production as the ruling form of social economy, on which the working class grows and thrives. In this respect, there is a basic historical difference between the bourgeoisie and the proletariat. The bourgeoisie develops and is carried in the womb of the feudal class system. Aspiring to assure triumph for capitalism as the form of production, and for itself as the ruling class, the bourgeoisie creates the modern state on the ruins of the feudal system. Within the bounds of the development of capitalism and the rule of the bourgeoisie, the proletariat is next to make itself heard politically—still as part of the bourgeois state. But the state was already from the beginning its natural womb, just as the shell of an egg is for the chicken. Therefore, historically speaking, the idea that the modern proletariat could do nothing as a separate and conscious class without first creating a new nation-state, is the same as saying that the bourgeoisie in any country should first of all establish a feudal system, if by some chance it did not come about normally by itself, or had taken on particular forms, as for instance in Russia. The historical mission of the bourgeoisie is the creation of a modern "national" state; but the historical task of the proletariat is the abolition of this state as a political form of capitalism, in which they themselves, as a conscious class, come into existence to establish the socialist system. The proletariat, as part of the whole society, can take part in national movements of the bourgeoisie, where the bourgeois development demands the creation of a "nation-state," as was the case, for example, in Germany. But then it follows the lead of the bourgeoisie, and does not act as an independent class with a separate political program. The national program of the German socialists in the forties advanced two ideas, directly opposing the national program of the bourgeoisie: unification with borders which would be based strictly on divisions of nationalities, and a republican form of government.

The interests of the proletariat on the nationality question are just the opposite of those of the bourgeoisie. The concern about guaranteeing an internal market for the industrialists of the "fatherland," and of acquiring new markets by means of conquest, by colonial or military policies-all these, which are the intentions of the bourgeoisie in creating a "national" state, cannot be the aims of a conscious proletariat.

The proletariat, as a legitimate child of capitalistic development, takes this development into account as a necessary historical background of its own growth and political maturation. Social Democracy itself reflects only the evolutionary side of capitalist development, whereas the ruling bourgeoisie looks after this development on behalf of reaction. Social Democracy nowhere considers its task to be the active support of industry or trade; rather it struggles against military, colonial, and customs protection, just as it combats the whole basic apparatus of the existing class state—its administration, legislature, school systems, etc.

The national policy of the proletariat, therefore, basically clashes with the bourgeois policy to the extent that in its essence it is only defensive, never offensive; it depends on the harmony of interests of all nationalities, not on conquest and subjugation of one by another. The conscious proletariat of every country needs for its proper development peaceful existence and cultural development of its own nationality, but by no means does it need the dominance of its nationality over others. Therefore, considering the matter from this point of view, the "nation"-state, as an apparatus of the domination and conquest of foreign nationalities, while it is indispensable for the bourgeoisie, has no meaning for the class interests of the proletariat.

Therefore, of these "three roots of the modern national idea," which Kautsky enumerated, for the proletariat as a class only the last two are important: democratic organization, and education of the populace. Vital for the working class as conditions of its political and spiritual maturity, are the freedom of using its own native language, and the unchecked and unwarped development of national culture (learning, literature, the arts) and normal education of the masses, unimpaired by the pressures of the nationalists—so far as these can be "normal" in the bourgeois system. It is indispensable for the working class to have the same equal national rights as other nationalities in the state enjoy. Political discrimination against a particular nationality is the strongest tool in the hands of the bourgeoisie, which is eager to mask class conflicts and mystify its own proletariat.

The advocates, Polish nationalists of the "very best" social condition state, at this point that, whatever the situation, the surest guarantee of cultural development and of the rights of every nationality is precisely the independence of the state, their own nation-state, and that therefore the nation-state is finally also an indispensable class interest of the proletariat. We are hardly concerned with determining what is or would be "the best" for the proletariat. Such observations have no practical value. Moreover, once the subject of "what would be the best" from the standpoint of the proletariat is approached in an abstract way, we would have to conclude that "the best" cure for national pressure, as well as for all types of disorders of a social nature, is undoubtedly the socialist system. A utopian argument must always lead to a utopian solution, if only by leaping to the "state of the future," whereas actually the problem should be solved within the framework of existing bourgeois reality.

Moreover, from the point of view of methods, the above reasoning contains still another historical misunderstanding. The argument that an independent nation-state is, after all "the best" guarantee of national existence and development involves operating with a conception of a nation-state as a completely abstract thing. The nation-state as seen only from a national point of view, only as a pledge and embodiment of freedom and independence, is simply a remnant of the decaying ideology of the petite bourgeoisie of Germany, Italy, Hungary—all of Central Europe in the first half of the nineteenth century. It is a phrase from the treasury of disintegrated bourgeois liberalism. Since then, the development of the bourgeoisie has proved unequivocally that a modern nation-state is more real and tangible than the vague idea of "freedom" or national "independence"; that it is indeed a definite historical reality, neither very alluring nor very pure. The substance and essence of the modern state comprise not freedom and independence of the "nation," but only the class dominance of the bourgeoisie, protectionist policy, indirect taxation, militarism, war, and conquest. The bourgeoisie used to use the obvious technique of trying to cover up this brutal historical truth with a light ideological gauze, by offering the purely negative happiness of "independence and national freedom." For a time this technique paid off. But today it is only necessary to recall the circumstances under which this contention was advanced, to understand that it is simply opposed to what can and should be the class position of the proletariat.

In this case, as in many others, anarchism, the supposed antagonist of bourgeois liberalism, proved to be its worthy child. Anarchism, with characteristic "revolutionary" seriousness, accepted at face value the phraseology of the liberal ideology and, like the latter, showed only contempt for the historical and social content of the nation-state, which it set down as nothing else than an embodiment of "freedom," of the "will of the people," and of similar empty words. Bakunin, for example, wrote in 1849 about the national movements of Central Europe:

"The first sign of life in the Revolution of 1848 was the cry of hatred toward the old oppression, a cry of sympathy and love for all oppressed nationalities ... 'Away with the oppressors!' reverberated as if from one breast; 'Salvation for the oppressed Poles, Italians, and all! No more wars of conquest; just one more war should be carried through to its end — a glorious revolutionary struggle with the purpose of eventual liberation for all peoples! Down with the artificial boundaries which have been forcibly erected by despotic congresses according to so-called historical, geographical, strategic necessities! There should no longer be any other barriers between the nations but those corresponding to nature, to justice, and those drawn in a democratic sense which the sovereign will of the people themselves traces on the basis of their national characteristics!' Such was the cry which rang out among all the peoples."

To these dithyrambics on the subject of national independence and "the will of the people" Marx answered:

"Here there is no mention of reality, or insofar as it is considered at all, it is represented as something falsely, artificially established by 'despots' and 'diplomats.' Against this wicked reality is pitted the alleged will of the people with its categorical imperative of an absolute demand for 'freedom,' 'justice,' and 'humanity.' ... They can demand 'freedom' of this or that a thousand times; if the thing is impossible, it will not take place, and in spite of everything it will remain an 'empty dream.' ... Just a word about the 'universal brotherhood of peoples' and the establishment of boundaries which are traced by 'the sovereign will of the people themselves on the basis of their national characteristics.' The United States and Mexico are two republics; in both of them the people are sovereign. Then how did it happen that between these republics, which, according to the moralistic theory should be 'brotherly' and 'federated,' a war broke out over Texas: that the 'sovereign will' of the American people, supported by the bravery of American volunteers, moved the American borders (established by nature itself) a few hundred miles further south, claiming this action to be from 'geographic, commercial, and strategic necessities'"?

Marx's answer to this ironic question is clear. "Nation-states," even in the form of republics, are not products or expressions of the "will of the people," as the liberal phraseology goes and the anarchist repeats. "Nation-states" are today the very same tools and forms of class rule of the bourgeoisie as the earlier, non-national states, and like them they are bent on conquest. The nation-states have the same tendencies toward conquest, war, and oppression—in other words, the tendencies to become "not-national." Therefore, among the "national" states there develop constant scuffles and conflicts of interests, and even if today, by some miracle, all states should be transformed to "national," then the next day they would already present the same common picture of war, conquest, and oppression. The example given by Marx is typical in this regard. Why and over what did the war between the United States and Mexico arise? California was indispensable for the capitalistic development of the United States, first, as a gold treasury in the literal sense, second, as a gateway to the Pacific Ocean. Only by the acquisition of this land could the capitalism of the United States extend from ocean to ocean, entrenching itself and opening for itself an outlet to the West as well as to the East. For the backward Mexicans, California was just a simple territorial possession. The interests of the bourgeoisie were decisive. The "nation-state," worshiped and idealized by the anarchists as the "will of the people," served as an efficient tool of conquest in the interests of capitalism.

But even more striking examples of this kind are produced by the history of modern South America. We have already mentioned the double-edged character of the "national" liberation of the Spanish and Portuguese colonies at the dawn of the nineteenth century. Here their further political history, already as independent "nation-states," interests us as a colorful illustration of anarchistic phrases of "national freedom" and the "will of the people."

Brazil gained her freedom from Portugal after a hard struggle in 1825. In that same year a war broke out between Brazil and Argentina (which had just been liberated from under the scepter of Spain) over the province of Banda Oriental. Both of these new "nation"-states wanted to scoop up this province, which finally won independence itself as the Republic of Uruguay, but thanks only to the armed intervention of European states which had colonial interests in South America. France and other European countries issued an ultimatum to Argentina, which obstinately refused to recognize the independence of Uruguay and Paraguay. As a consequence, in 1845 another war broke out with the participation of Paraguay, Uruguay, and Brazil. In 1850, again a war was unleashed between Brazil and Argentina, in which Brazil, with the help of Paraguay and Uruguay, first defeated Argentina and then actually conquered Uruguay. In 1864, she formally forced this "independent" Uruguay to submission by armed action. Paraguay rose up against this action and declared war on Brazil, which was joined by Argentina and Uruguay. This war, lasting from 1865 to 1870, finally assured Brazil, where there ruled not so much "the will of the people" as the will and interests of the coffee plantation owners, the position of a dominant Great Power in South America. History does not touch upon the rule of the whites in Brazil (who make up less than one-third of the population) over the Negroes and the mixed population, Only after internal struggles was the emancipation of the slaves announced in 1871, but with compensation to be paid to their owners from state funds. Parliament, however, being the instrument of the plantation owners, did not vote these funds and slavery was still practiced. In 1886 the freeing of slaves over seventy years of age was declared; the rest were supposed to wait another seventeen years for freedom. But in 1888 the dynastic party, struggling to hold the throne, forced through parliament the general abolition of slavery without compensation, and this was decisive for the future of the republican movement. The plantation owners stood behind the republican banner en masse, and in the military coup of 1889, Brazil was declared a republic.

This is how idyllic the internal conditions and events in South America look since the time of the rising of the "nation-states" and the establishment of the "will of the people." A beautiful complement to this picture is offered by the United States of Australia. Hardly had these states emerged from the position of English colonies and gained their freedom—the republican form of government or the federal system, the very ideal of Bakuninist phraseology—when they began an offensive policy in regard to New Hebrides, next door to New Guinea, and in skillful imitation of the United States of America, declared their own particular national doctrine: that "Australia should belong to the Australians." At the same time, the growing navy of the Australian Union is an emphatic commentary on this doctrine.

If, on the one hand, political independence, i.e., the nation-state, is necessary for capitalism and the class interest of the bourgeoisie just because a nation-state is a tool of domination (or control) and conquest, on the other hand, the working class is interested in the cultural and democratic content of nationalism, which is to say that the workers are interested in such political systems as assure a free development of culture and democracy in national life by means of defense, not conquest, and in the spirit of solidarity and cooperation of various nationalities which belong historically in the same bourgeois state. Equality before the law for nationalities and political organizations, and the assurance of national cultural development— such are the general forms of the program of the proletariat, a natural program resulting from its class position, in contrast to the nationalism of the bourgeoisie.

II

The classical confirmation and proof of these general principles is the most famous nationality problem within the framework of the Russian state—the Polish question.

In Poland, the national movement, right from the beginning, took on a completely different character from that of Western Europe. Those who search for a historical analogy for the Polish national idea in the history of today's Germany and Italy, betray their own misunderstanding of the true historical substance of the national movements in Germany and Italy as well as in Poland. With us Poles the national idea was a class idea of the nobility, never of the bourgeoisie. The material base of Polish national aspirations was determined not as in Central Europe in the nineteenth century, by modern capitalist development, but, on the contrary, by the nobility's idea of its social standing, rooted in the natural-feudal economy.

The national movements of Poland vanished together with these feudal relations; whereas the bourgeoisie, as the historical spokesman of capitalistic development, was with us, from the very beginning, a clearly anti-national factor. This was due not only to the specific origin of the nineteenth-century bourgeoisie, alien and heterogeneous, a product of colonization, an alien body transplanted into the Polish soil. Also decisive was the fact that Polish industry from its beginning, already in the 1820s and 1830s, was an export industry, even before it managed to control or even to create a domestic market within Poland. We will not quote here all the statistics of the industrial development of our country, but rather refer the reader to our treatise, *Die Industrielle Entwicklung Polens* (*The Industrial Development of Poland*) (published also in Russian), as well as to the work *Kwestja polska a ruch socjalistyczny* (*The Polish Question and the Socialist Movement*), Cracow 1905. Here we shall recall only the most important outlines of this development.

Export to Russia, especially of the basic branches of capitalist industry, i.e., the production of textiles, became the basis for the existence and development of Polish capitalism from its beginnings, and furthermore, also the basis of the Polish bourgeoisie. As a consequence, our bourgeoisie from the first showed political leanings, not toward the west, to the national unification of Galicia with the Crown, but toward the east: toward Russia. These leanings, after the withdrawal of the customs barrier between the Empire and the Polish Kingdom, increased with the development of big industry. However, the real rule of the bourgeois class in society began after the abortive January Insurrection in 1863. The new rule was inaugurated by the "program of organic work" which meant a renunciation of national independence. Moreover, the class rule of the bourgeoisie in Poland not only did not demand the creation of a united nation-state, as in Germany and Italy, but, on the contrary, it arose on the foundations of the conquest and division of Poland. The idea of unification and national independence did not draw its vital juices from capitalism; on the contrary, as capitalism developed, this idea became historically outlived. And that very circumstance, that particular historical relationship of the capitalistic bourgeoisie to the national idea in our country, became decisive also for the fate of that idea and defined its social character. In Germany, in Italy, as one half-century before in South America, the "national rebirth" carried with it all the traits of a revolutionary, progressive spirit. Capitalistic development embraced this national idea, and historically speaking, elevated it with the political ideals of the revolutionary bourgeoisie: democracy and liberalism. Exactly in this historical sense, the national idea was only a detail of the general class program of the bourgeoisie—of the modern bourgeois state. In Poland there arose an opposition between the national idea and the bourgeois development, which gave the former not only a utopian but also a reactionary character. This opposition is reflected in the three phases of the history of the idea of Polish national independence.

The first is the failure of the armed struggle of the Polish nobility. Not even the most ardent advocates of the theory of "violence and force" in the philosophy of history will explain the defeat of Polish insurrectionist movements as mere superiority of the Russian bayonets. Whoever knows anything about the modern economic and social history of Poland knows that the defeat of the military insurectionists was prepared by the same capitalistic market interest which elsewhere, in the words of Kautsky, comprised one of the main elements of the modern national idea. The endeavors of the bourgeoisie to secure for themselves conditions of large-scale capitalistic production did not involve the demand for a nation-state; on the contrary, the bourgeoisie sought to exploit the annexation, and to paralyze the national movement of the nobility. Thus in Poland, the idea of a nation-state, an idea essentially bourgeois, was sabotaged by the bourgeoisie, and met defeat in the January 1863 uprising.

The second phase was the inheritance of the Polish national idea by the petite bourgeoisie. In this incarnation, the national idea changed from an armed struggle to a policy of neutrality, and at the same time, began to show its weakness. After vegetating for twenty years away from society—in the eighties and nineties petit bourgeois nationalism lingered in emigration in the form of a half-dozen "all-Polish patriots"—finally, with the opening of the present revolutionary era, it has emerged as an active party on the political scene.

The National Democracy proclaimed its entrance into a politically active phase with a public renunciation of the program of national independence as an unrealizable utopia, and with writing into its program instead the double slogan of autonomy of the country and counter-revolution. Now, after throwing off the ballast of the traditional national program, "National Democracy" quickly becomes the true political force in the society. Having failed in its second petit bourgeois form, the program of the nation-state is replaced by a program which is practical and realizable on the basis of a bourgeois Poland—a program of autonomy.

Finally, the third and last phase in the history of the Polish national idea is its attempt to join the class movement of the proletariat. The twenty-year, social-patriotic experiment of the PPS was the only case in the history of the international workers' movement where the slogan of the nation-state was made part of a socialist program. And this singular experiment ended after twenty years in exactly the same kind of crisis and in the same manner as the petit bourgeois experiment. At the time of the outbreak of the Workers' Revolution in 1905 in Russia, the PPS, so as to secure for itself a part in active politics and in the life of the society, publicly renounced the program of rebuilding Poland. The National Democracy renounced this program so as to take an active part in the middle-class counter-revolution; the PPS did so to exert pressure for the proletarian revolution.

The crisis, decline, and fall of the PPS, brought on by this renunciation, constituted the third and last bankruptcy of the idea of the Polish nation-state — this time wearing the mantle of the proletariat. The current revolution, that mightiest social upheaval of modern times, which is calling all embryos of life to growth and maturity, and simultaneously tearing up the entire foundation of society with a giant plow, rejected the last trace of the idea of the Polish nation-state, as if it were an empty shell from which historical development had removed all content, and which could only roll about among the rubble of social traditions during the troubles of a period of reaction.

The historical career of Polish nationalism, however, has not yet come to an end. Indeed, it has ended its life as the idea of the nation-state, but it has simultaneously transformed itself from a utopian specter to a realistic factor of social life. The Polish bourgeois-capitalistic development fettered Poland to Russia and condemned the idea of national independence to utopianism and to defeat. But the other side of this bourgeois process is the revolutionary development of Polish society. All the manifestations and factors of social progress in Poland, above all its principal factor, the Polish position proletariat and its part in the general revolution in the Tsarist Empire, have grown out of the foundations of this same bourgeois-capitalistic development. The social progress and development of Poland are in this way united with the capitalistic process by unbreakable historical ties, which united Poland and Russia, and which buried the Polish national idea. Consequently, all separatist aspirations directed at raising an artificial barrier between Poland and Russia, are by nature directed against the interests of social progress and revolutionary development; or in other words, they are manifestations of reaction. But at the same time, the national idea, after the final failure of the program of the nation-state and national independence, was reduced to a general and undefined idea of national separation, and, as such, Polish nationalism became a form of social reaction blessed by tradition. The national idea became a collective ideological shield for the reactionary aspirations of the whole camp of bourgeois classes, nobility, middle class, and petite bourgeoisie. Historical dialectics also proved to be far more imaginative, supple, and inclined to variety than the minds of the politicians, caught in the grip of stereotypes, and speculating in the abstract wilderness of the "rights of nations." So many Russian, German, and other revolutionaries were, and still are, inclined to regard "national tradition" as a historic vessel, destined by nature for all times, to absorb and carry all sorts of revolutionary currents, as a sea conch, which, according to legend, when carried ashore and lifeless, will always repeat the distant roar of the sea waves when placed close to the ear. This "national tradition," in these concrete historical and social conditions which created today's Poland, becomes just the opposite: a vessel for all types of reaction, a natural shield for counter-revolution. Under the slogan of "national tradition" there took place the elections of the National Democracy to the first Duma, protected by the Cossacks from the criticisms and protests of the Polish proletariat. In the name of the "national idea" the National Democrats used bullets to chase away the Social Democratic workers from the pre-election meetings, and even killed several dozen workers in Warsaw, Lodz, and Pabianice. Under the national slogan, workers' "national unions" were organized by the National Democracy for counteraction against the economic struggle and the revolutionary action of the proletariat. Under the national slogan, National Democratic railroad workers broke the railroad strike, which had been started in December 1905 in Poland, forcing the striking workers to return to work at gun point. Under the national slogan. the National Democracy began a crusade against the general strike and other forms of strikes, claiming they were ruining the "country's industry and the national wealth." Under the national slogan, the Polish Circle in the Duma renounced participation in the Vyborg

Manifesto deliberations, and in the declaration of the Vyborg Manifesto itself, after the dispersion of the Duma.

Under the national slogan, the National Democracy organized so-called "Polish Falcons," or, rather, armed fighting squads destined for murdering socialists, making strikes impossible, and so on. Mr. Dmowski, the leader of the National Democracy, declared in its official organ that "socialists are outsiders" and are thus "foreign enemies," thereby justifying in advance the "national" murders of the socialists. And finally, in the name of the national idea, the future of the nation, and national defense, the Polish bourgeoisie, with the National Democracy at the head, publicly stood behind the banner of "neo-pan-Slavism," in the ranks of the hirelings of absolutism and the Russian "national idea," "with no reservations." The last vestige of the political "national" program—Poland's autonomy—was thus given up on the altar of counter-revolution. Mistreated by history, the Polish national idea moved through all stages of decline and fall. Having started its political career as a romantic, noble insurgent, glorified by international revolution, it now ends as a national hooligan—a volunteer of the Black Hundreds of Russian absolutism and imperialism.

3. Federation, Centralization, and Particularism

We must turn next to another proposed form of the solution of the nationality question, i.e., federation. Federalism has long been the favorite idea of revolutionaries of anarchic hue. During the 1848 revolution Bakunin wrote in his manifesto: "The revolution proclaimed by its own power the dissolution of despotic states, the dissolution of the Prussian state ... Austria ... Turkey ... the dissolution of the last stronghold of the despots, the Russian state ... and as a final goal—a universal federation of European Republics." From then on, federation has remained an ideal settlement of any nationality difficulties in the programs of socialist parties of a more or less utopian, petit bourgeois character; that is, parties which do not, like Social Democracy, take a historical approach but which traffic in subjective "ideals." Such, for example, is the party of Social Revolutionaries in Russia. Such was the PPS in its transitional phase, when it had ceased to demand the creation of a national state and was on the way to abandoning any philosophical approach. Such, finally, are a number of socialist groups in the Russian Empire, with which we will become acquainted more closely at the end of the present chapter.

If we ask why the slogan of federation enjoys such wide popularity among all revolutionaries of anarchistic coloring, the answer is not difficult to find: "Federation" combines □ at least in the revolutionary imagination of these socialists—"independence" and "equality" of nations with "fraternity." Consequently, there is already a certain concession from the standpoint of the law of nations and the nation-state in favor of hard reality, it is a sui generis, ideological, taking into account the circumstance, which cannot be overlooked that nations cannot live in the vacuum of their "rights" as separate and perfectly self-sufficient "nation-states," but that there exist between them some links. Historically developed connections between various nationalities, the material development which welded whole areas, irrespective of national differences, the centralization of bourgeois development—all this is reflected in the heads of those revolutionary improvisers; in place of "brute force" they place "voluntarism" in relations between nations. And since republicanism is self-evident in this because the very same "will of the people" which restores independence and equality to all nations obviously has so much good taste as to throw simultaneously with contempt to the dump of history all remnants of monarchism, consequently the existing bourgeois world is transformed at one stroke into a voluntary union of independent republics, i.e., federation. Here we have a sample of the same "revolutionary" historical caricature of reality by means of which the appetite of Tsarist Russia for the southern Slays was transformed, in Bakunin's phraseology, into the pan-Slavic ideal of anarchism, "a federation of Slavic Peoples." On a smaller scale, an application of this method of "revolutionary" alterations of reality was the program of the PPS adopted at its Eighth Congress in 1906: a republican federation of Poland with Russia. As long as the social-patriotic standpoint—in the pre-revolutionary period—was maintained in all its purity and consistency, the PPS recognized only the program of nation-states, and rejected with contempt and hatred the idea of federation offered, for instance, by the Russian Social Revolutionaries. When the outbreak of revolution all at once demolished its presuppositions, and the PPS saw itself forced to follow the road of concessions in favor of reality which could no longer be denied, in view of the obvious fact that Poland and Russia form one social entity, a manifestation of which was precisely the common revolution, the program of federation of Poland with Russia, previously held in contempt, became the form of that concession. At the same time, the PPS, as is usual with "revolutionaries" of this type, did not notice the following fact: when Social Democracy took for the historical basis of its program and tactics the joint capitalistic development of Poland and Russia, it merely stated an objective, historical fact, not depending on the will of the socialists. From this fact, the revolutionary conclusion should have been drawn in the form of a united class struggle of the Polish and Russian proletariat. The PPS, however, putting forward the program of federation of Poland with Russia, went much further: in place of the passive recognition of historical fate, it itself actively proposed a union of Poland with Russia and assumed responsibility for the union, and in lieu of the objective historical development, it placed the subjective consent of socialists in "revolutionary" form.

But federalism as a form of political organization has, like the "nation-state" itself, its definite historical content, quite different from, and independent of, the subjective ideology attached to that form. Therefore, the idea of federation can be evaluated from the class standpoint of the proletariat only when we examine the fate and role of that idea in modern socialist development.

II

An outstanding tendency of capitalistic development in all countries is indisputably an internal, economic, and capitalist centralization, i.e., an endeavor to concentrate and weld into one entity the state territory from the economic, legislative, administrative, judicial, military, etc. viewpoints. In the Middle Ages, when feudalism prevailed, the link between the parts and regions of one and the same state was extremely loose. Thus, each major city with its environs, itself produced the majority of objects of daily use to satisfy its needs; it also had its own legislation, its own government, its army; the bigger and wealthier cities in the West often waged wars on their own and concluded treaties with foreign powers. In the same way, bigger communities lived their own closed and isolated life, and each area of land of a feudal lord or even each area of knightly estates constituted in itself a small, almost independent state. The conditions of the time were characterized by a diminution and loosening of all state norms. Each town, each village, each region had different laws, different taxes: one and the same state was filled with legal and customs barriers separating one fragment of a state from another. This decentralization was a specific feature of the natural economy and the nascent artisan production of the time.

Within the framework of the pulverization of public life, connected with the natural economy, and of the weak cohesion between the parts of the state organism, territories and whole countries passed incessantly from hand to hand in Central and Western Europe throughout the Middle Ages. We note also the patching together of states by way of purchase, exchange, pawnings, inheritance, and marriage; the classical example is the Hapsburg monarchy.

The revolution in production and trade relations at the close of the Middle Ages, the increase of goods production and moneyed economy, together with the development of international trade and the simultaneous revolution in the military system, the decline of knighthood and the rise of standing armies, all these were factors that, in political relations, brought about the increase of monarchical power and the rise of absolutism. The main tendency of absolutism was the creation of a centralized state apparatus. The sixteenth and seventeenth centuries are a period of incessant struggle of the centralist tendency of absolutism against the remnants of feudalist particularism. Absolutism developed in two directions: absorbing the functions and attributes of the diets and provincial assemblies as well as of the self-governing municipalities, and standardizing administration in the whole area of the state by creating new central authorities in the administration and the judiciary, as well as a civil, penal, and commercial code. In the seventeenth century, centralism triumphed fully in Europe in the form of so-called "enlightened despotism," which soon passed into unenlightened, police-bureaucratic despotism.

As a result of the historical circumstance that absolutism was the first and principal promoter of modern state centralism, a superficial tendency developed to identify centralism in general with absolutism, i.e., with reaction. In reality, absolutism, insofar as, at the close of the Middle Ages, it combated feudal dispersion and particularism, was undoubtedly a manifestation of historical progress. This was perfectly well understood by Staszic, who pointed out that the Polish gentry commonwealth could not survive "in the midst of autocracies." On the other hand, absolutism itself played only the role of a "stirrup drink" (parting good wishes) with regard to the modern bourgeois society for which, politically and socially, it paved the way by toppling feudalism and founding a modern, uniform, great state on its ruins. Indeed, independent of absolutism, and after its historical demise, bourgeois society continued to carry through with undiminished force and consistency the centralist tendency. The present centralism of France as a political area is the work of the Great Revolution. The very name, "Great Revolution," exerted, everywhere its influence reached in Europe, a centralizing influence. Such a product of the Revolution's centralism was the "*République Helvétique*," in which, in 1798, suddenly the previously loosely confederated Swiss cantons were compressed. The first spontaneous action of the March 1848 revolution in Germany was the destruction by the popular masses of the so-called customs houses (*Mauthäuser*), the symbols of medieval particularism.

Capitalism, with its large-scale machine production, whose vital principle is concentration, swept away and continues to sweep away completely any survivals of medieval economic, political, and legal discrimination. Big industry needs markets and freedom of untrammeled trade in big areas. Industry and trade, geared to big areas, require uniform administration, uniform arrangement of roads and communications, uniform legislation and judiciary, as far as possible in the entire international market, but above all in the whole area inside each respective state. The abolition of the customs, and tax autonomy of the separate municipalities and gentry holdings, as well as of their autonomy in administering courts and law, were the first achievements of the modern bourgeoisie. Together with this went the creation of one big state machinery that would combine all functions: the administration in the hands of one central government; legislation in the hands of a legislative body—the parliament; the armed forces in the form of one centralized army subject to a central government; customs arrangements in the form of one tariff encompassing the entire state externally; a uniform currency in the whole state, etc. In accordance with this, the modern state also introduced in the area of spiritual life, as far as possible, a uniformity in education and schools, ecclesiastical conditions, etc., organized on the same principles in the entire state. In a word, as comprehensive a centralization as possible in all areas of social life is a prominent trend of capitalism. As capitalism develops, centralization increasingly pierces all obstacles and leads to a series of uniform institutions, not only within each major state, but in the entire capitalistic world, by means of international legislation. Postal and telegraphic services as well as railway communication have been for decades the object of international conventions.

This centralist tendency of capitalistic development is one of the main bases of the future socialist system, because through the highest concentration of production and exchange, the ground is prepared for a socialized economy conducted on a world-wide scale according to a uniform plan. On the other hand, only through consolidating and centralizing both the state power and the working class as a militant force does it eventually become possible for the proletariat to grasp the state power in order to introduce the dictatorship of the proletariat, a socialist revolution.

Consequently, the proper political framework in which the modern class struggle of the proletariat operates and can conquer is the big capitalistic state. Usually, in the socialist ranks, especially of the utopian trend, attention is paid only to the economic aspect of capitalistic development, and its categories—industry, exploitation, the proletariat, depressions—are regarded as indispensable prerequisites for socialism. In the political sphere, usually only democratic state institutions, parliamentarianism, and various "freedoms" are regarded as indispensable conditions of this movement. However, it is often overlooked that the modern big state is also an indispensable prerequisite for the development of the modern class struggle and a guarantee of the victory of socialism. The historical mission of the proletariat is not "socialism" applicable on every inch of ground separately, not dictatorship, but world revolution, whose point of departure is big-state development.

Therefore, the modern socialist movement, legitimate child of capitalist development, possesses the same eminently centralist characteristic as the bourgeois society and state. Consequently, Social Democracy is, in all countries, a determined opponent of particularism as well as of federalism. In Germany, Bavarian or Prussian particularism, i.e., a tendency to preserve Bavaria's or Prussia's political distinctiveness, their independence from the Reich in one respect or another, is always a screen for gentry or petit bourgeois reaction. German Social Democracy also combats, with full energies, the efforts, for instance, of South German particularists to preserve a separate railroad policy in Bavaria, Baden, Württemberg; it also energetically combats particularism in the conquered provinces of Alsace-Lorraine, where the petite bourgeoisie tries to separate itself, by its French nationalism, from political and spiritual community with the entire German Reich. Social Democracy in Germany is also a decided opponent of those survivals of the federal relationship among the German states inside the Reich which have still been preserved. The general trend of capitalist development tends not only toward the political union of the separate provinces within each state, but also toward the abolition of any state federations and the welding of loose state combinations into homogeneous, uniform states; or, wherever this is impossible, to their complete break-up.

An expression of this is the modern history of the Swiss Confederacy, as well as of the American Union; of the German Reich, as well as of Austria-Hungary.

III

The first centralist constitution of the integrated republic of Switzerland, created by the great revolution, was obliterated without a trace by the time of the Restoration, and reaction, which triumphed in Switzerland under the protection of the Holy Alliance, quickly returned to the independence of the cantons, to particularism and only a loose confederation. Domestically, this implementation of the ideal "of voluntary union of independent groups and state units" in the spirit of anarchists and other worshipers of "federation." involved the adoption of an aristocratic constitution (with the exclusion of the broad working masses) as well as the rule of Catholic clericalism.

A new opposition trend, toward the democratization and the centralization of the Swiss federation, was born in the period of revolutionary seething between the July 1830 and March 1848 revolutions, which was manifested in Switzerland in the form of a tendency to create a close state union in place of federation, and to abolish the political rule of noble families and of the Catholic clergy. Here, centralism and democracy initially went hand in hand, and encountered the opposition of the reaction which fought under the slogan of federation and particularism.

The first constitution of the present Swiss Confederation of 1848 was born out of a bitter struggle against the so-called "Sonderbund," i.e., a federation of seven Catholic cantons which, in 1847, undertook a revolt against the general confederation in the name of saving the independence of the cantons and their old aristocratic system, and clericalism. Although the rebels proudly waved the banner of "freedom and independence" of the cantons against the "despotism" of the Confederacy, in particular of "freedom of conscience" against Protestant intolerance (the ostensible cause of the conflict was the closing of the convents by the Democratic Radical parties), democratic and revolutionary Europe, undeceived by this, applauded wholeheartedly when the Confederacy, by brutal armed force, i.e., by "violence," forced the advocates of federalism to bow and surrender to the Confederate authority. And when Freiligrath, the bard of the *Neue Rheinische Zeitung*, triumphantly celebrated the victory of the bayonets of Swiss centralism as a reveille to the March revolution— "In the highlands the first shot was fired, in the highlands against the parsons" it was the absolutist government of Germany, the pillar of Metternich's reaction, that took up the cause of the federalists and the defenders of the old independence of the cantons. The later development of Switzerland up until the present has been marked by constant, progressive, legal and political centralization under the impact of the growth of big industry and international trade, railroads, and European militarism. Already the second Constitution of 1874 extended considerably the attributes of the central legislation, the central government authority, and particularly of a centralized judiciary in comparison with the Constitution of 1848. Since the Constitution was thoroughly revised in 1874, centralization has progressed continuously by the addition of ever new individual articles, enlarging the competence of the central institutions of the Confederacy. While the actual political life of Switzerland, with its development toward a modern capitalist state, is increasingly concentrated in the federal institutions, the autonomous life of the canton declines and becomes increasingly sterile. Matters have gone even further. When the federal organs of legislation and uniform government, originating from direct elections by the people (the so-called Nazionalrat and the so-called Bundesrat), assume increasingly more prestige and power, the organ of the federal representation, i.e., of the cantons (the so-called Ständerat), becomes more and more a survival, a form without content, condemned by the development of life to slow death. At the same time, this process of centralization is supplemented by another parallel process of making the cantonal constitutions uniform by means of constant revisions in the legislatures of the respective cantons and the mutual imitation and borrowing among them. As a result, the former variety of cantonal particularisms rapidly disappears. Until now, the main safeguard of this political separateness and independence of the cantons was their local civil and penal law which preserved the entire medley of its historical origin, tradition, and cantonal particularism. At present, even this stubbornly defended fortress of the cantons' independence has had to yield under the pressure of Switzerland's capitalist development—industry, trade, railroads and telegraphs, international relations—which passed like a leveling wave over the legal conditions of the cantons. As a result, the project of one common civil and penal code for the entire confederation has been already elaborated, while portions of the civil code have already been approved and implemented. These parallel currents of centralization and standardization, working from above and below and mutually supplementing each other, encounter, almost at every step, the opposition of the socially and economically most backward, most petit bourgeois French and Italian cantons. In a significant manner, the opposition of the Swiss decentralists and federalists even assumes the forms and colors of a nationality struggle for the French Swiss: the expansion of the power of the Confederacy at the expense of cantonal particularism is tantamount to the increase of the preponderance of the German element, and as such they, the French Swiss, openly combat it. No less characteristic is another circumstance, viz., the same French cantons which, in the name of federation and independence, combat state centralism, have internally the least developed communal self-government, while the most democratic self-governing institutions, a true rule of the people, prevail in those communes of the German cantons which advocate centralization of the Confederation. In this way, both at the very bottom and at the top of state institutions, both in the latest results of the development of present-day Switzerland and at its point of departure, centralism goes hand in hand with democracy and progress, while federalism and particularism are linked with reaction and backwardness.

In another form the same phenomena are repeated in the history of the United States of America.

The first nucleus of the Union of the English colonies in North America, which until then had been independent, which differed greatly from one another socially and politically, and which in many respects had divergent interests, was also created by revolution. The revolution was the advocate and creator of the process of political centralization which has never stopped up to the present day. Also, here, as in Switzerland, the initial, most immature form of development, was the same "voluntary federation" which, according to the conscious and unconscious adherents of anarchistic ideas, stands at the apex of modern social development as the crowning summit of democracy.

In the first Constitution of the United States, elaborated in the period 1777-1781, there triumphed completely the "freedom and independence of the several colonies, their complete right of self-determination." The union was loose and voluntary to such an extent that it practically did not possess any central executive and made possible, almost on the morrow of its establishment, a fratricidal customs war among its "free and equal" members, New York, New Jersey, Virginia, and Maryland, while in Massachusetts, under the blessing of complete "independence" and "self-determination," a civil war, an uprising of debt-encumbered farmers broke out, which aroused in the wealthy bourgeoisie of the states a vivid yearning for a strong central authority. This bourgeoisie was forcibly reminded that in a bourgeois society the most beautiful "national independence" has real substance and "value" only when it serves the independent utilization of the fruits of "internal order," i.e., the undisturbed rule of private property and exploitation.

The second Constitution of 1787 already created, in place of federation, a unified state with a central legislative authority and a central executive. However, centralism had still, for a long time, to combat the separatist tendencies of the states righters which finally erupted in the form of an open revolt of the Southern states, the famous 1861 war of secession Here we also see a striking repetition of the 1847 Swiss situation. As advocates of centralism, the Northern states acted representing the modern, big-capital development, machine industry, personal freedom and equality before the law, the true corollaries of the system of hired labor, bourgeois democracy, and bourgeois progress. On the other hand, the banner of separatism, federation, and particularism, the banner of each hamlet's "independence" and "right of self-determination" was raised by the plantation owners of the South, who represented the primitive exploitation of slave labor. In Switzerland as in America, centralism struggled against the separatist tendencies of federalism by means of armed force and physical coercion, to the unanimous acclaim of all progressive and democratic elements of Europe. It is significant that the last manifestation of slavery in modern society tried to save itself, as reaction always does, under the banner of particularism, and the abolition of slavery was the obverse of the victory of centralist capitalism. After the victorious war against the secessionists, the Constitution of the American Union underwent a new revision in the direction of centralism; the remainder was, from then on, achieved by big capital, big power, imperialist development: railroads, world trade, trusts, finally, in recent times, customs protectionism, imperialist wars, the colonial system, and the resulting re-organization of the military, of taxation, and so on. At present, the central executive in the person of the President of the Union possesses more extensive power, and the administration and judiciary are more centralized than in the majority of the monarchies of Western Europe. While in Switzerland the gradual expansion of the central functions at the expense of federalism takes place by means of amendments to the constitution, in America this takes place in a way of its own without any constitutional changes, through a liberal interpretation of the constitution by the judicial authorities.

The history of modern Austria presents a picture of incessant struggle between a centralist and federalist trend. The starting point of this history, the 1848 revolution, shows the following division of roles: the advocates of centralism are the German liberals and democrats, the then leaders of the revolution, while the obstruction under the banner of federalism is represented by the Slavic counter-revolutionary parties: the Galician nobility; the Czech, Moravian and Dalmatian diets; the pan-Slavists and, the admirers of Bakunin, that prophet and phrasemaker of the anarchist "autonomy of free peoples." Marx characterized the policy and role of the Czech federalists in the 1848 revolution as follows:

"The Czech and Croat pan-Slavists worked, some deliberately and some unknowingly, in accordance with the clear interests of Russia. They betrayed the cause of revolution for the shadow of a nationality which, in the best case, would have shared the fate of the Polish one. The Czech, Moravian, Dalmatian, and a part of the Polish delegates (the aristocracy) conducted a systematic struggle against the German element. The Germans and a part of the Poles (the impoverished gentry) were the main adherents of revolutionary progress; fighting against them, the mass of the Slavic delegates was not content to demonstrate in this way the reactionary tendencies of their entire movement, but even debased itself by scheming and plotting with the very same Austrian government which had dispersed their Prague congress. They received a well-deserved reward for their disgraceful behavior. They had supported the government during the October uprising, the outcome of which finally assured a majority to the Slavs. This now almost exclusively Slavic assembly was dispersed by the Austrian soldiery exactly as the Prague congress had been and the pan-Slavists were threatened with imprisonment if they dared to complain. They achieved only this: that the Slavic nationality is now everywhere threatened by Austrian centralism."

Marx wrote this in 1852 during the revival of absolutist rule in Austria after the final collapse of the revolution and of the first era of constitutionalism — "a result which they owe to their own fanaticism and blindness."

Such was the first appearance of federalism in the modern history of Austria.

In no state did the socio-historical content of the federalist program and the fallacy of the anarchist fantasies concerning the democratic or even revolutionary character of that slogan appear so emphatically also in later times, and, so to speak, symbolically, as in Austria. The progress of political centralization can be directly measured here by the program of the right to vote for the Vienna parliament, which, passing successively through four phases of gradual democratization, was increasingly becoming the main cement binding together the state structure of the Hapsburg monarchy. The October Patent of 1860, which inaugurated the second constitutional era in Austria, had created in the spirit of federalism a weak central legislative organ, and given the right of electing the delegations to it not to the people, but to the diets of the respective crownlands. However, already in 1873, it proved indispensable for breaking the opposition of the Slavic federalists, to introduce voting rights not by the diets, but by the people themselves, to the Central Parliament (*Reichsrat*) — although it was a class, unequal, and indirect voting system. Subsequently, the nationality struggle and the decentralist opposition of the Czechs, which threatened the very existence and integrity of the Hapsburg monarchy, forced, in 1896, the replacement of their class voting right by a universal one, through the addition of a fifth curia (the so-called universal election curia). Recently we witnessed the final reform of the electoral law in Austria in the direction of universal and equal voting rights as the only means of consolidating the state and breaking the centrifugal tendencies of the Slavic federalists. Especially characteristic in this respect is the role of Galicia. Already from the first session of the Viennese Reichsrat and the Galician Diet in April 1861, the Galician nobility came forward as an extreme opposition against the liberal cabinet of Schmerling, violently opposing the liberal reforms in the name of "national autonomy" and the right of nations to "self-determination," i.e., in the name of the autonomous rights of the Provincial Diet.

Soon the policy became crystallized in the Stanczyk program of the so-called Cracow party, the party of such men as Tarnowski, Popiel, Wodzicki, and Kozmian, and found its expression in the notorious "resolution" of the Galician Diet of September 28, 1868, which is a kind of Magna Carta of the "separation of Galicia." The resolution demanded such a broadening of the competence of the Provincial Diet that for the Central Parliament there remained only the most important all-monarchy matters; it completely abolished the central administration, handing it over exclusively to the crown land authorities, and in the end completely separating also the crown land judiciary. The state connection of Galicia with Austria was reduced here to such a flimsy shadow that sanguine minds, who did not yet know the flexibility of Polish nationalism, would be ready to see in this ideal program of federalism, "almost" national independence or at least a bold striving toward it. However, to prevent any such illusions, the Stanczyk party had announced its political credo and begun its public career in Austria not with the above program of federation but with the notorious address of the Diet of December 10, 1866, in which it proclaimed its classical formula: "Without fear of deserting the national idea and with faith in the mission of Austria we declare from the bottom of our hearts that we stand and wish to stand by Your Majesty." This was only a concise aphoristic formulation of the sanguinary crusade which the nobility party around Przeglad Polski (Polish Review) waged, after the January uprising, against the insurrection and the insurgents against the "conspiracy," "illusions," "criminal attempts", "foreign revolutionary influences," "the excesses of social anarchy," liquidating with cynical haste the last period of our national movements under the slogan of "organic work" and public renunciation of any solidarity with Russian-dominated Poland. Federalism and political separatism were not in reality an expression of national aspirations but were, rather, their simple negation and their public renunciation. The other harmonious complement of the

Stanczyk program of federation (read: separation) was opposition and obstruction in coalition with Czech and Moravian federalists and the German clerical-reactionary party against any liberal reforms in Austria: against the liberal communal law, against the liberal law concerning elementary schools, against the introduction of the law concerning direct elections by the people to the Central Parliament; on the other hand it supported the government in all reactionary projects, e.g., support of the military laws starting with Taaffe's Law, etc. This development has been coupled with extreme reaction also in provincial policies, the most glaring expression of which is the adamant opposition against the reform of elections to the Provincial Diet.

Finally, the third component of Galician federalism is the policy of the Polish nobility toward the Ruthenians. Quite analogous to the French federalists of Switzerland, the Galician advocates of a potential decentralization of the Austrian state have been strict centralists internally in relation to the Ruthenian population. The Galician nobility has from the beginning stubbornly combated the demand of autonomy for the Ruthenians, the administrative division of Galicia into Eastern and Western, and the granting of equal status to the Ruthenian language and script along with the Polish language. The program of "separation" and federalism suffered a decisive defeat in Austria as early as 1873, when direct elections to the Central Parliament were introduced, and from then on the Stanczyk party, in keeping with its opportunistic principles, abandoned the policy of obstruction and acquiesced in Austrian centralism. However, Galician federalism from then on appears on the stage if not as a program of realistic politics then as a means of parliamentary maneuvers each time that serious democratic reforms are considered. The last memorable appearance of the program of "separating" Galicia in the public arena is connected with the struggle of the Galician nobility against the most recent electoral reform, against the introduction of universal and equal voting rights for the Vienna Parliament. And as if to put stronger emphasis on the reactionary content of the federalist program, the deputies of Austrian Social Democracy, in April 1906, voted unanimously against the motion concerning the separation of Galicia. At their head in his character as representative of the Austrian Workers' Party, a representative of the all-monarchy proletarian policy spoke and voted against the separation of Galicia: this was Mr. Ignacy Daszynski, who, as a leader in the three parts of the patriotic

PPS, considers the separation of the Kingdom of Poland from Russia as his political program. The Austrian Social Democracy is a determined and open advocate of centralism, a conscious adherent of the state consolidation of Austria and consequently a conscious opponent of any separatist tendencies.

"The future of the Austrian state" says Kautsky — "depends on the strength and influence of Social Democracy. Precisely because it is revolutionary, it is in this case a party upholding the state (*eine staatserltaltende Partei*) in this sense; although this sounds strange, one may apply to the Red revolutionary Social Democracy the words which half a century ago Grillparzer addressed to the hero of the Red Yellow reaction, General Radetzky: 'In your camp is Austria.'" (*"In deinen Lager ist Osterreich"*) is just as in the matter of the "separation" of Galicia Austrian Social Democracy decisively rejects the program of the Czech Federalists, that is, the separation of Bohemia. Kautsky writes:

"The growth of the idea of autonomy for Bohemia is only a partial Manifestation of the general growth of reaction in all big states of the Continent. The program of "autonomy" would not yet make Bohemia an autonomous state. It would still remain a part of Austria. The Central Parliament would not be abolished by this. The most important matters (military affairs, customs, etc.) would remain in its competence. However, the separation of Bohemia would break the power of the Central Parliament, which today is very weak. It would break it not only in relation to the diets of the several nations but also in relation to the central government, on the model of the delegations. (The reference here is to delegations of Austria and Hungary which were elected by the Vienna and Budapest parliament and had as their task the arrangement of the so-called Austro-Hungarian compromise, that is, the mutual relationship or proportion contributed by both countries for the common expenses of the state and the settlement of certain matters affecting both.) The state council, that is, the Central Parliament of Austria, would have to be reduced to a miserable idol nodding its head to everything. The power of the central government in military and customs affairs, as well as foreign policy, would then become unrestricted. The separation of Bohemia would signify the strengthening of the rule of bourgeois peasant clericalism in the Alpine lands of the nobility and in Galicia; also that of the capitalist magnates in Bohemia. As long as these three strata must exercise their authority in the Central Parliament jointly, they cannot develop all their power because their interests are not identical; holding them together is no easy matter. Their strength will be increased if each of these strata can concentrate on a certain defined area. The clericals in Innsbruck and Linz, the Galician nobility in Cracow and Lemberg, the Bohemian Tories in Prague are more powerful separately than all together in Vienna. Just as in Germany, the reaction draws its strength from the particularism and weakness of the Central Parliament; here, just as there, giving one's moral support to particularism means working in favor of reaction. Here, just as there, we are obligated to resist strongly the present current tending to the weakening of the Central Parliament. (Kautsky ends with these words:) We must combat Bohemian states' rights (the program of separating off Bohemia) as a product of reaction and a means of its support. We must combat it since it means splitting the proletariat of Austria. The road from capitalism to socialism does not lead through feudalism. The program of separating off Bohemia is just as little a preliminary to the autonomy of peoples as anti-Semitism (that is, a unilateral struggle against Jewish capital) is a preliminary to Social Democracy."

Where the remnants of feudalism have been preserved to this day in Europe, they are everywhere a protection of monarchy. In Germany, a striking manifestation of this is the fact that the unity of the Reich is based on a universal equal voting right to Parliament, while all German states taken individually have much more reactionary state constitutions, from Prussia, with its (as Bismarck expressed it) "most monstrous" tri-class electoral law, up to Mecklenburg, which is still in general a medieval state with a purely class constitution.

The city of Hamburg itself is an even more striking example if we believe that progress and democracy are connected with centralism, and reaction with particularism and federalism. The city of Hamburg, which forms three electoral districts of the German Reich, is represented in Parliament on the basis of a universal voting right, exclusively by social Democratic deputies. On the basis of the Constitution of the Reich as a whole, the Workers' Party is, therefore, in Hamburg, the unique ruling party. But the very same city of Hamburg, as a separate little state, on the basis of its distinction, separateness, introduced for itself a new electoral law even more reactionary than the one in force until now, which makes it almost impossible to elect Social Democrats to the Hamburg Diet.

In Austria-Hungary we see the same. On the one hand, a federal relationship between Hungary and Austria is an expression not of freedom and progress but of monarchical reaction because it is known that the Austro-Hungarian dualism is maintained only by the dynastic interest of the Hapsburgs, and Austrian Social Democracy clearly declared itself in favor of the complete dissolution of that federation and the complete separation of Hungary from Austria.

However, this position resulted by no means from the inclinations of Austrian Social Democracy for decentralization in general, but just the reverse: it resulted from the fact that a federal connection between Hungary and Austria is an obstacle to an even greater political centralization inside Austria for the purpose of restoring and consolidating the latter, and here the very same Social Democratic Party is an advocate of as close a union of the crownlands as possible, and an opponent of any tendencies to the separation of Galicia, Bohemia, Trieste, the Trentino, and so on. In fact, the only center of political and democratic progress in Austria is her central policy, a Central Parliament in Vienna which, in its development, reached a universal equal-voting right, while the autonomous Diets Galician, Lower Austrian, Bohemian—are strongholds of the most savage reaction on the part of the nobility or bourgeoisie.

Finally, the last event in the history of federal relationships, the separation of Norway from Sweden, taken up in its time eagerly by the Polish social-patriotic parties (see the Cracow *Naprzod* (Forward)) as a joyous manifestation of strength and the progressiveness of separatist tendencies, soon changed into a new striking proof that federalism and state separations resulting from it are by no means an expression of progress or democracy. After the so-called Norwegian "revolutions," which consisted in the dethronement and the expulsion from Norway of the King of Sweden, the Norwegians quietly elected another king for themselves, having even formally, in a popular ballot, rejected the project of introducing a republic. That which superficial admirers of all national movements and all semblances of independence proclaimed as a "revolution" was a simple manifestation of peasant and bourgeois particularism, a desire to possess for their own money a "king of their own" instead of one imposed by the Swedish aristocracy, and, therefore, a movement which had nothing in common whatever with a revolutionary spirit. At the same time, the history of the disintegration of the Swedish-Norwegian union again proved how far, even here, the federation had been an expression of purely dynastic interests, that is, a form of monarchism and reaction.

IV

The idea of federalism as a solution of the nationality question, and in general, an "ideal" of the political system in international relations, raised sixty years ago by Bakunin and other anarchists, finds at present refuge with a number of socialist groups in Russia. A striking illustration of that idea, as well as of its relation to the class struggle of the proletariat at the present time, is given by the congress of those federalist groups of all Russia held during the recent 1905 revolution and whose deliberations have been published in a detailed report. (See the Proceedings of the Russian National Socialist Parties, April 16-20, 1907, *Knigoi Izdatielstvo*, Sejm (St. Petersburg: 1908).)

First of all, a characterization of the political complexion and of the "socialism" of these groups is interesting. In the Congress, there participated Georgian, Armenian, Byelo-Russian, Jewish, Polish, and Russian federalists. The Georgian Socialist Federalist Party operates mainly — according to its own report — not among the urban population but in the countryside, because only there does there exist in a compact mass the national Georgian element; these number about 1.2 million and are concentrated in the gubernias of Tiflis, Kutai, and partially, Batum. This party is almost completely recruited from peasants and petty gentry. "In its striving for an independent regulation of its life" — declares the delegate of the Georgian Socialist Federalist Party — "without counting on the centralist bureaucracy, whether this be absolutistic or constitutional or even social-democratic (!), the Georgian peasantry will probably find sympathy and help on the part of that petty Georgian gentry which lives on the land and by the size of its possessions and also its way of life differs little from the peasantry." Therefore, the party considers that "even independently of considerations of a basic (!) nature, merely the practical conditions of Georgian agriculture demand the treatment of the agrarian question as a class question, peasant or gentry only as an over-all national question, as a social (!) problem, as a problem of work(!)." Starting with these assumptions, the Georgian Federalists, in harmony with the Russian Social Revolutionaries, strive for the "socialization of land which is to be achieved under the rule of the capitalistic or bourgeois system." A beautiful addition to this program is the reservation that "socialization" cannot be extended to orchards, vineyards and other "special cultivations," or to farms, because these are areas "demanding a certain contribution of work and material means which cannot be returned in one year or in several years" and which would be difficult for a Georgian peasant to renounce." Consequently, there remains private property for "cultivations" and "socialism" for grain-planting—of which there is little in the Caucasus—as well as for dunes, marginal lands, bogs, and forests.

The main thing on which the Socialist Federalists put emphasis is the reservation that the agricultural question in Georgia should be decided not in a constituent assembly nor in a central parliament, but only in autonomous national institutions, because "however life will decide this question, in principle, only this is unquestionable, that the land in a Georgian territory should belong first of all to the Georgian people." The question, how it happens that the "socialist" party is joined, en masse, by the petty gentry and bourgeoisie, the delegates of the Georgian Federalists explained by saying that this happens only because "there is no other party which would formulate the demands of these strata."

The Armenian Revolutionary Federation, that is, Dashnaktsutyun, founded at the beginning of the 1890s for the purpose of liberating the Armenians from Turkey, was exclusively concerned with "militarizing the people," i.e., the preparation of fighting detachments and armed expeditions into Turkey, the import of weapons, the direction of attacks on Turkish troops, etc. Only recently, at the beginning of the current century, the Armenian Revolutionary Federation expanded its activity into the Caucasus and assumed at the same time a social aspect. The cause for the revolutionary outburst of the movement and the terroristic action in the Caucasus was the confiscation of the estates of the Armenian clergy for the tsarist treasury in 1903. Besides its main combat" action, the party began, against the background of those events, a propaganda among the rural population in the Caucasus as well as a struggle against tsardom. The agrarian program of Dashnaktsutyun demands the expropriation of gentry estates without compensation, and surrendering there to the communes for equal distribution. This reform is to be based on the still rather general communal property in the central part of the Transcaucasus. Recently, there arose a "young" trend among the Armenian Federalists maintaining that the Dashnaktsutyun party is simply a bourgeois, nationalistic organization of a rather doubtful socialistic aspect—an organization linking within itself completely heterogeneous social elements, and in its activity and action on completely heterogeneous socio-political territory, such as Turkey on the one side and the Caucasus on the other. This party recognizes, according to its own report, the principle of federalism both as a basis of nation-wide relations and the basis on which should be thoroughly reconstructed the conditions in the Caucasus, and finally, as an organizing principle for the party.

A Byelorussian organization was formed in 1903 under the name of the Byelorussian Revolutionary Hromada. Its cardinal programmatic demand was separation from Russia, and in the sphere of economics, the nationalization of the land. In 1906, this program underwent a revision and from then on the party has been demanding a federal republic in Russia, with territorial autonomy for Lithuania and a diet in Vilna, as well as a non-territorial national cultural autonomy for the remaining nationalities inhabiting Lithuania, while on the agrarian question the following demands were adopted: lands held by the treasury, by the church, and by the monasteries, as well as big landed property above eighty to one hundred dessiatins are to be confiscated and turned into a land fund out of which, first of all, the landless and small peasants should be supplied on the basis of hereditary property, with the aim of eliminating pauperism as well as developing the productive forces of the country. The socialization of land cannot yet be mentioned because of the low intellectual level of the Byelorussian peasant. Thus, the task of the party is the creation and maintenance of a peasant farm in a normal size of eight dessiatins, as well as the consolidation of lands. Furthermore, forests, bodies of water, and bogs are to be nationalized. Hronmada carries on its activity among the Byelorussian peasants who inhabit, to the number of about seven millions, the gubernias of Vilna, Minsk, Grodno, and part of Witebsk.

The Jewish Federalist group, "*Sierp*" ("The Sickle"), organized only a few years ago by Jewish dissidents from the Russian Social Revolutionary Party, demands non-territorial autonomy for all nationalities in the Russian state; out of them would be created voluntary state political associations combining together into a state federation, in order to strive in that way for its ultimate goal, territorial (!) autonomy for the Jews. It directs its activity mainly to the organizing of Jewish workers in Witebsk, Ekaterinoslav, Kiev, etc., and it expects the implementation of its program to arise from the victory of the socialist parties in the Russian state.

It is superfluous to characterize the remaining two organizations, the PPS "revolutionary faction," and the Russian Party of Social Revolutionaries, since they are sufficiently known by origin and character.

Thus appears that Diet of Federalists cultivating at present that antiquated idea of federation rejected by the class movement of the proletariat. It is a collection of only petit bourgeois parties for whom the nationalist program is the main concern and the socialist program an addition; it is a collection of parties mainly representing — with the exception of the revolutionary fraction of the Polish Socialist Party and the Jewish Federalists — the chaotic aspirations of a peasantry in opposition, and the respective class proletarian parties that came into being with the revolutionary storm, in clear opposition to the bourgeois parties. In this collection of petit bourgeois elements, the party of the Russian terrorists is a trend, not only the oldest one, but also the one furthest left. The others manifest, much more clearly, that they have in common with the class struggle of the proletariat.

The only common ground which links this variegated collection of nationalists has been the idea of federation, which all of them recognize as a basis of state and political, as well as party, relations. However, out of this strange harmony, antagonism arises immediately from all sides the moment the question turns to practical projects of realizing that common ideal. The Jewish Federalists bitterly complain of the "haughtiness" of the nations endowed by fate with a "territory" of their own, particularly the egoism of the Polish Social Patriots, who presented the greatest opposition to the project of non-territorial autonomy; at the very same time, these Jewish nationalists questioned in a melancholy way whether the Georgian Federalists would admit any other nationality to their territory, which they claimed as the exclusive possession of the Georgian nationality. The Russian Federalists, on the other hand, accuse the Jewish ones, saying that, from the standpoint of their exceptional situation, they want to impose on all nationalities a non-territorial autonomy. The Caucasian, Armenian, and Georgian Federalists cannot agree concerning the relationship of the nationalities in a future federal system, specifically on the question of whether other nationalities are to participate in the Georgian territorial autonomy, "or whether such counties as Akhalkalak, inhabited mainly by Armenians, or Barchabin, with a mixture of population, will form individual autonomous territories, or will create an autonomy for themselves according to the composition of their population." The Armenian Federalists, on their part, demand the exclusion of the city of Tiflis from the autonomous Georgian territory, inasmuch as it is a center primarily inhabited by Armenians. On the other hand, all the Georgian and Armenian Federalists recognize that at present, since the Tatar-Armenian slaughter, the Tatars must be excluded from the federation of autonomous Caucasian peoples as "a nationality immature from the cultural point of view"! Thus, the conglomeration of nationalists agreeing unanimously to the idea of federation changes into as many contradictory interests and tendencies; and the "ideal" of federalism, which constitutes in the theoretical and super-historical abstraction of anarchism, the most perfect solution of all nationality difficulties, on the first attempt at its implementation appears as a source of new contradictions and antagonisms. Here it is strikingly proved that the idea of federalism allegedly reconciling all nationalities is only an empty phrase, and that, among the various national groups, just because they don't stand on a historical basis, there is no essentially unifying idea which would create a common ground for the settlement of contradictory interests.

But the same federalism separated from the historical background demonstrates its absolute weakness and helplessness not only in view of the nationality antagonisms in practice but also in view of the nationality question in general. The Russian Congress had as its main theme an evaluation and elucidation of the nationality question and undertook it unrestricted by any "dogmas" or formulae of the "narrow doctrine of Marxism." What elucidation did it give to one of the most burning questions of present political life? "Over the whole history of mankind before the appearance of socialism" — proclaimed the representative of the Social Revolutionary Party in his speech at the opening of the Congress—"one may place as a motto the following words from the Holy Scripture: 'And they ordered him to say "shibboleth" and he said "sibboleth" and they massacred him at the ford of the river.' Indeed, the greatest amount of blood spilled in international struggle was spilled because of the fact that one nation pronounced 'shibboleth' and the other 'sibboleth.'" After this profound introduction from the philosophy of history, there followed a series of speeches maintained at the same level, and the debates about the nationality questions culminated in the memorandum of the Georgian Federalists which proclaimed:

"In primitive times, when the main task of people was hunting wild animals as well as creatures like themselves there were neither masters nor slaves. Equality in social relations was not violated; but later, when people came to know the cultivation of the soil, rather than killing and eating their captives they began to keep them in captivity. What, therefore, was the reason out of which slavery arose? Obviously not only material interests as such, but also this circumstance: that man was by his physical nature a hunter and a warrior(!). And despite the fact that man has already long since become an industrial animal, he is to this very day a predator, capable of tearing apart his neighbor for minor material considerations. This is the source of unending wars and the domination of classes. Naturally the origin of class domination was influenced also by other causes, for instance, man's ability to become accustomed to dependence. But undoubtedly if man were not a warrior, there would be no slavery."

There follows a bloody picture of the fate of the nationalities subject to tsardom and then again a theoretical elucidation:

"Somebody may tell us that bureaucratic rule rages not only in the borderlands but in Russia itself. From our point of view this is completely understandable. A nation subjugating other nations eventually falls into slavery itself. For instance, the more Rome expanded its domination, the more the plebeians were losing their freedom. Another example: during the great French Revolution the military victories of the Republican Army annihilated the fruit of the revolution — the Republic (!). The Russians themselves enjoyed incomparably greater freedom before they united in one powerful state, that is, at the time of the rule of die separate princes." Thus, the memorandum ends its historio-philosophical lecture; freedom does not agree with the clatter of arms. Conquest was the main cause which brought into being both slavery as well as the rule of some social classes over others.

That is all that the Federalists of the present time are able to say about the nationality question. It is literally the same phraseology from the standpoint of "justice", "fraternity", "morality" and similar beautiful things which already, sixty years ago, was proclaimed by Bakunin. And just as the father of anarchism was blind to the Revolution of 1848, its inner springs, its historical tasks, the present last of the Mohicans of federalism in Russia stand helpless and powerless before the revolution in the tsarist system.

The idea of federation, by its nature and historical substance reactionary, is today a pseudo-revolutionary sign of petit bourgeois nationalism, which constitutes a reaction against the united revolutionary class struggle of the proletariat in the entire Empire.

4. Centralization and Autonomy

We have noted the general centralizing tendency of capitalism in the bourgeois states. But local autonomy also grows simultaneously out of the objective development and out of the needs of bourgeois society.

Bourgeois economy requires as great a uniformity as possible in legislation, the judiciary, administration, the school system, etc., in the entire area of the state, and as far as possible, even in international relations. But the same bourgeois economy, in carrying out all these functions, demands accuracy and efficiency quite as much as uniformity. The centralism of the modern states is of necessity connected with a bureaucratic system. In the medieval state, in a serf economy, public functions were connected with landed property; these were the "concrete rights," a kind of land tax. The feudal lord of estates was at the same time and by the same token a civil and criminal judge, the head of the police administration, the chief of military forces in a certain territory, and collector of taxes. These functions connected with owning real estate were, like the land itself, the object of transactions, gift, sale, inheritance, and so on. Absolutism, which increased toward the end of the Middle Ages, paving the way for capitalism by its struggle against feudal dispersal of state authority, separated public functions from land ownership and created a new social category for the execution of these functions, namely crown officials. With the development of modern capitalistic states, the performance of public functions passed completely into the hands of paid hirelings. This social group increased numerically and created the modern state bureaucracy. On the one hand, the transfer of public functions to hired personnel — completely devoted to their work and directed by one powerful political center — corresponds with the spirit of bourgeois economy, which is based on specialization, division of labor, and a complete subordination of manpower to the purpose of maintaining the social mechanism: on the other hand, however, the centralist bureaucracy has serious drawbacks hampering the economy.

Capitalist production and exchange are characterized by the highest sensitivity and elasticity, by the capacity, and even the inclination for constant changes in connection with thousands of social influences which cause constant fluctuations and undulations in market conditions, and in the conditions of production themselves. As a result of these fluctuations, the bourgeois economy requires subtle, perceptive administration of public services such as the centralized bureaucracy, with its rigidity and routine, is not able to afford. Hence, already as a corrective to the centralism of the modern state, there develops, in bourgeois society, along with legislation by representative assemblies, a natural tendency toward local autonomy, giving the possibility of a better adjustment of the state apparatus to social needs. For local autonomy takes into account the manifold variety of local conditions and also brings about a direct influence and cooperation of society through its public functions.

However, more important than the deficiencies inseparable from the rule of bureaucracy, by which the theory of bourgeois liberalism usually explains the necessity for autonomy, there is another circumstance. The capitalist economy brought forth, from the moment of the inception of mass factory production, a whole series of entirely new social needs imperiously demanding satisfaction. Above all the penetration of big capital and the system of hired labor, having undermined and ruined the entire traditional social structure, created a plague unknown before, namely mass unemployment and pauperization for the proletariat. Since capital needs a reserve labor force and since public security must be preserved, society, in order to hold in check the proletarian masses deprived of means of livelihood and employment, cannot but take care of them. In this way, modern public welfare comes into being as a social function within the framework of capitalistic production.

The agglomeration of big masses of industrial proletarians in the worst material conditions in the modern industrial centers created for the adjacent bourgeois classes a threat of infectious diseases and brought about another urgent social need: public concern for health, and in connection with this, the whole management of the sewage system and supply of water as well as public regulation of building construction.

The requirements of capitalist production and of bourgeois society brought about for the first time the problem of popular education. The system of schools accessible to broad masses, not only in the big cities but also in the provinces and among the rural population, brought the idea that the creation and regulation of schools was a public function.

The movement of goods and persons in the whole area of the state as a normal phenomenon and a condition of the existence of capitalist production brought forth the need for constant public concern about roads and means of communication, not only in the form of trunk-line railroads and maritime traffic, important from the point of view of military strategy and world trade, but also of vehicular roads, highways, bridges, river navigation, and subsidiary railroads. The creation and maintenance of these indispensable conditions of internal communication became one of the most urgent economic needs of bourgeois society.

Finally, public safety of persons and property as a matter of general concern and social need is also a clearly modern product, connected with the requirements of capitalist economy. In medieval society, safety was guaranteed by some special areas of legal protection: for the rural population, the area of the respective feudal dominion, for the burghers, the protective walls of the city and the statutes and "freedoms" of each city separately. The knights were supposed to guarantee their own safety. Modern society, based on the production of goods, needs safety of persons and property as a universal social guarantee for everybody in the entire territory of the state without discrimination. The central government cannot satisfy all these needs. There are some the government cannot take care of at all, like the local affairs in the remote parts of the country; understandably, the government tends to transmit the expenses of managing such affairs to the local population.

Local autonomy, therefore, originates in all modern states very early, above all in the form of transferring the material burden of a series of social functions to the population itself.

On the other hand, capitalism stratifies and links into one economic and social organism the biggest state areas, and, to a certain extent, the entire world. At the same time, however, in order to promote its interests, to perfect and integrate the bourgeois economy, capitalism splits the autonomous states and creates new centers, new social organisms, as, for instance, big cities and provincial regions, etc. A contemporary modern city is tied by numberless economic and political bonds not only to the state but to the entire world. The accumulation of people, the development of municipal transportation and economy, turns the city into a separate small organism; its needs and public functions are more numerous and varied than were those of a medieval city, which with its handicraft production, was almost entirely independent both economically and politically.

The creation of different states and of new urban areas provided the framework for the modern municipal government—a product of new social needs. A municipal or provincial government is necessary in order to comply with the needs of these specific social organisms into which capitalism, following the economic principle of the contradictory interests of the city and the village, transformed the city on the one hand and the village on the other. Within the framework of the special capitalistic connection between industry and agriculture, that is, between city and village, within the framework of the close mutual dependence of their production and exchange, a thousand threads linking the daily interests of the population of each major city with the existence of the population of the neighboring villages there goes, in a natural way, a provincial autonomy as in France—departmental, cantonal, or communal. Modern autonomy in all these forms is by no means the abolition of state centralism but only its supplementation; together they constitute the characteristic form of the bourgeois state.

Besides political unification, state sovereignty, uniform legislation, and centralized state government, local autonomy became, in all these countries, one of the basic policy issues both of the liberals and of the bourgeois democracy. Local autonomy, growing out of the modern bourgeois system in the manner indicated, has nothing in common with federalism or particularism handed down from the medieval past. It is even its exact opposite. While the medieval particularism or federalism constitutes a separation of the political functions of the state, modern autonomy constitutes only an adaptation of the concentrated state functions to local needs and the participation in them of the people. While, therefore, communal particularism or federalism in the spirit of Bakunin's ideal is a plan for splitting the territory of a big state into small areas partly or completely independent of each other, modern autonomy is only a form of democratization of a centralized big state. The clearest illustration of this point of modern autonomy which grew in the chief modern states on the grave the former particularism and in clear opposition to it.

II

State administrative and bureaucratic centralism was initiated in France by absolutism during the ancien régime. By the suppression of communal independence in the cities, especially in Paris, by subjugating the largest feudal possessions and incorporating them into the crownlands, finally by concentrating administration in the hands of the state council and royal supervisors, there was created already in the time of Richelieu a powerful apparatus of state centralism. The former independent feudal fiefs were reduced to the condition of provinces; some of them were governed by assemblies whose power, however, was more and more of an illusion.

The Great Revolution undertook its work in two directions. On the one hand, continuing the tendency toward political centralization, it completely abolished the territorial remnants of feudalism; on the other, in place of the provincial administration of bureaucrats assigned by the government, it created a local administration with representatives elected by the people. The Constituent Assembly wiped from the map of France the historical division of the country into provinces, as well as the medieval division into administratively diverse cities and villages. On the tabula rasa which was thus left the Constituent Assembly, following the idea of Siéyès, introduced a new, simple, geometrical division into square departments. The departments, in turn, are subdivided into arrondissements, cantons, and communes, each governed by a body elected by public vote. The constitution of the Directory of the Year III made certain changes in details, maintaining however, the foundations of the great reform effected by the Constituent Assembly; it was this reform which had given to modern history an epoch-making model of modern autonomy, which grew up on the grave of feudal decentralization and was imbued with an entirely new idea, namely, democratic representation by election.

There followed a hundred years of change in the history of autonomy in France. This history and the whole political fate of democracy in the country oscillated, in a characteristic manner, between two poles. The slogan of the aristocratic, monarchical reaction is, throughout this time, decentralization, in the sense of returning to the independence of the former historical provinces, while the slogan of liberalism and democracy is close adherence to political centralism and at the same time, the rights of representation of the local population, especially in the commune. The first blow to the work of the Revolution in that field was dealt by Napoleon, who was crowned by the so-called Statute of Pluvois 28 of the year VIII (Feb. 17, 1800), his coup d'état of 18th Brumaire. This statute, taking advantage of the general confusion and chaos caused especially in the provinces by the counter-revolution during the time of the Directory, for which the democratic autonomy was blamed, hastily compressed the work of the Revolution into the framework of bureaucracy. Maintaining the new territorial division of France in line with political centralism, Napoleon abolished, by one stroke of the pen, any participation of the people in local autonomy and gave over the entire power into the hands of officials assigned by the central government: prefect, sub-prefect, and mayor. In the department, the Napoleonic prefect was, in a considerable measure, a resurrection of the supervisor from the happy times of the ancien régime. Napoleon expressed this reversion with characteristic frankness when he said, *"Avec mes préfets, mes gens d'armes et mes prêtres, je ferai tout ce que je voudrai."* ("With the help of my prefects, police, and priests I will do whatever I like.")

The Restoration kept the system of its predecessor in general, according to a current expression. "The Bourbons slept on a bed that had been made by Napoleon." However, as soon as the aristocratic emigration returned home its battle cry was decentralization, a return to the system of the provinces. The notorious chambre introuvable had scarcely assembled when one of the extreme Royalists, Barthe Lebastrie, at a meeting of January 13, 1816, solemnly announced the indispensability of decentralization. On many later occasions the leaders of the right, Corbière, De Bonald, La Bourdonnaye, de Villèle, Duvergier de Hauranne, argued "the impossibility of reconciling the monarchy with republican uniformity and equality." Under this standard, the aristocracy fought simply for a return to its former position in the provinces from the economic and political point of view. At the same time, it denounced political centralism as "a ground for revolution, a hotbed of innovations and agitation." Here we already hear literally the same arguments under cover of which the right, half a century later, tried to mobilize the provincial reaction against the revolutionary Paris Commune.

Therefore, the first timid attempt at the reform of the local administration with application of the principle of election, that is, the project of Martignaque, called forth a storm in the honorable pre-July assembly and was rejected clearly as the "beginning of revolution."

The enraged representatives of the landed aristocracy demanded only the broadening of the competence of the prefect and sub-prefect and making them dependent on the central authority. However, the days of the Restoration were already numbered and the defeat of Martignaque's project became the prologue of the July Revolution. The July Monarchy, which was only an improved edition of the Restoration in the spirit of the rule of the richest bourgeoisie, introduced insignificant changes in local autonomy; it provided a shadow of the system of election. The law of 1831 on the communes and the law of 1833 on the departments gave the right of suffrage for municipal and departmental councils to a small minority of the most highly taxed as well as to the bureaucracy and bourgeois intelligentsia, without, however, any broadening of the attributes of these councils.

The revolution of 1848 restored the work of its great predecessor, introduced universal suffrage for departmental councils, and made the meetings of the councils public. After the June days, the party of the aristocratic-clerical right violently demanded the return to decentralization as a weapon against the hydra of socialism. In 1849-1851, the departmental councils unanimously demanded the extension of their competence and extraordinary powers in case of civil war, for use against Paris. Thiers, at that time still a liberal, on the contrary, insisted on centralism as the most certain preventive means against socialism. (The very same Thiers, it is true, in 1871, himself waved the banner of federalism and decentralization to mobilize the provinces against the Paris Commune.) The Second Republic, in liquidating the work of the February Revolution, prepared in 1851 a project for the reform of local administration which restored completely the system of Napoleon I, with an all-powerful prefect, and in this way built here, as in general, a bridge on which Napoleon III entered. The latter undertook an even more thorough revision of the February achievements, put local administration even further back than the reforms of Napoleon I, and abolished the openness of the meetings of the departmental councils and their right to elect their own cabinet; from then on the government appointed mayors quite arbitrarily, i.e., not from within the communal council. Finally, Napoleon III expanded the power of the prefects (by the laws of 1852 and 1861) to such an extent that he made them completely independent of the government. These omnipresent departmental satraps, dependent directly on Louis Napoleon, became, by virtue of their function of "directors" of elections to Parliament, the main pillars of the Second Empire.

The course of the above history until the beginning of the Second Empire was characterized by Marx in broad strokes in his *The Eighteenth Brumaire of Louis Bonaparte* in the following way:

"This executive power with its enormous bureaucratic and military organization, with its ingenious state machinery, embracing wide strata, with a host of officials numbering half a million, besides an army of another half-million, this appalling parasitic body, which enmeshes the body of French society like a net and chokes all its pores, sprang up in the days of the absolute monarchy, with the decay of the feudal system, which it helped to hasten. The seignorial privileges of the landowners and towns became transformed into so many attributes of the state power, the feudal dignitaries into paid officials, and the motley pattern of conflicting medieval plenary powers into the regulated plan of a state authority whose work is divided and centralized as in a factory. The first French Revolution, with its task of breaking all separate local, territorial, urban, and provincial powers in order to create the civil unity of the nation, was bound to develop what the absolute monarchy had begun: centralization, but at the same time the extent, the attributes, and the agents of governmental power. Napoleon perfected this state machinery. The Legitimist Monarchy and the July Monarchy added nothing but a greater division of labor, growing in the same measure as the division of labor within bourgeois society created new groups of interests, and, therefore, new material for state administration. Every common interest was straightaway severed from society, counterposed to it as a higher general interest, snatched from the activity of society's members themselves and made an object of governmental activity, from a bridge, a schoolhouse, and the communal property of a village community to the railways, the national wealth, and the national university of France. Finally, in its struggle against the revolution, the parliamentary republic found itself compelled to strengthen, along with the repressive measures, the resources and centralization of governmental power. All revolutions perfected this machine instead of smashing it. The parties that contended in turn for domination regarded the possession of this huge state edifice as the principal spoils of the victor.

"But under the absolute monarchy, during the first Revolution, under Napoleon, bureaucracy was only the means of preparing the class rule of the bourgeoisie. Under the Restoration, under Louis Philippe, under the parliamentary republic, it was the instrument of the ruling class, however much it strove for power of its own.

"Only under the second Bonaparte does the state seem to have made itself completely independent. As against civil society, the state machine has consolidated its position so thoroughly that the chief of the Society of December 10 suffices for its head, an adventurer blown in from abroad, raised on the shield by a drunken soldiery, which he has bought with liquor and sausages, and which he must continually ply with sausage anew."

The bureaucratic system of Napoleon III stirred up, especially toward the end of his reign, a strong opposition; this opposition comes through clearly in the statements of certain local administrations. The most striking example was the famous "Nancy Manifesto," which demanded extreme decentralization and under whose banner there rallied, in 1865, the whole legitimist-clerical opposition of the last phase of the Empire. In the name of "freedom and order" the Manifesto demanded the liberation of the Commune from the super-vision of the prefect, the appointment of the mayor from among the communal councilors, and the complete elimination of the arrondissement councils. On the other hand, the Manifesto demanded establishing cantonal councils and assigning to them the distribution of taxes, and finally, revising the boundaries between departments in the spirit of returning to the historical boundaries of the provinces and making the departments so revised independent concerning budget and the entire administration. This program, which aimed "to create preventive measures against revolutions," to save "freedom compromised by three revolutions," was accepted by all liberal conservatives of the Odilon Barrot type, and its advocates were headed by all the leaders of legitimism, i.e., the Bourbon party: Béchard, Falioux, Count Montalembert, and finally, the Pretender to the crown himself, Count Chambord, who, in his Manifesto of 1871 raised "administrative decentralization" to the role of a leading programmatic demand on the banner of the white lilies.

The Nancy program provoked sharp resistance from two sides — from the Empire and from the extreme Left, Republicans, Democrats, and Socialists. The latter, condemning the counter-revolutionary tendency of legitimist "decentralization," said, in the words of Victor Hugo: "Gentlemen, you are forging a chain and you say: 'This is freedom.'" "Therefore," they exclaimed, "we do not want your departmental councils as a legislative authority, nor your permanent departmental commissions as administrative authority in which a triple feudalism would prevail: the landed interest, the church, and industry, interested in keeping the people in ignorance and misery." Under the pretext of freedom, France was to be handed over as prey to bishops, landed aristocracy, and factory owners—this is the opinion of contemporary democracy and socialists about the 1865 program. Louis Blanc was an especially inflexible opponent of decentralization, even to the departments, which he considered an artificial creation, though he fervently encouraged the widest self-government of the Commune as the natural historical organization and the foundation of the state.

In the revolutionary camp the advocates of decentralization, who indeed went further than the legitimists, were only adherents of Proudhon, such as Desmaret, who distinctly proclaimed the slogan of federalism both in application to "the United States of Europe" and to communes and districts within the state, as an ideal solution of the social question because it was a way of "annihilating power by dividing it." That the adherents of this anarchistic manner of disposing of the bourgeois state have not yet died out in France is proved by the book which appeared in 1899, *Le principe sauveur par un girondin* (Cited by Avalov, p.228), in which the author sharply polemicizes against the centralism and homogeneity of the modern state, advocating, instead of departmental autonomy, the complete dissolution of the state in the spirit of federation. New voices in the same spirit have been heard even in later years—and enthusiasts for "historical" decentralization still crop up from the camp of the Royalists, as is demonstrated by the legitimist pamphlet from the time of the Dreyfus affair, *La decentralization et la monarchie nationale*.

The opposition between the views of the contemporary socialists and the anarchistic Proudhon was formulated as early as 1851 by Louis Blanc in his pamphlet, *La République une et indivisible*, in which in a thunderous voice he warned the republic against the danger of federalism, opposing to the antagonisms of thirty-seven thousand tiny parliaments *"la grande tradition montagnarde en fait de centralization politique"* and *"une administration surveillée"*. As a matter of fact, France at that moment was less threatened by the danger of federalism than by its opposite: the coup d'etat of Louis Bonaparte and the absolute rule of his prefects.

The same grouping of parties with regard to local administration was also reflected in the notorious national assembly in Bordeaux after the fall of the Empire. After the destruction of the Paris Commune the main question concerning decentralization was whether it could serve as a preventitive against the revolutionary movements of the proletariat. First of all, the Third Republic hastened to expand the competence of the departments, equipping them—in accordance with the leading idea of reaction since the time of the Restoration—with special powers against the revolution. The so-called *"Loi Tréveneuc"* of February 15, 1872, bears the significant title *"Loi relative au rôle eventuel des conseils généraux dans des circonstances exceptionnelles."* On the other hand, the powers of the communes were, after a temporary expansion, again restricted: whereas in 1871 the communal councils had received the power of electing their mayor, after three years they were again deprived of this right, and the government of the Third Republic appointed thirty-seven thousand mayors through its prefects, thus showing itself a faithful exponent of the monarchical traditions.

However, in the foundation of the Third Republic there occurred certain social changes which, despite all external obstacles, pushed the matter of local autonomy on to completely new paths. Although the independence of the urban and rural communes might have been abhorrent to the bourgeois reaction, intimidated by the great traditions of the Paris Commune from 1793 to 1871, it eventually became an indispensable need, especially since the inception of big industry under the wings of the Second Empire. It was then that railroads began to be built on a large scale. The artificially fostered and protected big industry not only flourished in Paris but in the fifties and sixties it spread into the provinces and suburban areas where capitalism sought cheap factory sites and cheap labor. Enterprises, industrial centers, financial fortunes mushroomed in the hothouse temperature of the Empire, suppressing small industry and introducing mass factory labor of women and children. The Paris Stock Exchange occupied second place in Europe. Together with this explosion of "original accumulation," as yet unbridled by any protective law—there was still no factory inspection—or by labor organization and struggle, there took place in France an unparalleled accumulation of mass poverty, disease, and death. Suffice it to mention that there were cases when female factory workers were paid one sou, i.e., five centimes per day, in a period of general unparalleled high prices of the prime necessities of life. The short period of this exploiting economy made bourgeois society painfully aware of the lack of any public activity to prevent glaring poverty, infectious diseases, danger to life and property on public roads, etc. As early as 1856, much was written and spoken about the necessity of an official inquiry concerning pauperism in France. In 1858, such an inquiry "confidentially" ordered by the government predictably came to naught.

The state of public education corresponded more or less with these economic conditions. School courses for adults, subsidized by the government under Louis Philippe by the tiny sum of 478 francs on the average annually, were, during the Empire, deprived of this subsidy and neglected. A certain historian described the state of elementary schools in 1863 as follows:

"Thousands of communes are without schools for girls; villages are deprived of any schools at all; a large number of others stay briefly in school and do not learn anything useful; there are no schools for adults and not a single library in the villages; the annual figures show that there is more than 27 percent illiteracy; that living conditions of the male and female teachers are miserable; that 5,000 female teachers receive less than 400 francs annual wages, some receive seventy-five francs per year. Not a single one is entitled to retirement pay. Not a single male teacher enjoys a retirement pay which would assure him of one franc daily subsistence."

Among the workers in Paris, the inquiry ordered by the Chamber of Commerce in 1860 ascertained that fifty thousand, i.e., about 13 percent of the working population, was completely illiterate. The Third Republic, whose mission it was to build a durable home for the bourgeoisie and first of all to liquidate the bankrupt estate taken over from the Empire, found itself faced with a number of new tasks: military reform, and in connection with this, a health reform; also a reform, or rather creation of public education; reform of transportation, completely neglected by the Empire, which was solely occupied with decorating and reforming Paris to turn it into a model capital of the Monarchy. Moreover, the Third Republic faced the task of acquiring means for these reforms. This meant an increase of taxes. However, these went primarily for military expenditures, for colonial policy, and especially for the maintenance of the bureaucratic apparatus. Without the participation of the local population, above all of the communes, the Third Republic would never have been able to solve these tasks.

At the same time, big industry's revolutionizing of conditions under the Empire completely changed the role of the department. When Louis Blanc, in the national assembly in 1871, declared that the department is an artificial product of administrative geometry, this was doubtless an anachronistic view. Indeed, in their beginning, emerging from the hands of the constituent assembly, the departments were an entirely "free improvisation" of the genius of the Revolution, a simple network of symmetrical figures on the map of France; and it was exactly in this abolition of all historical boundaries of the provinces that the powerful innovating thought, that great *"tradition montagnarde"* consisted, which, on the ruins of the medieval system, created a politically unified modern France. For decades, during the Restoration and later, the departments did not have any life of their own; they were used by the central government only as branch offices, as the sphere of action of the clerk-prefect whose only palpable expression was the obligatory *"hôtels de préfecture"*. However, in modern France, new local needs have brought, in the course of time, new institutions surrounding these fortresses of the central bureaucracy. The new "departmental interests" which have gained increasing recognition are centered around shelters, hospitals, schools, local roads, and the procurement of "additional centimes" necessary to meet the costs.

The originally empty framework of the departments, drawn on the grave of the medieval particularism of the provinces, became in the course of time, through the development of bourgeois France, filled with new social content: the local interests of capitalism. The local administration of France by all-powerful prefects could suffice in the second half of the nineteenth century only for the artificial maintenance of the Empire. The Third Republic was eventually forced, in its own interests, to admit the local population to participation in this administration and to change the communes and departments from exclusive instruments of the central government into organs of democratic autonomy.

However, this shift could be effected only within the Third Republic. In the same way that the republican form of government was consolidated in France ultimately thanks only to circumstances which permitted the social nucleus of this clearly bourgeois political form to be husked from its ideological cocoon, from the illusion of "social republic" created by three revolutions in the course of almost half a century, so the local self-government had first to be liberated from the traditional ideology hostile to it. As late as the 1871 National Assembly, some advocates of liberalism abhorred the "reactionary" idea of autonomy which they persistently identified with feudal decentralization. The Monarchist, d'Haussonville, warned his party, reminding it that already during the Great Revolution the appearance of adhering to federalism was sufficient to send people to the guillotine, while Duvergier de Hauranne declared that France was faced with a dilemma: either uniform administration represented in each department by a prefect, or a federation of autonomous departments. These were the last reverberations of an opinion which weighed on people's minds for three-quarters of a century. Only when, with the fall of the Second Empire and the triumph of the Third Republic, the attempts of the aristocratic clerical reaction were defeated once and for all and the phantom of the federalism of the "historic provinces" was relegated to the realm of disembodied spirits did the idea of the relative independence of the departments cease to give an impression of federalism which frightened away bourgeois liberalism and democracy. And only when the last flicker of the Paris Commune revolutionary tradition died out in the cinders of the 1871 Commune and under the withered lawn of the "Confederates' Wall" ("*Mur des Fédérés*") at Père Lachaise, where the corpses and half-dead bodies of the Commune's heroes were dumped, only then did the idea of communal self-government cease to be synonymous with social upheaval in the minds of the bourgeoisie, and the Phrygian cap cease to be the symbol of the City Hall. In a word, only when both departmental and communal autonomy were able to demonstrate their proper historical social value as genuinely modern institutions of the bourgeois state, growing out of its own needs and serving its interests, did the progressive development of local autonomy in France become possible. The organic statute of 1871, supplemented by the law of 1899, at last authorized representatives of departments chosen by general elections of the people to participate in the administration with a determining voice, and the statute of 1884 gave a similar right to the communal councils, returning to them the power of choosing their own mayor. Slowly and reluctantly, and only in recent times, the modern autonomy of France has liberated itself from the iron bonds of bureaucracy.

The history of self-government in England followed entirely different paths. Instead of the revolutionary change-over from medieval to modern society, we sec here, on the contrary, an early compromise which has preserved to this day the old remnants of feudalism. Not so much by the shattering of old forms as by gradually filling them with new content, bourgeois England has carved out a place for itself in medieval England. And perhaps in no other area is this process so typical and interesting as in the area of local self-government. At first glance, and according to a commonplace expression, England appears as the country with the oldest local self-government, nay, as the cradle, the classical homeland of self-government, on which the liberalism of the continent sought to model itself. In reality, that age-old self-government of England belongs to the realm of myths, and the famous old English self-government has nothing in common with self-government in the modern sense. Self-government was simply a special system of local administration which originated at the time of the flowering of feudalism and bears all the hallmarks of its origin. The centers of that system are the county, a product of the feudal conditions after the Norman Conquest, and the parish, a product of medieval, ecclesiastical conditions; while the main person, the soul of the whole county administration, is the justice of the peace, an office created in the fourteenth century along with the three other county offices: the sheriff, conducting the elections to parliament, administering judgments in civil lawsuits, etc.; the coroner, conducting inquests in cases of violent death; and finally, the commander of the county militia. Among these officials only the secondary figure of the coroner is elective; all other officers are appointed by the Crown from among the local landed aristocracy. Only landed proprietors with a specified income could be appointed to the office of justice of the peace. All these officers fulfilled their duties without remuneration, and the purely medieval aspect is further indicated by the fact that in their competence they combined judicial and executive power. The justice of the peace did everything in the county as well as in the parish, as we shall presently see. He ran the courts, assigned taxes, issued administrative ordinances, in a word, he represented in his person the whole competence of public authority entirely in accordance with the feudal attributions of the landed proprietor; the only difference here was his appointment by the Crown. The justice of the peace, once appointed, became an omnipotent holder of public power: justices of the peace were entirely independent of the central government, and in general, not responsible, because the old system of English self-government obviously knows nothing of another basic feature of modern administration: the judicial responsibility of officials and the supervision by the central authority over local offices. Any participation of the local population in this administration was out of the question. If, therefore, the ancient English self-government may be regarded as a kind of autonomy, this can be done only in the sense that it was a system of unrestricted autonomy of the landed aristocracy, who held in their hands the complete public power in the county.

The first undermining of this medieval system of administration coincides with the reign of Elizabeth, i.e., the period of that shattering revolution in rural property relations which inaugurated the capitalistic era in England. Violent expropriations of the peasantry by the aristocracy on the broadest scale, the supersession of agriculture by sheep-herding, the secularization of church estates which were appropriated by the aristocracy, all this suddenly created an immense rural proletariat, and in consequence, poverty, beggary, and public robbery. The first triumphal steps of capital shook the foundations of the whole society and England was forced to face a new threat — pauperism. There began a crusade against vagrancy, beggary, and looting, which extends in a bloodstained streak until the middle of the nineteenth century. Since, however, prisons, branding with hot irons, and even the gallows proved an entirely insufficient medicine against the new plague, summary convictions came into being in England and also "public philanthropy"; next to the gallows at the cross-roads arose the parish workhouse. The modern phenomenon of mass pauperism was the first problem transcending the powers and means of the medieval system of administration as carried out by the self-government of the aristocracy. The solution adopted was to shift the new burden to new shoulders of the middle classes, the wealthy bourgeoisie. Now the mold-covered church parish was called to a new role — care of the poor. In the peculiar English administration, the parish is not only a rural but also an urban organization, so that to this day the parish system overlaps the modern administrative network in the big cities, creating a great chaos of competences.

At the end of the sixteenth century, a tax for the poor was introduced in the parish, and this tax gradually became the cornerstone of the tax system of the commune. The poor rates grew from £900,000 sterling at the end of the seventeenth century to £7,870,801 sterling in 1881. The collection and administration of these funds, the organization of assistance and workhouses, called forth a new organization of the communal office: and to it there also fell presently another important public function which was likewise caused b the needs of the nascent capitalist economy: supervision of roads. This organization also comprised, from then on, besides the rector who was at the head and two church wardens elected by the commune, two overseers of the poor, designated by the justice of the peace, and one surveyor of the highways, also designated by the justice of the peace. As we see, this was still the use of the old self-government apparatus for modern purposes. The landed aristocracy in the persons of the justices of the peace preserved power in their hands; only the material burden fell on the bourgeoisie. The commune had to carry the burden of the poor tax; however, it didn't have any voice in the apportionment of the tax. The latter function was an attribute of the justice of the peace and of the communal overseers subject to him.

In such a state the local administration survived until the nineteenth century. A few attempts at admitting the population to participation in this administration were undertaken at the beginning of that century but came to nothing.

In the meantime, capitalism in England entered new paths: big machine industry celebrated its triumphal entry and undertook an assault on the old fortress of self-government, which the crumbling structure could not withstand.

The violent growth of factory industry at the end of the eighteenth and the beginning of the nineteenth century caused a complete upheaval in the conditions of England's social life. The immense influx of the rural proletariat to the cities soon brought about such a concentration of people and such a housing shortage in the industrial cities that the workers' districts became abhorrent slums, dark, stinking, filthy, plague-ridden. Sickness among the population assumed terrifying proportions. In Scotland and Ireland an outbreak of typhoid took place regularly after each price increase and each industrial crisis. In Edinburgh and Glasgow, for instance as stated by Engels in his classic work, The Condition of the Working Class in England in 1844, in the year 1817, 6,000 persons fell ill; in 1826 and 1837, 10,000 each; in 1842, in Glasgow alone, 32,000, i.e., 12 percent of the entire population. In Ireland, in 1817, 39,000 persons fell ill with typhoid, in 1819, 60,000; in the main industrial cities of counties Cork and Limerick, one-seventh and one-fourth respectively of the entire population fell victim in those years to the epidemic. In London and Manchester, malaria was endemic. In the latter city, it was officially stated that three-quarters of the population needed medical help every year, and mortality among children up to five reached, in the industrial city of Leeds in 1832, the terrifying figure of 5,286 out of a population of 100,000. The lack of hospitals and medical help, housing shortages, and undernourishment of the proletariat became a public threat.

In no less a degree, the intellectual neglect of the mass of the people became a public plague when big industry, having concentrated immense crowds of the proletariat under its command, made them a prey of spiritual savages. The textile industry especially, which was the first to introduce mass labor of women and children at the lowest age and which made impossible any home education, however rudimentary, made the filling of this gap, i.e., the creation of elementary schools, a public need. However, the state performed these tasks to a minimal degree. At the beginning of the fourth decade of the century, out of the budget of England amounting to £55 million, public education is allotted the ridiculous sum of £40,000. Education was left mainly to private initiative, especially of the church, and became mostly an instrument of bigotry and a weapon of sectarian struggle. In Sunday schools, the only ones accessible to working-class children, the latter were often not even taught reading and writing, as occupations unworthy of Sunday; while in the private schools, as was demonstrated by a parliamentary inquiry, the teachers themselves often did not know how to read or write. In general, the picture revealed by the famous Children Employment Commission showed the new capitalistic England as a scene of ruin and destruction, a wreckage of the entire antiquated, traditional, social structure. The great social reform was accomplished for the purpose of establishing tolerable living conditions for the new host, i.e., for the capitalistic bourgeoisie. The elimination of the most threatening symptoms of pauperism, the provision of public hygiene, elementary education, etc. became an urgent task. However, this task could be achieved only when both in state policy and in the entire administration the exclusive rule of the landed aristocracy was abolished and yielded to the rule of the industrial bourgeoisie. The election reform of 1832, which broke the political power of the Tories, is also the date from which begins self-government in England in the modern sense, i.e., self-government based on the participation of the population in the local administration, and on paid, responsible officials in the role of executor of its will under the supervision and control of the central authority. The medieval division of the state into counties and parishes corresponded to the new grouping of the population and local needs and interests as little as the medieval offices of the justice of the peace and parish councils. But while the revolutionary French liberalism swept from the country the historic provinces and in their place erected a homogeneous France with new administrative divisions, the conservative English liberalism created only a new administrative network—inside, beside, and through the old divisions, without formally abolishing them. The peculiarity of English self-government consists in the fact that, unable to utilize the completely in adequate framework of traditional self-government, it created a new kind of base: special communal associations of the population for each of the basic functions of self government.

Thus, the law of 1834 establishes new "poor law unions", comprising several parishes whose population jointly elects, on the basis of a six-class electoral law, in accordance with the taxes paid, a separate board of guardians for each union. This body decides the whole matter of welfare, building of workhouses, issuing doles, etc.; it also hires and pays the officials who carry out its decisions. The old office of the parish overseer of the poor changed from an honorary to a paid one, and was reduced to the function of imposing and collecting taxes assigned by the board.

According to the same model, but quite independently, the law of 1847 created a new, broad organization to take care of public health and supervision of buildings, cleanliness of streets and houses, water supply, and food marketing. Also for this purpose new associations of the local population with representatives elected by it were established. On the basis of the Public Health Act of 1875, England—with the exception of the capital—is divided into urban and rural sanitary districts. The organ of representation is, in the urban districts, the city council; in the boroughs, special local boards of health; and in the rural districts health is supervised by the board of guardians. All these boards decide all matters pertaining to health and hire salaried officers who carry out the resolutions of the board.

The administration of local transportation also followed the same lines but independently of the two bodies mentioned above. For this purpose, highway districts were created, composed of several parishes whose population elects separate highway boards. In many rural districts, transportation is the concern of the local board of health, or the board of guardians which administers both transportation and poor relief. The highway boards or the boards of guardians decide about transportation enterprises and hire a paid district-surveyor as the official carrying out their orders. And so the office of the former honorary highway surveyor vanished.

Finally, education was also entrusted to a special self-governing organization. Individual parishes, cities and the capital form as many school districts. However, the board of education of the council of state has the right to combine several urban parishes into one district. Every district elects a school board entrusted with supervision of elementary education: it makes decisions concerning tuition-free schooling and the hiring of officials and teachers.

In this way there came into being, quite independently from the old organization of self-government, new, multiple, autonomous organizations which, precisely because they originated not by way of a bold revolutionary reform but as discrete patchwork, formed an extremely complex and involved system of often overlapping areas of competence. However, it is characteristic for the classic country of capitalist economy that the axis around which this modern self-government was crystallized—so far clearly on the lowest level in the rural commune—was the organization of public welfare, the organization for combating pauperism: the "poor" was, in England, to the middle of the nineteenth century, the official synonym for the worker, just as in a later time of orderly and modernized conditions, the sober expression "hands" became such a synonym. Beside this new organization of self-government, the old counties with their justices of the peace became a relic. The justice of the peace fell to the subordinate role of participant in the local council, and supervision of administration was left him only to a certain extent in matters of highways. When, however, the local administration passed from the hands of the justice appointed by the Crown to the elected representatives of the local population, the administrative decentralization by no means increased, but on the contrary, was eliminated. If, in the old days, the justice of the peace was an all-powerful master in the council, entirely independent of the central government, at present, the local government is subject on the one hand to the uniform parliamentary legislation, and on the other to strict control by the central administrative authorities. The Local Government Board specially created for this purpose controls the activity of the local boards of guardians and boards of health through visiting inspectors, while the school boards are subject to the board of education of the state council.

Also, urban self-government in England is a product of most recent times. Only slight traces survived to modern times of the communal independence of the medieval city. The modern city, an outcome of the capitalist economy of the nineteenth century, made a new urban organization indispensable: initiated by the law of 1835, it was not finally established until 1882.

The history of self-government in Germany and Austria lacks such distinctive features as that of France or England; however, it generally followed the same lines. In both countries, the division into cities and rural communes resulting from the medieval development brought about a highly developed self-government of the cities and their political independence, and also created the political split, perhaps the greatest in Europe, of the state territory into independent feudal areas. After the sixteenth century, and especially in the eighteenth century, during the time of enlightened absolutism, the cities completely lost their independence and fell under the authority of the state. At the same time, the rural communes lost their traditional self-governing institutions, having completely fallen, through the growth of serfdom, under the authority of landowners. Although much later than in France, absolutism nevertheless, as the creator of a unified state authority and territory, triumphed in Germany in the eighteenth century. At the beginning of the nineteenth century, bureaucratic centralism is everywhere victorious.

However, before long, in connection with the rising big-industrial production and the aspiration of the bourgeoisie to introduce modern conditions into the state, the development of local self-government on new principles begins. The first general law of this kind originated in Austria during the March Revolution. Actually, however, the foundations of the present self-government were laid in Austria by the statute of 1862; in the respective crownlands, particular communal laws came into being later through legislation of the Diet.

In Germany, there prevails French law, partly derived from Napoleonic times, which does not distinguish between the urban and rural commune: for instance, in the Rhineland, in the Bavarian Palatinate, Hesse, Thuringia, etc. On the other hind, the Prussian model prevailing in western and eastern Germany is an independent product. Although the Prussian urban law dates already from 1808, the actual period of the development of the present self-government in Prussia fell in the sixties and the main reforms in the seventies and eighties. Among the main areas of urban administration—province, district (*Kreis*), and commune—only the last has well-developed, self-governing institutions, i.e., extensive power of the representatives elected by the population; in the remaining ones, representative bodies (*Kreistag, Provinzallandtag*) exist but they are rather modernized, medieval class diets and their competence is extremely limited by the competence of officials appointed by the Crown, such as Regierungspräsident in the province, and Landrat in the district.

Local self-government in Russia constitutes one of the most outstanding attempts of absolutism which, in the famous "liberal reforms" after the Sebastopol catastrophe, aimed at adjusting the institutions of oriental despotism to the social needs of modern capitalist economy. Between the peasant reform and the reform of the courts at the threshold of the "renewed" Russia of Alexander II, stands the law which created the territorial institutions. Modeled on the newly established self-governing institutions of Prussia, the system of the Russian "zemstvo" is a parody of English self-government; it entrusts the entire local administration to the wealthy nobility, and at the same time subjects this self-government of the nobility to strict police supervision and the decisive authority of tsarist bureaucracy.

The law governing elections to the county and gubernial territorial councils happily combines, in the tri-curial system and indirect elections, the class principle with the census principle. It makes the county marshal of the nobility the ex-officio chairman in the district council, and securing in it to the nobility curia half of the seats suspends over all resolutions of the council, like a Damocles sword, the threatening veto of the governor.

As a result of this peculiarity of Russia's social development, which, in the period before 1905 made not the urban bourgeoisie, but certain strata of the nobility the advocates of "liberal dreams" however pale, even this parody of self-governing institutions represented by the Russian zemstvos has become, in the hands of the nobility, a framework for serious social and cultural activity.

However, the sharp clash that immediately arose between liberalism, nestling in the territorial administration, on the one hand, and the bureaucracy and government on the other, glaringly illuminated the genuine contradiction between modern self-government and the medieval state apparatus of absolutism. Beginning a few years after the introduction of the zemstvos, the collision with the power of the governors extends like a red thread through the history of self-government in Russia, oscillating between the deportation of recalcitrant council chairmen to more or less distant regions; and the boldest dreams of Russian liberals in the form of an all-Russian Congress of zemstvos which was supposed to be transformed into a constituent assembly that would abolish absolutism in a peaceful manner.

The few years of the action of the 1905 revolution solved this historical collision, violently moving the Russian nobility to the side of reaction and depriving the parody of territorial self-government of any mystifying resemblances to liberalism. Thus was clearly demonstrated the impossibility of reconciling the democratic self-government indispensable In a bourgeois society with the rule of absolutism, as well as the impossibility of grafting modern bourgeois democracy onto the class action of the territorial nobility and its institutions. Local self-government in the modern sense in only one of the details of the general political program whose implementation in the entire state constitutes the task of the revolution.

In particular, the Kingdom of Poland and Lithuania must participate in this political reform. This Kingdom is at sent a unique example of a country with a highly developed bourgeois economy which, however, is deprived of any traces of local self-government.

In ancient Poland, a country of natural economy and gentry rule, there obviously was no local self-government. Polish district and provincial councils possessed only functions connected with elections to the sejm. Although cities possessed their Magdeburg laws, imported from Germany and standing outside the national law, in the seventeenth and eighteenth centuries, with the complete decline of cities, the majority of them fell under the law of serfdom or regressed to the status of rural settlements and communes, and in consequence urban self-government disappeared.

The Duchy of Warsaw, which was an experiment of Napoleon, was endowed with a system of self-government bodily transferred from France, not the one which was the product of revolution, but a self-government squeezed in the clamps of the Statute of Pluvois 28. The Duchy was divided into departments, counties, and communes with "municipal" self-governments and "prefects" who appointed municipal councillors from a list of candidates elected at county diets, which was a slavish copy of the Napoleonic "*listes de confiance*" in the department. These bodies, destined mainly to impose state taxes, had only advisory functions otherwise, and lacked any executive organs.

In the Congress Kingdom, the French apparatus was completely abolished; only the departments remained, renamed "voyvodship." However, they still had no self-governing functions, only a certain influence on the election of judges and administrative officials. After the November Insurrection of 1830, even this remnant of self-governing forms was abolished, and with the exception of the short period of Wielopolski's experiment in 1861, when provincial and county as well as urban councils were created on the basis of indirect, multilevel elections and without any executive organs, the country to this day remains without any form of self-government. A weak class commune crippled by the government is the only relic in this field. Consequently, the Kingdom of Poland represents at present, after a hundred years of the operation of Russian absolutism, some analogy to that tabula rasa which the Great Revolution created in France in order to erect on this ground a radical and democratic reform of self-government unrestricted by any historical survivals.

III

Karl Kautsky characterizes the basic attitude of Social Democracy to the question of autonomy as follows:

"The centralization of the legislative process did not by any means involve the complete centralization of administration. On the contrary. The same classes which needed unification of the laws were obliged thereafter to bring the state power under their control. However, this took place only incompletely under the parliamentary form of government, in which the government is dependent on the legislature. The administration, with the whole bureaucratic apparatus at its disposal, was nominally subordinate to the central legislature, but the executive often turned out to be stronger in practice. The administration influences the voters in the legislature through its bureaucracy and through its power in local matters; it corrupts the legislators through its power to do them favors. However, the strongly centralized bureaucracy shows itself less and less able to cope with the increasing tasks of the state administration. It is overcome by them. The results are: fumbling, delays, postponing the most important matters, complete misunderstanding of the rapidly changing needs of practical life, massive waste of time and labor in superfluous pencil work. These are the rapidly increasing shortcomings of bureaucratic centralism.

"Thus there arises, along with the striving for uniformity of legislation, after the several provincial legislatures have been superseded by a central parliament, a striving for decentralization of administration, for local administration of the provinces and communes. The one and the other are characteristic of the modern state.

"This self-government does not mean the restoration of medieval particularism. The commune (*Gemeinde*) and likewise the province) does not become a self-sufficient entity as it once was. It remains a component part of the great whole, the nation, (Here used as synonymous with "state." — Kautsky) and has to work for it and within the limits that it sets. The rights and duties of the individual communes as against the state are not laid down in special treaties. They are a product of the general system of laws, determined for all by the central power of the state; they are determined by the interests of the whole state or the nation, not by those of the several communes." — K. Kautsky, *Der Parlamentarismus, die Volksgesetzgebung und die Sozialdemokratie*, p.48.

"If Comrade Stampfer will keep separate the centralization of administration and the centralization of the legislative process, he will find that the paths being followed by German and Austrian Social Democracy respectively are not diverging at all, but are going in the same direction as the whole of modern democracy. Opposition to all special privileges in the country, strengthening of the central legislature at the expense of the provincial parliaments as well as of the government administration; weakening of the central administration both through the strengthening of the central legislature and through the devolution of self-administration to the communes and provinces — this latter process taking, in Austria, in accordance with its own local conditions, the form of self-administration of the nationalities — but a self-administration regulated for the whole country by the central legislature along uniform lines: that is, in spite of all historical and other social differences, in Germany and Austria the position of Social Democracy on the question of centralism and particularism."

We have quoted the above extensive argument of Kautsky on the question we are examining but not because we unreservedly share his views. The leading idea of this argument: the division of modern state centralism into administrative and legislative, the rejection of the former and the absolute reognition of the latter, appears to us somewhat too formalistic and not quite precise. Local autonomy — provincial, municipal, and communal — does not at all do away with administrative centralism: autonomy covers only strictly local matters, while the administration of the state as a whole -mains in the hands of the central authority, which, even in such democratic states as Switzerland, shows a constant tendency to extend its competence.

An outstanding feature of modern administration in contradistinction to medieval particularism is precisely the strict supervision by central institutions and the subordination of the local administration to the uniform direction and control the state authorities. A typical illustration of this arrangement is the dependence of the modern self-governing officials in England on the central offices and even the special creation over them of a central Local Government Board which eliminates genuine administrative decentralization represented by the old system in which, it will be recalled, the all-powerful justices of the peace were entirely independent of the central government. In the same way, the most recent development of self-government in France paves anew the way to democratization, and at the same time gradually eliminates the independence of the prefect from the central ministries, a system that had characterized the government of the Second Empire.

The above phenomenon also completely corresponds to the general direction of political development. A strong central government is an institution peculiar not only to the epoch of absolutism at the dawn of bourgeois development but also to bourgeois society itself in its highest stage, flowering, and decline. The more external policy — commercial, aggressive, colonial — becomes the axis of the life of capitalism, the more we enter into the period of imperialistic "global" policy, which is a normal phase of the development of bourgeois economy, and the more capitalism needs a strong authority, a powerful central government which concentrates in its hands all the resources of the state for the protection of its interests outside. Hence, modern autonomy, even in its widest application, finds definite barriers in all those attributes of power which are related to the foreign policy of a state.

On the other hand, autonomy itself puts up barriers to legislative centralization, because without certain legislative competences, even narrowly outlined and purely local, no self-government is possible. The power of issuing within a certain sphere, on its own initiative, laws binding for the population, and not merely supervising the execution of laws issued by the central legislative body, constitutes precisely the soul and core of self-government in the modern democratic sense—it forms the basic function of municipal and communal councils as well as of provincial diets or departmental councils. Only when the latter in France acquired the right of deciding in the last instance about their problems instead of submitting their opinions in a consultative capacity, and particularly when they acquired the right of drafting their independent budget, only from that time dates the real beginning of the autonomy of the departments. In the same way, the foundation of urban self-government in Germany is the right of establishing the budget of the towns, and in connection with this the independent fixing of supplements to the state taxes and also the introduction of new communal taxes (although within limits fixed by state law). Further, when, for instance, the city council of Berlin or Paris issues binding regulations concerning the building code, insurance duties for home industry, employment and unemployment aid, the city sewage-disposal system, communications, etc., all these are legislative activities. The axis of the incessant struggle between local representatives and organs of the central administration is the democratic tendency constantly to expand the legislative competence of the elected organs and to reduce the administrative competence of the appointed organs.

The attitude to local autonomy—its legislative and administrative functions—constitutes the theoretical basis of the political fight which has been going on for a long time between Social Democracy on the one hand and the government and the bourgeois parties on the other. The latter hold a uniform view on the matter in question except for a small group of extreme-left progressives. While the theory of bourgeois reaction maintains that local self-government is, by its nature, only a localization of state administrations, that the commune, district, or province as a financial unit is called to administer the state property, Social Democracy defends the view that a commune, district, or province is a social body called upon to take care—in a local sphere—of a number of social matters and not only financial ones. The practical conclusion of these two theories is that the bourgeois parties insist that electoral rights to self-governing bodies should be limited by a property qualification, while Social Democracy calls for a universal and equal electoral right for the whole population. Generally speaking, the progress of modern self government toward democracy can be measured by the expansion of the groups of population which participate in self-government by way of elections, as well as by the degree to which their representative bodies extend their competence. The transfer of some activities from the administration to the legislative, representative bodies is a measure extending the latter's competence. It seems therefore that the centralized state apparatus can be separated from local self-government, and modern self-government from feudal and petit bourgeois particularism. This can be done, in our opinion, not by a formalistic approach, whereby the legislative and the administrative powers are separated, but by separating some spheres of social life— namely those which constitute the core of a capitalist economy and of a big bourgeois state—from the sphere of local interests.

In particular, Kautsky's formula including national autonomy under the general heading of local self-government would, in view of his theory about legislative centralization lead Social Democracy to refuse to recognize regional diets on the ground that they were a manifestation of legislative decentralization, i.e., medieval particularism. Kautsky's arguments are in their essence extremely valuable as an indication concerning the general tendency in Social Democratic policy, concerning its basic standpoint toward centralism and big power policy on the one hand and particularistic tendencies on the other. But precisely from the same foundations from which, in all capitalistic states, grows local self-government, there also grows in certain conditions national autonomy, with local legislation as an independent manifestation of modern social development, which has as little in common with medieval particularism as the present-day city council has with a parliament of the ancient Hanseatic republic.

5. The National Question and Autonomy

Capitalism transforms social life from the material foundations up to the top—the cultural aspects. It has produced a whole series of entirely new economic phenomena: big industry, machine production, proletarization, concentration of property, industrial crises, capitalist monopolies, modern industry, labor of women and children, etc. Capitalism has produced a new center of social life: the big city, as well as a new social class: the professional intelligentsia. Capitalist economy with its highly developed division of labor and constant progress of technology needs a large specialized staff of employees with technical training: engineers, chemists, architects, electricians, etc. Capitalist industry and commerce need a whole army of lawyers: attorneys, notaries, judges, etc. Bourgeois management, especially in big cities, has made health a public matter and developed for its service large numbers of physicians, pharmacists, midwives, dentists, as well as public hospitals with appropriate staffs. Capitalist production requires not only specially trained production managers but universal, elementary, popular education, both to raise the general cultural level of the people which creates ever growing needs, and consequently demand for mass articles, and to develop a properly educated and intelligent worker capable of operating large-scale industry. Hence, bourgeois society everywhere, popular education and vocational training are indispensable. Consequently we see public schools and numerous elementary, secondary, and college teachers, libraries, reading rooms, etc.

Capitalistic production and participation in the world market are impossible without appropriately extensive, speedy, and constant communication—both material and cultural. Bourgeois society has thus created on the one hand railroads and modern postal and telegraph services, and on the other based on these material foundations—a periodical press, a social phenomenon which before was entirely unknown. To work for the press there has come into being in bourgeois society a numerous category of professional journalists and publicists. Capitalism has made any manifestation of human energy, including artistic creativity, an object of commerce, while on the other hand, by making art objects accessible to the broad masses of the people through mass production, it has made art an everyday need of at least urban society. Theater, music, painting, sculpture, which, in the period of natural economy had been a monopoly and private luxury of individual, powerful sponsors, are in bourgeois society a public institution and part and parcel of the normal daily life of the urban population. The worker's cultural needs are met in the taverns or beer gardens and by cheap book illustrations and junky ornaments; he adorns his person and his lodging with artistic tawdriness, while the bourgeoisie has at its disposal philharmonics, first-rate theaters, works of genius, and objects of elegance. However, the one and the other kind of consumption calls forth a numerous class of artists and artistic producers.

In this way capitalism creates a whole new culture: public education, development of science, the flowering of learning, journalism, a specifically geared art. However, these are not just mechanical appendages to the bare process of production or mechanically separated lifeless parts. The culture of bourgeois society itself constitutes a living and to some extent autonomous entity. In order to exist or develop, this society not only needs certain relationships of production, exchange, and communication, but it also creates a certain set of intellectual relations within the framework of contradictory class interests. If the class struggle is a natural product of the capitalist economy then its natural needs are the conditions that mike this class struggle possible; hence not only modern political forms, democracy, parliamentarianism, but also open public life, with an open exchange of views and conflicting convictions, an intense intellectual life, which alone makes the struggle of classes and parties possible. Popular education, journalism, science, art—growing at first within the framework of capitalist production—become in themselves an indispensable need and condition of existence of modern society. Schools, libraries, newspapers, theaters, public lectures, public discussions grow into the normal conditions of life, into the indispensable intellectual atmosphere of each member of the modern, particularly urban society, even outside the connection of these phenomena with economic conditions. In a word, the vulgar material process of capitalism creates a whole new ideological "superstructure" with an existence and development which are to some extent autonomous.

However, capitalism does not create that intellectual spirit in the air or in the theoretical void of abstraction, but in a definite territory, a definite social environment, a definite language, within the framework of certain traditions, in a word, within definite national forms. Consequently, by that very culture it sets apart a certain territory and a certain population as a cultural national entity in which it creates a special, closer cohesion and connection of intellectual interests.

Any ideology is basically only a superstructure of the material and class conditions of a given epoch. However, at the same time, the ideology of each epoch harks back to the ideological results of the preceding epochs, while on the other hand it has its own logical development in a certain area. This is illustrated by the sciences as well as by religion, philosophy, and art.

The cultural and aesthetic values created by capitalism in a given environment not only assume a certain national quality through the main organ of cultural production, i.e., the language, but merge with the traditional culture of society, whose history becomes saturated with its distinct cultural characteristics; in a word, this culture turns into a national culture with an existence and development of its own. The basic features and foundations of modern culture in all bourgeois countries are common, international, and the tendency of contemporary development is doubtless toward an ever greater community of international culture. However, within the framework of this highly cosmopolitan, bourgeois culture, French is clearly distinguished from English culture, German from Dutch, Polish from Russian, as so many separate types.

The borderlines of historical stages and the historical "seams" are least detectable in the development of an ideology. Because the modern capitalist culture is an heir to and continuator of earlier cultures, what develops is the continuity and monolithic quality of a national culture which, on the surface, shows no connection with the period of capitalist economy and bourgeois rule. For the phrasemonger of the "National Democracy," or mindless "sociologist" of social patriotism, the culture of present-day Poland is, in its core, the same unchanged "culture of the Polish nation" as at the time of Batory or Stanislas Augustus, while Straszewicz, Swiatochowski, and Sienkiewicz are direct-line spiritual heirs of Rey of Nagtowice, Pasek, and Mickiewicz. In fact, however, the literature and the press in modern, bourgeois Poland are appallingly trivial; Polish science and the entire Polish culture are appallingly poor: they belong in a new historical stage completely alien in spirit and content to the old culture of feudal Poland, mirrored in its last monumental work, Pan Tadeusz. Present-day Polish culture, in all its destitution, is a modern product of the same capitalist development that chained Poland to Russia and placed at the head of society, in the role of ruling class, a rabble of heterogeneous money-makers without a past, without a revolutionary tradition, and professional traitors to the national cause. The present-day bourgeois learning, art, and journalism of Poland are in spirit and content ideological hieroglyphs from which a materialist historian reads the history of the fall of gentry Poland, the history of "organic work," conciliation, National Democracy, deputations, memoranda, up to the "national" elections to the tsarist Duma under a state of emergency, and "national" teens to murder Polish Socialist workers. Capitalism created modern Polish national culture, annihilating in the same process Polish national independence.

Capitalism annihilated Polish national independence but at the same time created modern Polish national culture. This national culture is a product indispensable within the frame-work of bourgeois Poland; its existence and development are a historical necessity, connected with the capitalistic development itself. The development of capitalism, which chained Poland to Russia by socio-economic ties, undermined Russian absolutism, united and revolutionized the Russian and Polish proletariat as a class called upon to overthrow absolutism, and in this way created, under the Tsars, the indispensable preconditions for achieving political freedom. But within the framework and against the background of this general tendency toward the democratization of the state, capitalism at the same time knit more closely the socio-economic and cultural-national life of the Polish kingdom, thus preparing the objective conditions for the realization of Polish national autonomy.

As we have seen, the requirements of the capitalist system lead with historic necessity in all modern states to the development of local self-government through the participation of the people in carrying out socio-political functions on all levels, from the commune to the district and province. Where, however, inside a modern state there exist distinct nationality districts constituting at the same time territories with certain economic and social distinctions, the same requirements of the bourgeois economy make self-government on the highest, country-wide level, indispensable. On this level, local self-government is also transformed, as a result of a new factor, national-cultural distinctness, into a special type of democratic institution applicable only in quite specific conditions.

The Moscow-Vladimir industrial district, with its economic achievements, local specific interests, and concentration of population, differs certainly as much from the vast Russian space surrounding it as does the Kingdom of Poland. However, the factor distinguishing our country from the central district of Russia in a decisive way, is the distinctness of the cultural-national existence, which creates a whole sphere of separate common interests besides purely economic and social ones. Just as an urban or village commune, district, department or gubernia, province or region must possess, in keeping with the spirit of modern self-government, a certain range of local legislation contained within the framework of state laws, national self-government, in the spirit of democracy, must be based on the representation of the people and their power of local legislation within the framework of state laws, to satisfy the national socio-economic and cultural-national needs.

The entire modern culture is, above all, a class, bourgeois culture. Learning and art, school and theater, professional intelligentsia, the press—all primarily serve the bourgeois society, are imbued with its principles, its spirit, its tendency. But the institutions of the bourgeois system, like the capitalist development itself, are, in the spirit of the historical dialectic, twofold, double-edged phenomena: the means of class development and rule are at the same time so many means for the rise of the proletariat as a class to the struggle for emancipation, for the abolition of bourgeois rule. Political freedom, parliamentarianism are, in all present-day states, tools for building up capitalism and the interests of the bourgeoisie as the ruling class. However, the same democratic institutions and bourgeois parliamentarianism are, at a certain level, an indispensable school of the proletariat's political and class maturity, a condition of organizing it into a Social Democratic party, of training it in open class struggle.

The same applies to the sphere of the intellect. The basic school, elementary education, is necessary for bourgeois society in order to create appropriate mass consumption as well as an appropriate contingent of able working hands. But the same school and education become the basic tools of the proletariat as a revolutionary class. The social, historical, philosophical, and natural sciences are today the ideological products of the bourgeoisie and expressions of its needs and class tendencies. But on a certain level of its development the working class recognizes that for it also "knowledge is power"—not in the tasteless sense of bourgeois individualism and its preachings of "industriousness and diligence" as a means of achieving "happiness," but in the sense of knowledge as a lever of class struggle, as the revolutionary consciousness of the working masses. Finally, socialism, which links the interest of the workers as a class with the development and future of mankind as a great cultural brotherhood, produces a particular affinity of the proletarian struggle with the interests of culture as a whole, and causes the seemingly contradictory and paradoxical phenomenon that the conscious proletariat is today in all countries the most ardent and idealistic advocate of the interests of learning and art, the same bourgeois culture of which it is today the disinherited stepchild.

The national autonomy of the Kingdom of Poland is primarily necessary for the Polish bourgeoisie to strengthen its class rule and to develop its institutions in order to exploit and oppress with no restrictions whatsoever. In the same way as the modern state-political parliamentary institutions, and, as their corollary, the institutions of local self-government are on a certain level an indispensable tool of bourgeois rule and a close harmonization of all state and social functions with the interests of the bourgeoisie, in a narrower sense, national autonomy is an indispensable tool of the strict application of the social functions in a certain territory to the special bourgeois interests of that territory. Absolutism, which safe-guarded the crudest although the most important vital interest of the ruling classes, viz., the limitless exploitation of the working strata, naturally, at the same time, sacrificed to its own interests and working methods all subtle interests and forms of bourgeois rule, i.e., treated them with Asiatic ruthlessness. Political liberty and self-government will eventually give the Polish bourgeoisie the possibility of utilizing a number of presently neglected social functions — schools, religious worship, and the entire cultural-spiritual life of the country — for its own class interests. By manning all offices of the administration, judiciary, and politics, the bourgeoisie will be able to assimilate genuinely these natural organs of class rule with the spirit and home needs of bourgeois society, and so turn them into flexible, accurate, and subtle tools of the Polish ruling classes. National autonomy, as a part of all-state political freedom, is, in a word, the most mature political form of bourgeois rule in Poland.

However, precisely for this reason, autonomy is an indispensable class need of the Polish proletariat. The riper the bourgeois institutions grow, the deeper they penetrate the social functions, the more ground they cover within the variegated intellectual and aesthetic sphere, the broader grows the battlefield and the bigger the number of firing lines wherefrom the proletariat conducts the class struggle. The more unrestrictedly and efficiently the development of bourgeois society proceeds, the more courageously and surely advances the consciousness, political maturity, and unification of the proletariat as a class.

The Polish proletariat needs for its class struggle all the components of which a spiritual culture is made; primarily, its interests, essentially based on the solidarity of nations and striving toward it, require the elimination of national oppression, and guarantees against such oppression worked out in the course of social development. Moreover, a normal, broad, and unrestricted cultural life of the country is just as indispensable for the development of the proletariat's class struggle as for the existence of bourgeois society itself.

National autonomy has the same aims as are contained in the political program of the Polish proletariat: the overthrow of absolutism and the achievement of political freedom in the country at large; this is but a part of the program resulting both from the progressive trends of capitalist development and from the class interests of. the proletariat.

II

The national separateness of a certain territory in a modern state is not by itself a sufficient basis for autonomy; the relationship between nationality and political life is precisely what calls for closer examination. Theoreticians of nationalism usually consider nationality in general as a natural, unchangeable phenomenon, outside social development, a conservative phenomenon resisting all historical vicissitudes, In accordance with this view bourgeois nationalism finds the main sources of national vitality and strength not in the modern historical formation, i.e., urban, bourgeois culture, but, on the contrary, in the traditional forms of life of the rural population. The peasant mass with its social conservatism appears to the romantics of nationalism as the only genuine mainstay of the national culture, an unshakable fortress of national distinctness, the stronghold of the proper national genius and spirit. When, in the middle of the last century, there began to flourish, in connection with the nationalist trend in the politics of Central Europe, so-called folklorism, it turned above all to the traditional forms of peasant culture as to the treasury in which every nation deposits "the threads of its thoughts and the flowers of its feelings." In the same way at present, the recently awakened Lithuanian, Byelorussian, and Ukrainian nationalism bases itself entirely on the rural population and its conservative forms of existence, significantly starting the cultivation of this age-old and virgin national field with spreading primers and the Holy Scripture in the national language and national orthography. Already, in the 1880s, when the pseudo-socialistic and pseudo-revolutionary *Glos* (Voice) was published in Warsaw, the Polish National Democracy too, following its infallible reactionary instinct, turned its peculiar national sentiments, happily married to the anti-Semitism of the urban bourgeoisie, toward the rural population. Finally, in the same way, the most re-cent "nationalist" current in Russia, the party of Mr. Korfanty and Company, is based mainly on the conservatism of the rural population of Upper Silesia, exploited as a foundation for economic and political success by the reactionary Polish petite bourgeoisie.

On the other hand, the problem of which social strata constitute the proper guardians of national culture has recently caused an interesting exchange of views in the Social Democratic camp.

In the study of the "nationality question, " quoted by us several times, Karl Kautsky, criticizing the work of the Austrian party publicist Otto Bauer on the same subject, says:

"Class differences lead Bauer to the paradoxical opinion that only those portions of a nation constitute a nation which participate in the culture: consequently, until now, only the ruling and exploiting classes."

"In the period of the Staufers" — writes Bauer — "the nation existed only in the cultural community of knighthood ... A homogeneous national character produced by the homogeneity of cultural influences, was only the character of one class of the nation ... The peasant did not share in anything that united the nation. Therefore the German peasants do not at all constitute the nation; they are the Hintersassen of the nation. In a society based on the private ownership of the means of production, the ruling classes constitute the nation — formerly the knighthood, today the educated people, as a community of people in whom uniform education developed by the nation's history, with the help of a common language and national education, develops an affinity of characters. On the other hand the broad popular masses do not constitute the nation."

According to Bauer only the socialist system, by making the masses of the working people participants in the entirety of the culture, will turn these masses into a nation. Kautsky replies to these arguments as follows:

"This is a very subtle thought with a very right core but in the nationality question it leads to a false road, for it treats the concept of nation in such a way as to make simply impossible the understanding of the force of the national thought in all classes in the present, and the bases of the present national contradictions of entire nations. Bauer conflicts here with the observation made by Renner that it is precisely the peasant who is the preserver of nationality. Renner demonstrates that in Austria (including Hungary), during the last century, a number of cities changed their nationality, becoming Hungarian or Czech rather than German. On the other hand German cities, specifically Vienna, absorbed an immense influx of foreign nationalities and assimilated them to the German nation. However, in the countryside the linguistic boundaries have practically not shifted. Actually, in Austria's major cities, the process of Germanization has achieved its goal; at the beginning of the nineteenth century they had all been German cities, with the exception at the most of Galicia, Croatia, and the Italian towns. By contrast, the peasant population is the one that remained national; the tendencies toward making Austria a national state shattered against the peasantry. The peasant firmly adheres to his nationality as to any tradition, while the city dweller, especially the educated one, assimilates much more easily."

In the course of his study, Kautsky is forced to considerably revise his reasoning. Examining more closely the foundations of modern national movements, he points out that precisely the bourgeois development calling into existence a new social class, the professional intelligentsia, creates in this form the main fact of the contemporary national idea and a pillar of national life. It is true that the same development simultaneously leads the social and cultural life of present-day nationalities, and particularly of the intelligentsia to international paths, and from this standpoint Kautsky rightly reverses the perspective outlined by Bauer, by explaining that the task of the great socialist reform in the future will not be the nationalization, i.e., the national separation of the working masses, but, on the contrary, blazing the trail for one universal, international culture in which distinct nationalities will disappear. However, in present-day conditions, the role of the urban, or strictly speaking, bourgeois element, is decisive for the fate of nationalities. If Kautsky in agreement with Renner points to a whole series of Slavic critics Germanized at the beginning of the nineteenth century in the Hapsburg monarchy as an example of the national non-resistance of the urban element, these facts may actually serve only as an illustration of the petit bourgeois conditions of the pre-capitalist era by which doubtless the urban life in the Slavic lands of Austria was characterized at the beginning of the nineteenth century. The further development of events, a definite swing of the same type of critics to their own nationality in the last few decades, which is confirmed by Kautsky and Renner, is, on the other hand, a striking example of how far the rise of its own bourgeois development in a country, its own industry, its own big city life, its own "national" bourgeoisie and intelligentsia, as it occurred for example in Bohemia, can form the basis for a resistant national policy and for an active political life connected with it.

The emphasis on the peasant element in connection with the fate of nationality is correct so far as the quite passive preservation of national peculiarities in the ethnic group is concerned: speech, mores, dress, and also, usually in close connection with this, a certain religion. The conservatism of peasant life makes possible the preservation of nationality within these narrow bounds and explains the resistance for centuries to any denationalization policy, regardless of either the ruthlessness of the methods or the cultural superiority of the aggressive foreign nationality. This is proved by the preservation of speech and national type among the South Slavic tribes of Turkey and Hungary, the preservation of the peculiarities of the Byelorussians, Ruthenians, Lithuanians in the Russian empire, of the Masurians and Lithuanians in East Prussia, or the Poles in Upper Silesia, etc.

However, a national culture preserved in this traditional-peasant manner is incapable of playing the role of an active element in contemporary political-social life, precisely because it is entirely a product of tradition, is rooted in past conditions, because — to use the words of Marx — the peasant class stands in today's bourgeois society outside of culture, constituting rather a "piece of barbarism" surviving in that culture. The peasant, as a national "outpost," is always and a priori a culture of social barbarism, a basis of political reaction, doomed by historical evolution. No serious political-national movement in present-day conditions is possible solely on a national peasant foundation. And only when the present urban classes-bourgeoisie, petite bourgeoisie, and bourgeois-intelligentsia—become the promoters of the national movement, will it be possible to develop, in certain defined circumstances, the seeming phenomenon of the national contradictions and national aspirations of "entire nations," referred to by Kautsky.

Thus, local autonomy in the sense of the self-government of a certain nationality territory is only possible where the respective nationality possesses its own bourgeois development, urban life, intelligentsia, its own literary and scholarly life. The Congress Kingdom demonstrates all these conditions. Its population is nationally homogeneous because the Polish element has a decisive preponderance over other nationalities in the country's whole area, with the exception of the Suwalki gubernia in which the Lithuanians prevail. Out of the overall population of 9,402,253 the Poles constitute 6,755,503, while of the remaining nationalities the Jews and Germans are mainly concentrated in the cities where, however, they do not represent a foreign bourgeois intelligentsia, but, on the contrary, are considerably assimilated by Polish cultural life, while the Russians, except in the Lublin and Siedlce regions, represent mainly the influx of bureaucratic elements alien to Polish society. The percentage of total population of these nationalities in the respective provinces, with the exception of Suwalki, appears, according to the census of 1897, as follows:

Gubernia	Poles	Jews	Germans	Russians
Kalisz	83.9%	7.6	7.3	1.1
Kielce	87.6	10.9	—	1.2
Lublin	61.3	12.7	0.2	21.0
Lomza	77.4	15.8	0.8	5.5
Piotrokow	71.9	15.2	10.6	1.6
Plock	80.4	9.6	6.7	3.3
Radom	83.8	13.8	1.1	1.4
Siedlce	66.1	15.5	1.4	16.5
Warsaw	73.6	16.4	4.0	5.4

Thus, in all the gubernias except two, and in the country as a whole, the Polish element constitutes more than 70 percent of the population; it is, moreover, the decisive element in the socio-cultural development of the country.

However, the situation looks different when we turn to the Jewish nationality.

Jewish national autonomy, not in the sense of freedom of school, religion, place of residence, and equal civic rights, but in the sense of the political self-government of the Jewish population with its own legislation and administration, as it were parallel to the autonomy of the Congress Kingdom, is an entirely utopian idea. Strangely, this conviction prevails also in the camp of extreme Polish nationalists, e.g., in the so-called "Revolutionary Faction" of the PPS, where it is based on the simple circumstance that the Jewish nationality does not possess a "territory of its own" within the Russian empire. But national autonomy conceived in accordance with that group's own standpoint, i.e., as the sum of freedoms and rights to self-determination of a certain group of people linked by language, tradition, and psychology, is in itself a construction lying beyond historical conditions, fluttering in mid-air, and therefore one that can be easily conceived, as it were, "in the air," i.e., without any definite territory. On the other hand, an autonomy that grows historically together with local self-government, on the basis of modern bourgeois-democratic development, is actually as inseparable from a certain territory as the bourgeois state itself, and cannot be imagined without it to the same extent as "non-territorial" communal or urban self-government. It is true that the Jewish population was completely under the influence of modern capitalistic development in the Russian empire and shares the economic, political, and spiritual interests of particular groups in that society. But on the one hand, these interests were never territorially separated so as to become specifically Jewish capitalist interests; rather, they are common interests of the Jewish and other people in the country at large. On the other hand, this capitalist development does not lead to a separation of bourgeois Jewish culture, but acts in an exactly opposite direction, leading to the assimilation of the Jewish bourgeois, urban intelligentsia, to their absorption by the Polish or Russian people. If the national distinctness of the Lithuanians or Byelorussians is based on the backward peasant people, the Jewish national distinctness in Russia and Poland is based on the socially backward petite bourgeoisie, on small production, small trade, small-town life, and—let us add parenthetically—on the close relation of the nationality in question to religion. In view of the above, the national distinctness of the Jews, which is supposed to be the basis of non-territorial Jewish autonomy, is manifested not in the form of metropolitan bourgeois culture, but in the form of small-town lack of culture. Obviously any efforts toward "developing Jewish culture" at the initiative of a handful of Yiddish publicists and translators cannot be taken seriously.

The only manifestation of genuine modern culture in the Russian framework is the Social Democratic movement of the Russian proletariat which, because of its nature, can best replace the historical lack of bourgeois national culture of the Jews, since it is itself a phase of genuinely international and proletarian culture.

Different, though no less complicated, is the question of autonomy in Lithuania. For nationalist utopians, obviously the existence of a certain territory inhabited by a population of distinct nationality is a sufficient reason to demand for the nationality in question, in the name of the right of all nationalities to self-determination, either an independent republic, or one federated with Russia, or the "broadest autonomy." Each of these programs was advanced in turn by the former "Lithuanian Social Democracy," then by the PPS in its federative phase, and finally by the recently organized "Byelorussian Socialist Commune" which, at its Second Congress in 1906, adopted a somewhat vague program of a "federal republic in Russia with a territorial-autonomous diet in Vilna for the territory of the Western country." Whether the "Byelorussian Commune" demands the proclamation of the "Western country" as one of the republics into which the Russian Empire is to be split, or a "territorial autonomy" for that "Western country" is difficult to figure out; since an "autonomous" diet is demanded for Vilna, it would seem that the latter version is intended, or else, what is in complete harmony with the whole utopian-abstract treatment of the question, no basic distinctions are made between an independent republic, a federal system, and autonomy, but only qualitative distinctions. Let us examine the matter from the standpoint of territorial autonomy. The "Western country," according to the terminology in the Russian administrative division, is a preponderantly agrarian and small-industry district comprising areas with considerable variations in conditions. Apart from the local interests of the rural, municipal, and provincial self-governments, this territory is much less of as distinct production and trading district, with a less distinctive character and a less distinct grouping of interests, than the Kingdom of Poland or the industrial Moscow district. On the other hand it is a distinct nationality district. But it is precisely with regard to this question of nationality that the greatest difficulties arise from the standpoint of potential autonomy. The "Western country," i.e., the territory of former Lithuania, is an area occupied by several different nationalities, and the first question that arises is: which nationality is to be served by the territorial-national autonomy that is at stake, which language, which nationality is to be decisive in the schools, cultural institutions, the judiciary, legislation, and in filling local offices? The Lithuanian nationalists obviously demand autonomy for the Lithuanian nationality. Let us look at the actual conditions of that nationality.

According to the census of 1897—the last one that has taken place and whose results in the area of nationality relations have been available to the public since 1905—the genuine Lithuanian nationality in the Russian empire numbers 1,210,510 people. This population inhabits mainly the Vilna, Kovno, Grodno, and Suwalki gubernias. Besides, there live almost exclusively in the Kovno gubernia, 448,000 persons of Samogitian nationality, who by no means identify with the Lithuanians. If we were to outline the territory that might serve as a basis for an autonomous Lithuania, we would have to eliminate part of the present "Western country," and on the other hand go beyond its borders and include the Suwalki gubernia which today belongs to the Congress Kingdom. We would obtain a territory approximately corresponding to the voyvodship of Vilna and Troki which, in pre-partition Poland, constituted "Lithuania proper." The Lithuanian population is distributed in that territory as follows: out of the sum total of 1,200,000 Lithuanians almost half, i.e., 574,853, are concentrated in the Kovno gubernia. The second place with regard to the concentration of Lithuanians is occupied by the Suwalki gubernia, where 305,548 live; somewhat fewer are to be found in the Vilna gubernia, viz., 297,720 persons; finally, an insignificant number of Lithuanians, about 3,500, inhabit the northern portion of the Grodno gubernia. Actually, the Lithuanian population is doubtless more numerous, because in the census the language used by the respective populations was the main point taken into consideration, while a sizable proportion of Lithuanians use the Polish language in everyday life. However, in the present case, from the standpoint of nationality as a basis of national autonomy, obviously only the population wherein national distinctness is expressed in a distinct native language can be taken into account.

The distribution of the Lithuanian population becomes apparent only when we ascertain its numerical ratio to the remaining population in the same territory. The over-all population figure in the gubernias mentioned (always according to the 1897 census) is as follows:

Percent
Lithuanians
In the Kovno gubernia   1,544,569 37.0
In the Vilna gubernia 1,591,207 17.0
In the Grodno gubernia 1,603,409 0.2
In the Suwalki gubernia   582,913 52.0

Out of a total population of 5,322,093 in that territory, the Lithuanians constitute less than 23 percent. Even if we were to include, as do the Lithuanian nationalists, the entire Samogitian population with the Lithuanians, we would obtain the ratio of 31 percent, i.e., less than a third of the total population. Obviously, setting up the former "Lithuania proper" as the area of the Lithuanian nationality is, in present-day conditions, an entirely arbitrary and artificial construction.

The total population of the four "north-western" gubernias included because of the Byelorussian nationality is as follows:

Minsk gubernia   2,147,621
Mogilev gubernia 1,686,764
Witebsk gubernia 1,489,246
Smolensk gubernia 1,525,279

Together with the population of the four gubernias inhabited by Lithuanians, this adds up to the considerable figure of 12,171,007. However, among this population, the Byelorussians constitute less than half, i.e., about 5.85 million (5,855,547). Even considering only the figures, the idea of fitting Lithuania's autonomy to the Byelorussian nationality seems questionable. However, this difficulty becomes much greater if we take into consideration the socio-economic conditions of the respective nationalities.

In the territory inhabited by them the Byelorussians constitute an exclusively rural, agrarian element. Their cultural level is extremely low. Illiteracy is so widespread that the "Byelorussian Commune" was forced to establish an "Education Department" to spread elementary education among the Byelorussian peasants. The complete lack of a Byelorussian bourgeoisie, an urban intelligentsia, and an independent scholarly and literary life in the Byelorussian language, renders the idea of a national Byelorussian autonomy simply impractical.

The social conditions among the Lithuanian nationals are similar. To a preponderant degree farming is the occupation of the Lithuanians. In the cultural heart of Lithuania, the Vilna gubernia, the Lithuanians constitute 19.8 percent of the total population, and 3.1 percent of the urban population. In the Suwalki gubernia, the next with regard to Lithuanian concentration, the Lithuanians constitute as much as 52.2 percent of the gubernia population, but only 9.2 per-cent of the urban population. It is true that the cultural conditions among the Lithuanians are quite different from those in Byelorussia. The education of the Lithuanian population is on a relatively high level, and the percentage of illiterates is almost the lowest in the Russian Empire. But the education of Lithuanians is preponderantly a Polish education, and the Polish language, not the Lithuanian, is here the instrument of culture, which fact is closely connected with the fact that the possessing classes, the rural landed gentry, and the urban intelligentsia are genuinely Polish or Polonized to a high degree. The same situation prevails to a considerable degree in Ruthenia. Indeed, in Lithuania and Ruthenia the only nationality culturally fit to manage national autonomy is the Polish, with its urban population and its intelligentsia. Therefore, if the national autonomy of the "Western country" were to be considered, it would have to be neither a Lithuanian nor a Byelorussian autonomy, but a Polish one: the Polish language, the Polish school, Poles in public offices would be the natural expression of the autonomous institutions of the country.

Given this situation, culturally and nationally, Lithuania and Ruthenia would constitute only an extension of the Kingdom, not a separate autonomous region; they would form, with the Kingdom, a natural and historical region, with Polish autonomy over the Kingdom plus Lithuania.

Such a solution of the question is opposed by several decisive considerations. First of all, from the purely national point of view, this would be the rule of a small Polish minority over a majority of Lithuanians, Byelorussians, Jews, and others. In Lithuania and Ruthenia, the Jews and the Poles make up most of the urban population; together they occupy what would be the natural social centers of autonomous institutions. But the Jewish population decisively outnumbers the Polish, whereas in the Congress Kingdom there are 6,880,000 Poles (according to the 1897 census) and only 1,300,000 Jews. The percentage of each in the four gubernias of Lithuania proper in terms of the over-all population is as follows:

Gubernia Poles Jews
Suwalki 22.99 10.14
Kovno 9.04 13.73
Vilna 8.17 12.72
Grodno 10.08 17.37

Only in the Suwalki gubernia is the Jewish population smaller than the Polish, but even here this ratio is quite different when we take the towns into consideration: then the Poles constitute 27 percent, the Jews 40 percent of the urban population. It should also be taken into consideration that Jews in the Kingdom, if assimilated—more so in the urban areas—reinforce the Polish nationality; whereas in Lithuania the assimilation process, which is anyway much slower, occurs—when it does at all—among Jews who belong to the Russian culture; in both cases confusion among nationalities grows and the question of autonomy becomes more and more entangled. Suffice it to say that in the heart of Lithuania and the seat of the planned autonomous diet, Vilna, out of the 227 schools counted in 1900, 182 are Jewish!

Another consideration no less important is the circumstance that the Polish nationality is in Lithuania and Ruthenia precisely the nationality of the ruling strata: the gentry landowners and the bourgeoisie; while the Lithuanian and particularly the Byelorussian nationality is represented mostly by landless peasantry. Therefore, the nationality relationship is here—generally speaking—a relationship of social classes. Handing over the country's autonomous institutions to the Polish nationality would here mean the creation of a new powerful instrument of class domination without a corresponding strengthening of the position of the exploited classes, and would cause conditions of the kind that would be brought about by the proposed autonomy of Galicia for the Ruthenians.

Consequently, both for nationality and for social reasons the joining of Lithuania to the autonomous territory of the Kingdom or the separation of Lithuania and Ruthenia into an autonomous region with an unavoidable preponderance of the Polish element is a project which Social Democracy must combat in principle. In this form, the project of Lithuania's national autonomy altogether falls through as utopian, in view of the numerical and social relations of the nationalities involved.

III

Another outstanding example of the difficulties encountered by the problem of nationality autonomy in practice is to be found in the Caucasus. No corner of the earth presents such a picture of nationality intermixture in one territory as the Caucasus, the ancient historical trail of the great migrations of peoples between Asia and Europe, strewn with fragments and splinters of those peoples. That territory's population of over nine million is composed (according to the 1897 census) of the following racial and nationality groups:

In Thousands
Russians   2,192.3
Germans   21.5
Greeks   57.3
Armenians   975.0
Ossetians   157.1
Kurds   100.0
Chechens   243.4
Circassians   111.5
Abkhaz   72.4
Lezgins   613.8
Georgians, Imeretins,
Mingrels, etc. Kartvelian 1,201.2
Jews   43.4
Tatars 1,139.6
Kumyks   100.8
Turks Turco-Tatars   70.2
Nogays   55.4
Karaches   22.0
Kalmuks   11.8
Estonians
Mordvinians   1.4

The territorial distribution of the largest nationalities involved is as follows: The Russians, who constitute the most numerous group in the whole Caucasus, are concentrated in the north, in the Kuban and Black Sea districts and in the northwest part of Tersk. Moving southward, in the western part of the Caucasus the Kartvelians are located; they occupy the Kutai and the south-eastern part of the Tiflis gubernias. Still further south, the central territory is occupied by the Armenians in the southern portion of the Tiflis, the eastern portion of the Kars and the northern portion of the Erivan gubernias, squeezed between the Georgians in the north, the Turks in the west and the Tatars in the east and south, in the Baku, Elizabetpol and Erivan gubernias. In the east and in the mountains are located mountain tribes, while other minor groups such as Jews and Germans live, intermingled with the autochthonous population, mainly in the cities. The complexity of the nationality problem appears particularly in the linguistic conditions because in the Caucasus there exist, besides Russian, Ossetian, and Armenian, about a half-dozen languages, four Lezgin dialects, several Chechen, several Circassian, Mingrel, Georgian, Sudanese, and a number of others. And these are by no means dialects, but mostly independent languages incomprehensible to the rest of the population.

From the standpoint of the problem of autonomy, obviously only three nationalities enter into consideration: Georgians, Armenians, and Tatars, because the Russians inhabiting the northern part of the Caucasus constitute, with regard to nationality, a continuation of the state territory of the purely Russian population.

The relatively most numerous nationality group besides the Russians are the Georgians, if we include among them all varieties of Kartvelians. The historical territory of the Georgians is represented by the gubernias of Tiflis and Kutai and the districts of Sukhum and Sakatali, with a population of 2,110,490. However, the Georgian nationality constitutes only slightly more than half of that number, i.e., 1,200,000; the remainder is composed of Armenians to the number of about 220,000, concentrated mainly in the Akhalkalats county of the Tiflis gubernia, where they constitute over 70 percent of the population; Tatars to the number of 100,000; Ossetians, over 70,000; Lezgins represent half of the population in the Sakatali district; and Abkhazes are preponderant in the Sukham district; while in the Borchalin county of the Tiflis gubernia a mixture of various nationalities holds a majority over the Georgian population.

In view of these figures the project of Georgian nationality autonomy presents manifold difficulties. Georgia's historical territory, taken as a whole, represents such a numerically insignificant population—scarcely 1,200,000—that it seems insufficient as a basis of independent autonomous life in the modern sense, with its cultural needs and socio-economic functions. In an autonomous Georgia, with its historical boundaries, a nationality that comprises only slightly more than half of the entire population would be called on to dominate in public institutions, schools, and political life. The impossibility of this situation is felt so well by the Georgian nationalists of revolutionary hue that they, a priori, relinquish the historical boundaries and plan to curtail the autonomous territory to an area corresponding to the actual preponderance of the Georgian nationality.

According to that plan, only sixteen of Georgia's counties would be the basis of the Georgian autonomy, while the fate of the four remaining ones with a preponderance of other nationalities would be decided by a "plebiscite" of those nationalities. This plan looks highly democratic and revolutionary; but like most anarchist-inspired plans which seek to solve all historic difficulties by means of the "will of nations" it has a defect, which is that in practice the plebiscite plan is even more difficult to implement than the autonomy of historical Georgia. The area specified in the Georgian plan would include scarcely 1,400,000 people, i.e., a figure corresponding to the population of a big modern city. This area, cut out quite arbitrarily from Georgia's traditional framework and present socio-economic status, is not only an extremely small basis for autonomous life but moreover does not represent any organic entity, any sphere of material life and economic and cultural interests, besides the abstract interests of the Georgian nationality.

However, even in this area, the Georgians' nationality claims cannot be interpreted as an active expression of autonomous life, in view of the circumstance that their numerical preponderance is linked with their pre-eminently agrarian character.

In the very heart of Georgia, the former capital, Tiflis, and a number of smaller cities have an eminently international character, with the Armenians, who represent the bourgeois stratum, as the preponderant element. Out of Tiflis's population of 160,000 the Armenians constitute 55,000, the Georgians and Russians 20,000 each; the balance is composed of Tatars, Persians, Jews, Greeks, etc. The natural centers of political and administrative life as well as of education and spiritual culture are here, as in Lithuania, seats of foreign nationalities. This circumstance, which makes Georgia's nationality autonomy an insoluble problem, impinges simultaneously on another Caucasian problem: the question of the autonomy of the Armenians.

The exclusion of Tiflis and other cities from the autonomous Georgian territory is as impossible from the standpoint of Georgia's socio-economic conditions as is their inclusion into that territory from the standpoint of the Armenian nationality. If we took as a basis the numerical preponderance of Armenians in the population, we would obtain a territory artificially patched together from a few fragments: two southern counties of Tiflis gubernia, the northern part of Erivan gubernia, and the north-eastern part of Kars gubernia, i.e., a territory cut off from the main cities inhabited by the Armenians, which is senseless both from the historical standpoint and from the standpoint of the present economic conditions, while the size of the putative autonomous area would be limited to some 800,000. If we went beyond the counties having a numerical preponderance of Armenians we would find the Armenians inextricably mixed in the north with the Georgians; in the south—in the Baku and Elizabetpol gubernias— with the Tatars; and in the west, in the Kars gubernia, with the Turks. The Armenians play, in relation to the mostly agrarian Tatar population which lives in rather backward conditions, partly the role of a bourgeois element.

Thus, the drawing of a boundary between the main nationalities of the Caucasus is an insoluble task. But even more difficult is the problem of autonomy in relation to the remaining multiple nationalities of the Caucasian mountaineers. Both their territorial intermingling and the small numerical size of the respective nationalities, and finally the socio-economic conditions which remain mostly on the level of largely nomadic pastoralism, or primitive farming, without an urban life of their own and with no intellectual creativity in their native language, make the functioning of modern autonomy entirely inapplicable.

Just as in Lithuania, the only method of settling the nationality question in the Caucasus, in the democratic spirit, securing to all nationalities freedom of cultural existence without any among them dominating the remaining ones, and at the same time meeting the recognized need for modern development, is to disregard ethnographic boundaries, and to introduce broad local self-government—communal, urban, district, and provincial—without a definite nationality character, that is, giving no privileges to any nationality. Only such a self-government will make it possible to unite various nationalities to jointly take care of the local economic and social interests, and on the other hand, to take into consideration in a natural way the different proportions of the nationalities in each county and each commune.

Communal, district, provincial self-government will make it possible for each nationality, by means of a majority decision in the organs of local administration, to establish its schools and cultural institutions in those districts or communes where it possesses numerical preponderance. At the same time a separate, empire-wide, linguistic law guarding the interests of the minority can establish a norm in virtue of which national minorities, beginning with a certain numerical minimum, can constitute a basis for the compulsory founding of schools in their national languages in the commune, district, or province; and their language can be established in local public and administrative institutions, courts, etc., at the side of the language of the preponderant nationality (the official language). Such a solution would be workable, if indeed any solution is possible within the framework of capitalism, and given the historical conditions. This solution would combine the general principle of local self-government with special legislative measures to guarantee cultural development and equality of rights of the nationalities through their close co-operation, and not their mutual separation by barriers of national autonomy.

IV

An interesting example of a purely formalistic settlement of the nationality question for the entire Russian empire is provided by the project of a certain K. Fortunatov published by the group "*Trud i Borba*" (Work and Struggle), an attempt at a practical solution of the problem in accordance with the principles of the Russian revolutionary socialists. On the basis of the census, the author first arranges a map of the empire according to nationalities, taking as a basis the numerical preponderance of each nationality in the respective gubernias and counties. The numerically strongest nationality is the Great Russians who are preponderant in thirty gubernias of European Russia. They are followed by the Little Russians who have a majority in the Ukraine in the gubernias of Poltawa, Podolia, Kharkov, Kiev, and Volhynia, and are represented also in the gubernias of Ekaterinoslav, Chernigov, Kherson, Kuban, and Taurida, while in Bessarabia the Moldavians and in the Crimea the Tatars are preponderant. Apart from the Poles, the third nationality is the Byelorussians, who have a majority in five gubernias: Mogilev, Minsk, Vilna, Witebsk, and Grodno, with the exception of eight counties (Bialystok, inhabited mainly by Poles; Bielsk, Brzesc, and Kobryn, in which the Little Russians are preponderant; the Dzwinsk, Rezyca, and Lucin counties, where the Latvians are in the majority; and finally Troki, in which the Lithuanians prevail). On the other hand, the Krasne county of Smolensk gubernia has to be included in Byelorussia because of the preponderance of that nationality. The Lithuanians and Samogitians prevail in the Kovno and Suwalki gubernias, with the exception of the Suwalki and Augustow counties in which the Poles are in the majority. The Latvians in Courland and the Estonians in Estonia have a decisive majority, and between them they divide Livonia into practically two equal parts, southern and northern. Including the Congress Kingdom, with the exception of the Suwalki gubernia, we obtain, in sixty-two gubernias of European Russia, the following picture of nationality relations:

Great Russians preponderant in 30 gubernias
Little Russians 10 gubernias
Byelorussians 5 gubernias
Poles 9 gubernias
Lithuanians 2 gubernias
Latvians 2 gubernias
Estonians 1 gubernia
Moldavians 1 gubernia
Tatars 2 gubernias

Having examined the territorial distribution of nationalities in the Caucasus according to gubernias and counties, the author in turn moves to Asiatic Russia. In Siberia, the Russian element is in a decisive majority, forming 80.9 percent of the population besides the Buriats, 5 percent; Yakuts, 4 per-cent; Tatars, 3.6 percent; other nationalities, 6.5 percent. Only in the Yakut gubernia do the Russians constitute a minority of 11.5 percent while the Yakuts form 82.2 percent of the whole. In Central Asia, the most numerous nationalities are the Kirgis, who are in a majority in all gubernias with the exception of the three southern ones: Trans-Caspia, in which the Turkomans number 65 percent, Samarkana, inhabited by the Uzbekhs

(58.8 percent) and Tadzikhs (26.9 percent), and the Fergan Valley, in which the Sarts form half, the Uzbekhs 9.7 percent, the Kirgis 12.8 percent of the population.

Thus, taking as a basis the gubernias and counties with a preponderance of one nationality or another, Mr. Fortunatov ranges the following scheme of nationality districts in the whole empire, as shown in the appendix below.

In this scheme we are struck by great numerical differences, e.g., between the tremendous Great Russian and Little Russian districts and such tiny ones as the Lithuanian, Estonian, or individual Caucasian, let alone the Yakut. This circumstance apparently offends the sense of symmetry of the admirers of the principle of "Federation." It also evokes in them some doubts as to whether nationalities so unequal in strength and size could enter into idyllic coexistence as autonomous districts possessing equal rights. Therefore, our statistician, without much thought, obviates the evil with scissors and glue by combining several small districts into one and simultaneously dismembering two big ones into smaller ones. Apparently taking a population of six to nine million as a normal measure of a nationality district—although it is unknown on what basis—he considers that it is "easy" to split the Little Russian district into three and the Great Russian into seven, separating for instance the Don, Astrakhazan, Kuban, Stavropol, and Black Sea gubernias and two counties of Tersk with a population of 6.7 million as a "Cossack" district, and the Kazan, Ufa, Orenburg, Samar gubernias and two counties of Symbir gubernia with nine million population as a Tatar Bashkir district, finally simply dividing the remaining territory of twenty-five gubernias with forty-two million people into five more or less symmetrical parts with eight million people, with no regard to the nationality principle.

In this way we obtain the plan of the division of the whole of Russia into the following sixteen "states" or autonomous districts on the basis of nationalities:

1 Poland with a population of   8,696,000
1 Byelorussia with a population of   7,328,000
1 Baltic with a population of   5,046,000
3 Little Russia with a population of 27,228,000

a. South-western (Podolia, Volhynia and Kiev, and 3 counties of Grodno) with a population of 10,133,000

b. Little Russia Proper (Poltawa, Kharkov, Chernigov without the northern counties as well as the Little Russian counties of Kursk and Voronezh gubernia) with a population of 8,451,000

c. New Russia (Bessarabia, Kherson, Taurida, Ekaternoslav and Taganrog county) with a population of 8,644,000

1 Caucasus (without the Russian counties) 6,157,000

1 Kirgis in Central Asia (without 2 counties of Akmolin province) with a population of 7,490,000

1 Siberia (with 2 counties of Akmolin province) with a population of 6,015,000

7 Great Russia with a population of 57,680,000

In setting up the above scheme the author was obviously not restrained by any historical or economic considerations, or by the divisions of production or commercial communication created by modern development and natural conditions. It is well known that such pedestrian considerations can only hamper the political concoctions of people professing the "Marxist" doctrine and a materialistic world view. They do not exist for the theorists and politicians of "truly revolutionary socialism," who have in mind only the "rights" of nations, freedom, equality, and other such lofty matters. The separation of two Lithuanian gubernias—Kovno and Suwalki—with the exclusion of the Polish counties—from the historico-cultural heart of Lithuania, the Vilna gubernia and other neighboring regions with which economic relations were of long standing, and on the other hand the joining of these two curtailed gubernias with Livonia, Courland, and Estonia, with which the historical links, as well as present-day economic ones, are quite loose, clearly demonstrates this point. Although the cutting up of the Ukraine for the sake of symmetry into various divisions, despite the continuity of its natural and economic character, and on the other hand, combining into one autonomous region of Siberia a country comprising 12.5 million square kilometers, i.e., by one-third bigger than the whole of Europe, a country representing the greatest natural economic and cultural contrasts, is a demonstration that that method is free of any "dogmas." At the same time, the nationality autonomy in this scheme is treated free of any connection with the economic and social structure of the given nationality. From this standpoint other peoples are equally prepared for regional autonomy—that is, they evince a certain permanent territory and administration, legislation, and cultural life centralized in that territory. There are, on the one hand, the Poles, and on the other the Kirgis, the Yakuts, and the Buriats, who are still partly nomadic and are still living according to the traditions of tribal organization, thwarting to this very day the efforts of the territorial administration of Russian absolutism. The autonomous regional construction, in accordance with the "socialist-revolutionary" views, is thus entirely "free," unconnected with any real bases in time and space, and all the existing historical, economic, and cultural conditions play only the role of material out of which, by means of "revolutionary" scissors, artful nationality plots are to be cut out.

What is the result of this solely and exclusively ethnographic method of the political dismemberment of Russia? Mr. Fortunatov's scheme reduces the principle of nationality to an absurdity. Although the Lithuanians are cut off from the Polish nationality with which they coalesce culturally, still they are linked on the basis of ethnographic affinity into one "Baltic" nationality with the Latvians and the Estonians with whom they identify as little as with the Poles: thus they gravitate toward the completely Germanized cultural centers of Livonia and Estonia. Combining the Georgians, Armenians, Tatars, and a few dozen other tribes of the Caucasus into one "Caucasian" nationality smacks of a malicious satire against national autonomous aspirations. No greater regard for these aspirations is evidenced by the inclusion of the Moldavians, situated in Bessarabia, in the Little Russian nationality, of the Crimean Tatars in the very same nationality, and finally by the combining of Samoyeds, Ostiaks, Tunguz, Buriats, Yakuts, Chuckchees, Kamchadals, and many other tribes, each living an entirely separate life, differing among themselves in the level of cultural development, language, religion, even partly race, with the Russian population of Siberia into one mysterious "Siberian" nationality with common legislative, administrative, and cultural institutions. Fortunatov's scheme is basically a simple negation of the nationality principle. It is also interesting as an example of the anarchistic approach to nationalism, unrestricted as it is by any considerations of objective social development. Having thrown its weight around in that valley of tears, it eventually returns to the results, very much resembling the same ugly history of reality which it had undertaken "to correct," i.e., the systematic violations of the "nationality rights" and their equality. The whole difference consists in the fact that the trampling of the "rights" of nationalities imagined by the ideology of liberalism and anarchism is, in reality, the result of the process of historical development which has its inner sense and what is more important — its revolutionary dialectic, while revolutionary-nationalistic bungling tends, in its zealous cutting up of what had grown together socially, and in its gluing of what socially cannot be glued together, to trample eventually the nationality "rights" celebrated by it, merely for the sake of schematic pedantry deprived of any sense and blown up with political buffoonery.

Down With Reformist Illusions — Hail the Revolutionary Class Struggle!

(1913)

When May Day demonstrations were held for the first time, the vanguard of the International, the German working class, was just at the point of breaking the chains of a disgraceful Exception Law and of entering upon the path of a free, legal development. The period of prolonged depression in the world market, since the crash of the seventies, had been overcome and capitalist economy had entered directly upon an era of resplendent development that was to last almost a decade. Likewise the world had recovered, after twenty years of uninterrupted peace, from recollections of that war period in which the modern European state system had received its bloody christening. The path appeared free for a quiet cultural development. Illusions, hopes for a peaceful settlement between capital and labor sprouted forth luxuriantly among the ranks of the Socialists. Proposals to hold out "the open hand to good will" marked the beginning of the nineties; promises of an inperceptible, "gradual evolution" into Socialism marked their end. Crises, wars, and revolutions were considered outworn theories, mere swaddling clothes of modern society; parliamentarism and trade unionism, democracy in the State and democracy in the industry were to open the gates to a new and better order.

The actual course of events played frightful havoc with all these illusions. In place of the promised mild social-reformist development of culture there has set in since the end of the nineties a period of the most violent, extreme sharpening of capitalist conflicts, a period of storm and stress, of crashes and turmoil, of tottering and trembling in the very foundations of society. The ten-year period of the economic upward curve of development was compensated for in the following decade by two world-convulsing crises. After two decades of world peace there followed in the last decade of last century six bloody wars and in the first decade of the new century four bloody revolutions. Instead of social reforms—sedition bills, imprisonment bills and jailings; instead of industrial democracy—the powerful concentration of capital in cartels and employers' associations and the international practice of giant lockouts. And instead of the new upward development of democracy in the State a miserable collapse of the last remnants of bourgeois liberalism and bourgeois democracy. In Germany alone the destinies of the bourgeois parties since the nineties have brought: the rise and immediate hopeless dissolution of the National Social Party, the break-up of the liberal opposition and the re-uniting of its fragments in the morass of reaction, and finally the transformation of the Center from a radical people's party to a conservative government party. And the shifting in party development in other capitalist countries has been similar. Everywhere the revolutionary working class today sees itself alone confronted by the compact, hostile reaction of the ruling classes and by their energetic attacks, which are aimed at them alone.

The "sign" under which this whole development on the economic and political field has been carried out, the formula according to which its results may be traced back is: *imperialism*. This is not a new element, not an unexpected veering in the general historical course of capitalist society. Military preparations and wars, international conflicts and colonial policies have accompanied the history of capital from its cradle. It is the extreme augmentation of these elements, the concentration and gigantic outburst of these conflicts, which have resulted in a new epoch in the development of present-day society. In dialectic reciprocal action—at the same time result and cause of the powerful accumulation of capital and of the consequent sharpening and intensifying of the contradiction between capital and labor within and between the capitalist States without—has Imperialism entered upon its final phase, the violent division of the world by the assault of capital. A chain of continual, unprecedented competitive military preparations on land and sea in all capitalist countries, a chain of bloody wars, which have spread from Africa to Europe and which any moment may fan the glowing sparks to a world conflagration; in addition, for years the phantom of the high cost of living, of mass hunger throughout the whole capitalist world, which can no longer be banished—these are the "signs" under which labor's world holiday will soon celebrate the twenty-fifth anniversary of its existence. And each of these "signs" is a flaming testimonial to the living truth and power of the ideas of the May Day celebration.

The brilliant main idea of the May Day celebration is the independent action of the proletarian masses, is the political mass action of the millions of workers, who otherwise can give expression to their own will only through petty parliamentary action, separated by State boundaries and consisting for the most part only in voting for representatives. The excellent proposal of the Frenchman Lavigne at the international congress in Paris combined this indirect parliamentary manifestation of the will of the proletariat with a direct international mass manifestation, the laying down of tools as a demonstration and fighting tactic for the eight-hour day, world peace, and Socialism.

No wonder the whole development, the aggregate tendency of imperialism in the last decade has been to bring ever plainer and more tangibly before the eyes of the international working class that only the independent action of the broadest masses, their own political action, mass demonstrations, mass strikes, which must sooner or later break forth into a period of revolutionary struggles for State power, can give the correct answer of the proletariat to the unprecedented pressure of imperialist politics. At this moment of frenzied military preparations and of war orgies it is only the resolute fighting stand of the working masses, their ability and readiness for powerful mass action, which still maintains world peace, which can still postpone the threatening world conflagration. And the more the May Day idea, the idea of resolute mass action as demonstrations of international solidarity and as a fighting tactic for peace and for Socialism even in the strongest section of the International, the German working class, strikes root, the greater guaranty we shall have that from the world war, which will inevitably take place sooner or later, there will result an ultimately victorious settlement between the world of labor and that of capital.

Leipzig, April 30, 1913.